Educators Queering Academia

SOCIAL JUSTICE ACROSS CONTEXTS IN EDUCATION

sj Miller & Leslie David Burns
GENERAL EDITORS

Vol. 4

The Social Justice Across Contexts in Education series is part of the Peter Lang Education list.
Every volume is peer reviewed and meets the highest quality standards for content and production.

PETER LANG
New York • Bern • Frankfurt • Berlin
Brussels • Vienna • Oxford • Warsaw

Educators Queering Academia

Critical Memoirs

Edited by sj Miller and Nelson M. Rodriguez

PETER LANG
New York • Bern • Frankfurt • Berlin
Brussels • Vienna • Oxford • Warsaw

Library of Congress Cataloging-in-Publication Data

Names: Miller, sj, editor. | Rodriguez, Nelson M., editor.
Title: Educators queering academia: critical memoirs /
edited by sj Miller, Nelson M. Rodriguez.
Description: New York: Peter Lang, 2016.
Series: Social justice across contexts in education; v. 4
ISSN 2372-6849 (print) | ISSN 2372-6857 (online)
Includes bibliographical references.
Identifiers: LCCN 2016019532 | ISBN 978-1-4331-3431-9 (hardcover: alk. paper)
ISBN 978-1-4331-3430-2 (paperback: alk. paper) | ISBN 978-1-4539-1877-7 (ebook pdf)
ISBN 978-1-4331-3620-7 (epub) | ISBN978-1-4331-3621-4 (mobi)
Subjects: LCSH: Homosexuality and education. | Gays in higher education.
Gay college teachers. | Gay and lesbian studies.
Classification: LCC LC192.6 .E48 2016 | DDC 378.0086/64—dc23
LC record available at https://lccn.loc.gov/2016019532

Bibliographic information published by **Die Deutsche Nationalbibliothek.**
Die Deutsche Nationalbibliothek lists this publication in the "Deutsche Nationalbibliografie"; detailed bibliographic data are available on the Internet at http://dnb.d-nb.de/.

29 Broadway, 18th floor, New York, NY 10006
www.peterlang.com

When you are born into a world you don't fit in:
It's because you were born to help create a new one.
—Anonymous

Table of Contents

Foreword

JEN GILBERT

I don't know who I would have become had I not, more than 20 years ago, applied to grad school. I was not a particularly good student, my family was happily surprised that I went to university at all, but in my final year I took an English course on gay drama. We traveled from Vancouver to Seattle to see the touring production of *Angels in America*; we drank wine and ate cheese at our professor's bungalow in Surrey, and I wrote an essay about John Guare's play, *Six Degrees of Separation*. I imagine I did this, in part, because something about my own struggles at the university seemed illuminated in the scheming and lovable conman, Paul, who convinces a wealthy Upper-West Side family that he is the son of Sidney Poitier—a familiar feeling, perhaps, given the well-documented alienation of gender, sexual, class, and racial minorities in the university. I received an A+ on the paper—the highest grade I had ever received—and so decided to con my way in the grad school. Now, many years later, the university is my home, but I still sometimes feel I got away with something, that I could be asked to give back my degrees, and that exiled from the university, I could easily find myself homeless.

The university is a fickle home for many of the contributors to this volume—it is at once the ground for our emergence as scholars. That we write here, in a book devoted to exploring the experiences of LGBTQ academics, marks our debt to the university and the texts, ideas, and relationships we encounter there. But contributors also painfully note the ways the university fails to offer a welcoming home to LGBTQ people, ideas, and communities. I suspect this contradiction sits at the heart of much scholarship. Contributors to this volume have all made enormous political, social, and emotional commitments to the university; they trace the ways their thinking and erotic selves are indebted to institutional life, and yet, the casualties pile up: the rise of precarious labor, racist microaggressions, violence against trans* students and faculty, the corporatization of the university, ongoing hostility toward queer studies and scholars. It is an ambivalent relation.

In the memoirs collected here, we find stories of love and alienation. At their best, these narratives come close to what Janet Miller (2005) describes as "autobiography as a queer curriculum practice"—stories that shift "from modernist emphasis on producing predictable, stable, and normative identities … [toward] a consideration of 'selves' and curricula as sites of 'permanent openness'" (p. 302). Noticing how one can go to graduate school and fall in love—belatedly, reservedly—with Foucault, and then also feel betrayed by the university's failure to protect the rights of trans* students, Kristen Renn, in this volume, uses memoir to reimagine her becoming as a scholar as an ongoing, open process of understanding her alienation and privilege. In another chapter, Catherine Lugg describes how her life as a queer scholar was enfranchised by the university—as an assistant professor, a mentor encouraged her to pursue a queer research agenda—and then both imperiled and restored by institutional logics of the university after a tenure scare. Caught always within the machinations of institutional life, these memoirs create a space to "help us dis-identify with ourselves and others" (Miller, p. 303); the memoir can expose what Britzman (1997) calls "the tangles of implication." Through the memoir, we can begin to notice ourselves noticing the world. One of the challenges, then, that these memoirs pose for readers and the field of educational scholarship is that as some of us find and make our home in the university, we must remember those struggles and communities that can get tossed aside when we only celebrate the steady march of "progress." The professional lives of queer scholars of color, increasing the visibility of trans* students and faculty, the poverty of adjunct professors, and the rise of discourses of accountability in schools—a new research and activist agenda for LGBTQ scholars would put these communities and issues at the center of our efforts.

REFERENCES

Britzman, D. (1997). The tangles of implication. *International Journal of Qualitative Studies in Education, 10*(1), 31–37.

Miller, J. L. (2005). *Sounds of silence breaking: Women, autobiography, curriculum.* New York: Peter Lang.

Acknowledgments

Queers have been part of the academy since its creation. Fear and institutional policies, however, have created constraints that have kept those academics from being their authentic selves. Our work attempts to document part of that process and bring voice to those scholars who refuse to let past be prelude to future. We are deeply honored to have amassed such brave and forthright scholars who honor us, the field, and each other to advance collective understanding and empathy toward those we work with in the academy, the students we serve, the colleagues with whom we interact, and those coming into and being mentored and apprenticed to serve within the academy. We hope these memoirs offer healing to those who have been traumatized by institutional neglect and overt abuse and hope to the now and future of all those beautiful souls currently in and coming into education.

sj thanks Nelson, one of the most fabulous, passionate, and queer intellectuals sj has ever met. Thank you for inviting me to work and learn alongside you. Nelson thanks sj for being, well, amazing. What an honor and privilege it has been to work with someone as talented, thoughtful, and brilliant as sj Miller. sj also wants to thank my chosen family: Cynthia Tyson, JA Alston, Shirley Steinberg, Eelco Buitenhuls, Susan Groenke, Kevin Kumashiro, Nicole Sieben, Amber Kim, Alison and Jason Boardman, Nicole Plotkin, Kristen Renn, Cynthia Lewis, Penny Pence, Les Burns, David Kirkland, Yolanda Sealey-Ruiz, Jessica Zacher, Amanda Godley, Amanda Thein, Ebony Thomas, Darrell Hucks, David Carlson, Stephanie Shelton, Maryann Shaening, Ron Pokrasso, Lynne Canning, Danielle Gothie, Penny

Pence, Betsy Noll, Don Zancanella, Glenabah Martinez, Sue Hopewell, Kathy Escamilla, Channell Wilson-Segura, Rachel Hess, Mike Wenk, Janet Alsup, Lisa Eckert, Sandy Lassen, Eliot Lew, Briann and Mel Shear, Margaret Sheehy, Kevin Leander, Chris Iddings, Tonya Perry, Cathy Fleisher, Cathy Compton-Lilly, Todd and Diane Smith, Nelson Graff, Bettina Love, and Cris Mayo.

sj Miller and Nelson M. Rodriguez

Introduction

The Critical Praxis of Queer Memoirs in Education

sj MILLER AND NELSON M. RODRIGUEZ

When we initially conceived the idea for *Educators Queering Academia: Critical Memoirs*, it came from a space of *remembering*. As tenured queer educators not only did we want to remember those who forged diverse paths that have created the conditions for many of us in the present to be able to do queer work in academia, we also wanted to honor their tenacious and indomitable spirits. Their efforts, to be sure, have been formative for us in so many impactful ways that we were called to archive as many of our queer educational histories as possible that demonstrate diverse lineages and intersectionalities. From this perspective, we reached out to at least several dozen queer educators, including former, current, those new to the profession, and even those still yet-to-come, to share with us the ways in which they have queered, are queering, or will queer academia. What we compiled represents a cross-section of memoirs of those who responded to the call.

For this book, we utilize "queer" as an umbrella category referencing lesbian, gay, bisexual, transgender, intersex, and emerging categories (LGBTI+), as well as work specifically in queer theory arising out of poststructuralism and the postmodern turn in sexuality studies. We recognize that embedded in this usage are theoretical and political tensions between identitarian and non-identitarian approaches to thinking about gender/sexual identities and categories and their intersections with other categories of social difference. Nevertheless, we have opted for this usage because some of the authors in this volume identify with more "conventional" categories, such as gay or lesbian, but who also adopt a queer approach to their curriculum and/or pedagogy. Others might adopt queer as a nonbinary identification but be committed, for political reasons, to teaching about more "stable" LGBTI, histories, and subjects. And others in this volume might, concomitantly, blend their support for identity politics with a queer sense of self (e.g., queerly lesbian) … and so on. Thus, we identify *queer* not as relegated to lesbian, gay, bisexual, trans*[1]/ transgender, intersex, (a)gender/(a)sexual,[2] gender creative, expansive or fluid,[3] and questioning (LGBT*IAGCQ) people, but inclusive of a broad range of identities, experiences, and approaches to teaching and research that ultimately aims to interrogate and disrupt what is perceived as (hetero and cis)normative structures within academia. In this way, our use of queer embraces the freedom to move beyond, between, or even away from, yet even to later return to (myriad) identity categories that support the perpetual reinvention of the self within the context and concerns of an antihegemonic queer politics and praxis.

Informed by this broad and ever-expanding definition of queer, this collection represents a cross-section of critical reflections by a queerly diverse set of individuals on their experiences inhabiting a variety of spaces within the field of education. In their stories, the authors share how they queered and are continuing to queer the academy in relation to questions of teaching, research, policy, and/or administration. Their memoirs speak across generations of queer educators and scholars including the senior, mid, and junior levels, postdocs, as well as the doctoral level, and collectively their work highlights an array of theoretical perspectives and methodological approaches. As snapshots in time, the memoirs can be taken up as archives and studied in order to gain perspective on the issues facing queers in the academy across various intersections of identities related to ethnicity, culture, language, national origin, (a)gender, (a)sexuality, sexual orientation, disability, ability, socioeconomic status, religion, spirituality, age, veteran status, health status, height, weight, and so forth. By way of the memoirs in this volume, a richer body of queer knowledge is offered that can be pulled from and infused into the academic and personal contexts of the work of educators queering academia.

The volume is organized into six parts with various themes: (1) Queer Paranoia: To Risk or Not to Risk; (2) Queered Tensions: Beyond the Academy; (3) Queering Academic Spaces: Renarrating Lives; (4) Misrecognition: From Invisibility into Visibility; (5) The Political Is Personal; and (6) Queered All the Way Through. Each theme is described below and includes a cluster of chapters representing that theme. We welcome and hope that our readers will critically reflect along with the memoirs in each part. Indeed, educators, scholars, students, activists, artists, and other cultural workers in the academy (and beyond) with an interest in the general topic of queering education, and with an interest in the more specific topic of queering academia, will find this book useful, especially in light of the ongoing centrality and developments of lesbian, gay, bisexual, transgender, intersex, queer, and the ever-emerging issues within and beyond academia and on a global scale. Our long-term hope is that our volume will inspire and spur other interested folks to continue the work of archiving the narratives of educators/queers queering academia.

PART 1: QUEER PARANOIA: TO RISK OR NOT TO RISK

The chapters in this first part express authors' different concerns about whether or not to be out in the academy and how they reconcile their choices, a topic many of us face. We often fear how others might perceive us and/or how we might be unfairly treated and even denied opportunities. Such emotional labor can generate cognitive dissonance and force people to create a rewarding and deeply needed, queerly affirming life filled with "rejuvenation strategies" outside of academia. Taken to heart, the authors in part I guide readers to think about how they can forge, negotiate, and survive their way through the academy and consciously decide whether or not to come out.

To start off, Adam J. Greteman, in chapter 1, "Contingent Labor, Contingently Queer," takes us into his questioning about if one is queer in the academy, does one also need a fulfilling work life outside it—in his case, doing retail. He asks us to ponder with him, if working on the outside as a space to experience queer is a "consequence of being queer in academia."

In Chapter 2, "Queer Paranoia: Worrying About and Through a Queer Dissertation Study," Summer Pennell discusses her self-doubts throughout her dissertation study focused on a middle school elective called Math for a Cause, designed to draw upon queer pedagogy and methodologies. Pennell worried that her work was not "queer enough" and that her curriculum, driven by a combination of her own paranoia about taking on queer topics while also wanting students to have choice, made her capitulate into—that is, "come out" in support of—a curricular focus on heteronormative marriage.

Ryan Burns and Janet D. Johnson, in chapter 3, "Reconciling the Personal and Professional: Coming Out From the Classroom Closet," take us into two critical incidents during Burns's teaching journey as he sought personal and professional safety in his identity as a gay man teaching for social justice. Together, they explore and reconcile how the classroom closet affected Burns's personal and professional membership in dominant groups and the toll that took on his identities.

PART 2: QUEERED TENSIONS: BEYOND THE ACADEMY

Chapters in this second part unveil how lives outside of the academy can be strengthened by different social and cultural communities. These authors share intimate moments where their lives outside the academy experienced "flow," yet when entering the academy, they had to shut down and minimalize those critical pieces of themselves.

In chapter 4, "Remaining Stubbornly Faithful: What Queering Academia Does to Queer Teacher-Scholars," Sara Staley and Bethy Leonardi take up the affective-emotional dimensions of queering academia as teachers-scholars. What does queering *feel* like when engaging in the complex work of queering education across a number of different research contexts? Utilizing narrative inquiry as a research method, along with drawing from affect studies as a critical perspective, Staley and Leonardi argue for the importance of including, rather than avoiding, "felt experiences" as an object of analysis in queer research in education.

Michael Borgstrom, in chapter 5, "Inside. Out. Queer Time in Midcareer," situates his memoir within recent queer critiques of time. He describes as queer his experience of time inside academia as it unfolds "in terms that complicate traditional [expected] chronologies," particularly across the categories of teaching, research, and administration. Exploring the normative chronologies of academic culture in relation to the "temporal disjunctions" of being queer both inside and outside the academy, Borgstrom highlights the contradictory messiness and overlap of queer time in midcareer, that is, the nonlinear personal and professional experiences that inevitably constitute a career in higher education.

In chapter 6, "How I Met Foucault: An Intellectual Career in, Around, and Near Queer Theory," Kristen Renn draws on Critical Trans Politics (CTP) as a perspective through which to reflect on her experiences with "neoliberal higher education systems," in which she (as with many of us) has been embedded across her career. A cornerstone of CTP—the questioning of "its own effectiveness, engaging in constant reflection and self-evaluation"—Renn utilizes this perspective to reflect on her own identity as a white lesbian cisgender woman working as a university administrator and academic, from "'dean of queer students' at Brown to professor of education at Michigan State University." Organizing her memoir as a reflection on practices and processes within several moments in her career, Renn examines her role "in challenging, sometimes interrupting, but also in overlooking, ignoring, and perpetuating" hegemonic circuits of power in relation to queer and trans issues in the academy, while at the same time recommitting to working both within and against the system of higher education in the future.

PART 3: QUEERING ACADEMIC SPACES: RENARRATING LIVES

When the academy doesn't explicitly say, "We welcome queers, we want you here," queer academics must be their own advocates in carving out spaces for their queer work and for their relationships to thrive. These authors share how they shifted themselves within different academic spaces while simultaneously renarrating their own stories as they traversed the academy.

Leading off part 3, Nelson M. Rodriguez, in chapter 7, "From Doctoral Student to Dr. Sweetie Darling: My Queer(ing) Journey in Academia," reflects on the shifts in his institutional-intellectual location in academia, starting from being a doctoral student of critical pedagogy and cultural studies at the Pennsylvania State University in the mid-1990s. His memoir then shifts to a primary focus on his past 12 years at The College of New Jersey (TCNJ), that is, on his movement from being a professor of education to his current position teaching mostly sexuality and queer studies courses within the context of a women's, gender, and sexuality studies department. Utilizing several courses he currently teaches, Rodriguez considers what queering academia has meant during this period by making use of a number of concepts to think with, including affect/emotion, border crossing, criticality, and (queer) Eros. In relation to scholarship and teaching, Rodriguez concludes his memoir with a discussion of the next phase of his work of queering academia.

In chapter 8, "Working *With* and *Within*: *Weaving* Queer Spaces With Cycles of Resistance," Jenny Kassen and Alicia Lapointe take up the limitations of particular discourses of "safety and inclusion" in challenging (hetero/cis)normativity in education. Specifically, they center their critique on a Faculty of Education's mobilization of a privileged language of "individualized accounts of homophobia and transphobia," rather than of "systemic deconstruction." Offering a set of counternarratives, Kassen and Lapointe describe how they, as undergraduate/graduate queer students, "worked *with* and *within* an institution's (hetero/cis)normative fabric to establish and nurture queer intellectual and physical spaces through cycles of resistance."

In chapter 9, "Adopting a Queer Pedagogy as a Teaching Assistant," Stephanie Anne Shelton focuses on the struggle of being a teaching assistant (TA) who is actively committed to "incorporating queer topics and queer-ing work into the curriculum." Despite her commitment, however, Shelton notes that in terms of research literature and support networks there is "almost no consideration of what it means for TAs to enact queer pedagogies." This is a problem within a context of the significant presence of TAs to the teaching force coupled with an equally ever-growing presence of queer students and queer issues in higher education today. Utilizing autoethnography along with a queer perspective, Shelton's memoir describes, with wit and humor, the challenges she faced, along with the successes she experienced, in adopting a queer pedagogy as a queer-identified teaching assistant within the context of teacher education courses.

Closing out part 3, Michael Wenk, in chapter 10, "Sanctioning Unsanctioned Texts: The True Story of a Gay Writer," deploys narrative ethnography to explore the possibilities that were available to him to engage with queer literacies as a resource for queer identity formation as a teenager, closeted gay teacher, and doctoral student. In his memoir, he examines the role that sanctioned and unsanctioned texts have played both in his professional and personal sense of self, that is, as a developing writer and gay man. Wenk describes his dissertation study and participants as providing the queer literacy needed to understand his own "true story of a gay writer," noting, "I put words to page that, for the first time in my life, revealed real and important insights about the identities I had struggled with, as well as wished to become."

PART 4: MISRECOGNITION: FROM INVISIBILITY INTO VISIBILITY

In the academy, when academics are misrecognized, it is altogether difficult to hold a positive self-perception. The authors of the memoirs in part 4 understand this yet refuse to be made invisible. Such acts of courage have been seen by peers, students, friends, and family as motivational stances that encourage others to be seen and recognized as they are, and not for who they are. These four authors show us what courage means as they labor to be made visible.

For example, in chapter 11, "(Un)Becoming Trans*: Every Breath You Take and Every … ," sj Miller (dis)entangles what it means to be a trans* academic by splitting trans*ness from untrans*ness as a political strategy that embodies the personal, pedagogical, and theoretical. While surveilled and policed into expected bodied constructs, these stratagems paved multiple pathways for survival. Miller shares interstories about (un)becoming a trans* academic and constructing recognition strategies grounded in a theory of trans*ness and posttrans*ness.

In chapter 12, "Queering the Inquiry Body: Critical Science Teaching From the Margins," Kerrita K. Mayfield asks us to ponder, "How can a neutral scientific inquiry be mediated by a queer educator's embodiment?" To address this question, Mayfield presents a series of content-based and pedagogical engagements to explicate how the act of intentionally queering science curriculum promotes a form of queer praxis. She purposefully connects this to what we know as the definition of "teacher" as caring, to reaffirm that to embody queer instruction is a form of caring for self and other—indeed, that they are concomitant.

Darrell Cleveland Hucks, in chapter 13, "Intersectional Warrior: Battling the Onslaught of Layered Microaggressions in the Academy," questions the root and even consequences (for not doing the work) of the academy's intention to diversify hires. He accurately notes that while racial diversity is an overt focus in the academy, because people tend to presuppose identity based on skin color alone, race has turned into proxy, placating the academy with diversity quotas. The moral consequences for those with intersectional identities force people often into an unwelcomed silence, from whence they are positioned and made invisible. Hucks, through a series of vignettes, critically examines ways to authentically address bolstering institutional diversity on multiple levels.

In the final chapter of part 4, Erich N. Pitcher, in chapter 14, "Undone and (Mis)Recognized: Disorienting Experiences of a Queer, Trans* Educator," asks: "How can I complicate my lived experiences as a queer and trans* academic using *Queer Phenomenology?*" As a scholar-practitioner engaged in queer and trans* research, teaching, and service, Pitcher, "think[ing] with theory," uses autoethnography to elucidate his experiences over the last several years to describe his sedimentation and disorientation processes.

PART 5: THE POLITICAL IS PERSONAL

The political shapes and polices what queer bodies can and can't do in the academy. Certainly, there can be movement and challenges, but oftentimes victories are small and limited. Small victories do and can add up to larger moral and political victories, and these authors share how their academic experiences and victories have been shaped and constructed by policies and how they struggled with these external controls.

Starting us off, Catherine Lugg, in chapter 15, "Slam Dunk on Tenure? Not So Fast … ," maps out her experiences at Rutgers University as an untenured assistant professor of education working in educational administration and policy. She shares a story of her defining moment when she was denied tenure in the spring of 2002. Lugg discusses the strategies that she and her colleagues used to overturn this decision and then closes with thoughts about the lingering effects this experience has had on her personally as well as on her career.

In chapter 16, "Queering South Mississippi: Simple and Seemingly Impossible Work," Kamden Strunk, Douglas Bristol, and William Takewell describe the much-needed work for queer-positive policy and spaces at the University of Southern Mississippi from 2013 to 2015. They share how spaces for such work opened and closed and how administrators positioned queer-positive work as necessarily taking resources from other "diversity" initiatives. They describe the process of working with administrators, gathering data to support queer-positive policy, the later resistance and delay tactics of administrators, the trajectory of LGBTQ-inclusive policy at the university, and how work that was initially simple became, over time, seemingly impossible.

In chapter 17, "Smear the Queer: A Critical Memoir," Scotty M. Secrist, reflects on the personal and professional experiences that have shaped his orientation toward scholarly, administrative, and academic work. Through recalling specific discussions with supervisors and mentors about professionalism and name, coupled with the way that his ever-changing body has worked to either affirm or contradict his work as a queer higher education administrator and scholar, he argues for the need to take up a queer political stance to destabilize longstanding institutionalized and hegemonic norms in the academy.

In the closing piece for part 5, Thabo Msibi, in chapter 18, "'I Heard It From a Good Source'": Queer Desire and Homophobia in a South African Higher Education Institution," presents an autoethnographic account of how, in front of a class of students, a colleague falsely accused him of improperly using his power and authority to abuse a student—who happened to be Msibi's partner. This accusation threatened both his career and life. His account provokes questions about how queer academics are surveilled, policed, and tactfully controlled within higher education spaces and discourses. In exploring these events, Msibi unpacks how techniques of power operate at individual and institutional levels to legitimize heteronormativity at the expense of queer desire and human dignity. The chapter concludes with a call for the troubling of heterosexual privilege in higher education spaces so as to trouble institutional cultures that collude with the normalization of homophobic practices and actions.

PART 6: QUEERED ALL THE WAY THROUGH

Authors in this final part of *Educators Queering Academia* share how their queer journeys were always explicitly shared to both themselves and others. Their unwavering strength provides stories of hope that can be models for all who want to be "360-degree queer."

In chapter 19, "A Profound Moment of Passing," David Lee Carlson conducts an autoethnography of his experiences in higher education. He uses experimental narrative writing to reflect on pivotal moments in his life that have influenced his understanding of teacher education, queerness, sexuality and desire, and their ongoing intersections. More specifically, in making connections between his personal life as a gay man and his professional life as an educator and scholar doing queer studies work in the field of education, Carlson critically reflects on what it has meant to live and enact a queer life personally and professionally and, drawing on such reflections, wonders what queering academia will entail over the next decade of his career.

Dana M. Stachowiak, in chapter 20, "*Being* Queer in Academia ←→ Queer*ing* Academia," offers a set of queer stories about her life and work, "from her pre-academia life to her current life in academia as an assistant professor of diversity/multicultural education." Across these stories, Stachowiak blurs the boundary between *being* queer in academia and queer*ing* academia, thus creating the conditions to queer traditional academic writing, thought, and format. Stachowiak's different stories potentially suggest that what might be most important to us queer academics isn't necessarily *being* queer in academia but rather being able to queer it *as* queer.

Closing out the collection, in chapter 21, "The Constant in My Life," William F. Pinar chronicles his queer journey from "coming of age in politically conservative Westerville, Ohio" in the 1950s to returning to queer theory in late career. Pinar suggests that (queer) desire has always been imprinted across much of his personal and professional life, informing everything "pre" and "during" his scholarly life. Study, for Pinar, has been the constant in his life, a window into an ever-present queer sexuality that no doubt will remain central to his praxis as he considers assembling next, "between two covers, queer pieces now scattered here and there."

NOTES

1. Trans* is a prefix or adjective used as an abbreviation of transgender, derived from the Greek word meaning "across from" or "on the other side of." Many consider trans* to be an inclusive and useful umbrella term. Trans (without the asterisk) is most often applied to trans men and trans women, and the asterisk is used more broadly to refer to all non-cisgender gender identities, such as agender, cross-dresser, bigender, genderfluid, genderf**k, genderless, genderqueer, nonbinary, nongendered, third gender, trans man, trans woman, transgender, transsexual, and two-spirit.
2. (A)gender is a rejection of gender as a biological or social construct altogether and refusal to identify with gender. The lower case (a) in parenthesis does not nullify gender; it is a way of combining the terms so both gender refusal and gender are collapsed into one word. (A)sexual, does not nullify sexual orientation; it is a way of combining the terms so a refusal or rejection of the sexual body can be collapsed into one word.
3. Gender creative, expansive, and/or fluid means expressing gender in a way that demonstrates individual freedom of expression and that does not conform to any specific notion or essentialization of gender.

Part 1:
Queer Paranoia: To Risk or Not to Risk

CHAPTER ONE

Contingent Labor, Contingently Queer

ADAM J. GRETEMAN

People are always telling me to make practicable suggestions. You might as well tell me to suggest what people are doing already, or at least suggest improvements which may be incorporated with the wrong methods at present in use.

—JEAN-JACQUES ROUSSEAU

INTRODUCTION

Folding cashmere sweaters is an important skill for a Ph.D. these days, at least in my experience. According to the American Association of University Professors, more than 40% of all postsecondary education classes are taught by nontenure stream faculty, which is to say, professors who make, on average, according to the Coalition on the Academic Workforce, $2,700 per course. I am one of these faculty members—called a "lecturer" at one school and an "affiliated faculty member" at another. What connects both is the contingent nature of such labor. I have been living this way—contingently—for a number of years. And I enjoy the institutions I call home, the students I teach, and the faculties I work with. However, as we read stories like that of Margaret Mary Vojtko who died in poverty after teaching as an adjunct for 25 years, the state of higher education and the contingent labor of adjuncts seem ever more pressing to document and engage.

We are "Roads" scholars, often with no job security, limited access to employee-based healthcare, and no office space. We are the new normal in education. We are nomads wandering from school to school to teach a course here or there and everywhere. And at times, days before the term begins, we are informed that we are not needed due to enrollment. This leaves us scrambling, looking for other possible teaching gigs or other routes to pay our bills, all the while staying cool, calm, and collected.

I have titled this *critical memoir*, as such, "Contingent Labor, Contingently Queer" to speak to the contingency of queering academia in the midst of such realities. If queerness's contingency was forcefully exposed in the midst of AIDS, deroutinizing the time of those who survived as Sedgwick (1993) pointed out, and academia's contingency has been exposed in the midst of neoliberal policies, deroutinizing the lives of academicians, queering academia would seem to be a persistent challenge. Particularly so since the academy, as an institution, constantly creates new habits, norms, and policies that can produce and reproduce its purposes. Queerness and queering pierce or seek to pierce such norms both inside and outside institutional frameworks. Queer emphasizes breaking habits, rules, and norms to make life survivable and thrivable.

BEGINNING WITH MOMENTS

A memoir is a collection of moments, moments that are collected by an author to tell a particular story about that author's life. And a critical memoir is one that is critical of moments that one memoir-izes. I, as an author, must choose moments that speak to "educators queering academia," while being critical of such moments. The "moment" or moments collected here are in the "past," in that they have happened. But they also, in being moments, speak to future readers that encounter such moments in their present. A misalignment may very likely occur as the moments collected become outdated or unintelligible or naïve in the ever-changing worlds experienced by readers. Queering may very well be a fleeing matter, but capturing such moments in writing allows such fleetingness to leave traces for future readers. Queer indeed, then, are the processes of writing, reading, and having one's writing about moments "queering" academia be read.

Queerness is recognized in moments … moments of misalignment among subjects, objects, and the norms present in those moments. Such moments of misalignment cause all sorts of issues—from excitement to violence to confusion to even boredom. Queerness, as a temporal concept, is not static. What was once queer may not always be queer. So a memoir about queering upon being written and published will, as Eve Sedgwick noted about the printed word, become anachronistic. But "that's the wonderful thing about the printed word," Sedgwick argues, "it can't be updated instantly. It's allowed to remain anachronistic in relation to the culture at the *moment*" (italics added; Barber & Clark, 2002, p. 253). As an educator queering academia, or perhaps attempting to do so, I realize at the beginning of collecting such moments that my work is a holding on to things that have passed—both *what* have passed as "advances" in queer studies/politics and *who* has passed in the midst of violence perpetrated against queers in the academy or by the academy. Clearly, queers will keep coming in the ongoing moments of life that seek to "straighten" out subjects, but what do the memories of such momentary comings offer? Surely, it must be something more than self-shattering.

CONTINGENT MATTERS

There is a great level of contingency in writing, thinking, and educating. Contingency is a rather queer concept that speaks to the radical uncertainty of possibilities—a good thing. Queering academia, like queering society, is not nor can it be a proposed plan to put in place with various institutional initiatives, despite the ongoing attempts to institutionalize critical discourses (Ahmed, 2012; Ferguson, 2012). Rather, queering academia would seemingly be a contingent enterprise with pleasurable and serious aftereffects and affects. Foucault (1997) notes the danger of thinking in programmatic terms, particularly with regard to "liberation," writing,

> The idea of a program of proposals is dangerous. As soon as a program is presented, it becomes a law, and there's a prohibition against inventing. There ought to be an inventiveness special to a situation like ours and to these feelings. … We have to dig deeply to show how things have been historically *contingent*, for such and such reason intelligible but not necessary. We must make the intelligible appear against a background of emptiness and deny its necessity. We must think that what exists is far from filling all possible spaces. (pp. 139–140)

Contingency, with Foucault, is central to a project connected to queerness and how relations between subjects are invented, as opposed to relationships that have always existed or that are "natural" or that emerge out of programs. Richard Ford (2005) argues as much:

> Social identities are processes, possibilities, contingencies, or conceptual frameworks that organize thought and action; they are not only contingent on social practices but they themselves *are* social practices such that they are never formed but always in process of formation and reformation that is never complete. (p. 61)

There is with contingency a process, a becoming, that is never settled, but instead contested, challenged, and undone. Becoming, as Judith Butler (2004) argues, is unbecoming and such processes are contingent on the moments we are in the midst of living. We experience moments and interpret, reflect on, describe, and analyze such moments after the fact of their happening using languages, affects, and more to do so. And these moments are embedded and embodied in histories of violence, phobias, and -isms. To write of moments in a memoir then speaks to surviving enough moments to sit in the silence of one's thoughts and to write out, about, and through such moments so that they might be captured and, in being captured, speak to the deadly routines that threaten, have threatened, and might threaten the contingency of history, queerness, and education. My moments are here captured while many others are lost, in having not survived, and haunt my moments.

Moments that threaten, have threatened, and may threaten queerness, however, cannot rue the day. There is and must be attention also to the pleasures of queerness that emerge within our contingent times after or despite threats. There must be queerness beyond shame (Halperin & Traub, 2010), self-shattering (Bersani, 1987), and melancholy (Butler, 1997)—three concepts that have dominated certain psychoanalytically informed approaches to queer theory. Contingency matters not only to surviving threats but also thriving in the midst of and beyond survival. This might be related to Snediker's (2009) attempt "to clear space for the possible generosities and generativities of queer optimism" (p. 4). This is not your everyday optimism, but an optimism reformulated queerly to affirm persons living queerly—contingently engaging the social norms buoyantly, flamboyantly, with extra sugar in their tanks.

Contingency is not simple then as it both speaks to the possibilities to invent new ways of becoming a subject and the very threats contingency brings subjects and ways of being not yet intelligible. Contingency is, conceptually, central to the process of inventing and making alternatives thinkable within milieus embedded in violence and trauma. Yet, it also operates within the neoliberal present to define the relations between subjects—limiting what can be thought as the materiality of contingency. As Dean Spade (2011) calls attention to in *Normal Life*, the trends of neoliberalism have presented

> a significant shift in the relationships of workers to owners, producing a decrease in real wages, an increase in contingent labor, and the decline of labor unions; the dismantling of welfare programs; trade liberalization (sometimes called "gloablization"); and increasing criminalization and immigration enforcement. (p. 50)

Contingent labor—a hallmark of the 21st academy—comes head to head with contingent subjects that push up against and make possible other ways of becoming "self" in the world of ever-changing norms. Caught in contingent labor relations leaves little time for those, myself included, trapped in its claws even as such laborers might find joy in contingent possibilities, such as queering academia. I may seek to invent alternatives by refusing various normative ideas, but I am simultaneously thwarted from living fully due to my current precariousness as a contingent laborer. This may change—for the better or for the worse.

COLLECTING EXPERIENTIAL MOMENTS

As part of the contingent labor pool, I fold cashmere by day and teach Foucault by night. Talking and writing about my multiple jobs is awkward, but they represent two broad labor moments in my life. People do not expect such moments. In retail, I talk to customers while folding their purchases and at times my other role as a professor comes up. This is often amusing as there is a moment of realization that "I" am not some vapid gay man and the customer decides to see me in a different, more "reputable" light. There is a growing interest in what I teach and a moment where "I" become respectable. While these interactions ensure that I am more than a mere salesperson, these interactions also wound, insulting my sweater-folding comrades and me. These are the teaching moments about khakis and the current economics of higher education, followed by a more light-hearted comment that the discount is nice. I do, after all, have to keep my customers happy and my body gaily clothed.

When I walk into the classroom, the curiosity of my retail life takes on a different form. Students see me as approachable because, like them, I work in the service industry. I may have a Ph.D.; I may be a good teacher (if I am to believe my evaluations), but, in their minds, I have not succumbed to the ivory tower completely. It is a moment of recognition that "I" am like them. Faculty who make triple my salary for teaching half my courses respond in any number of other ways. Some express bewilderment that I have time to teach 4 to 5 courses a term, write for publication, and work a part-time job (10–15 hours a week). Others express a sense of solidarity concerned about my well-being, yet often can do nothing but throw up their hands in anxiety at the adjunctization of their worksites. And still some express a sense that I must have done something wrong—studied the wrong thing or gone to the wrong university—to land in such a state of affairs. I am seen by them as a fashionable gay man who has no place in the academy.

My relationship to academia is at the time of this writing defined by being a contingent laborer who is contingently queer. The moments, ever-passing in my daily existence, are defined, in part, by the larger social, economic, sexual, and historical contingencies that are coming to define the 21st century. Such moments are complex and complicated as they are for all of us (contingent laborers or not) who have to make ends meet and must struggle with the psychic demands of doing so.

Are such struggles—daily, mundane, material—the stuff of queering academia or the consequences of being queer in academia (or elsewhere)? Queer in its various forms—noun, verb, adjective, adverb—may very well contest one another. Can I be queer, given I am a white gay male with a Ph.D. living amid the new homonormativity where I have gained access to seemingly "all-important" social institutions—like the military and marriage? Am I queering such realities by refusing to join them and writing through them "here"? Do my labored realities as an adjunct and salesperson queer my seemingly normalized gay appearances or confirm them or both? Is writing about such things "here" for "there" in the future a way of exposing some of the complex workings involved in queering the 21st century academy? Of this, I am not sure …

Perhaps I should have listened to that professor in my first year of graduate studies who told me *straight* away that I should refocus my work and do something that is marketable. I should, he said, wait until I get tenure to do "queer" work. The security of tenure would have protected me from the risks of queer work, it seemed. Such advice was my first encounter with practical, albeit queer-phobic, advice. It was perhaps a common queer moment whereby a senior faculty member, with good intentions,[1] advised a young scholar to do different work that fit in and may lead to a more lucrative or successful career reproducing work that "matters." Had I listened to that faculty member, would things have been different for me now and would my work matter differently? Fantasies say yes, realities are not so sure. Timing matters, of course, and that advice came in 2006 at the start of my graduate studies and before the economic collapse of 2008.

After 2008, the game changed and nothing was certain—tenure track jobs were scarce as part-time positions flourished. Contingency bore its materiality and perhaps lost its luster as a theoretical idea. With full-time jobs scarce and the future uncertain (more so than usual, it felt), I realized that perhaps it didn't matter what I studied, wrote, and researched. Perhaps it never did. Maybe Edelman (2004) was right proclaiming "no future" for queers. Perhaps I was naïve? Or simply not good enough? Colleagues who did the work I had been told to do were no better off. Or so I told myself. Misery loves company, after all. Anyhow, I continued on my queer path—working with and through the emerging literatures on "queer," be they grounded in literary studies, sociology, philosophy, or education. I sought then as a graduate student (another form of contingent labor) to understand and contribute to "queer theory" with the support of a small contingent of other grad students and faculty members. One's experience in graduate school is, it would seem, already contingent—contingent on the people one enters with and meets and the time one enters such work. There is no ideal set-up or time, just a real contingent set of variables.

In the emerging depressions—economic and psychic—of the late 2000s, I sought to embrace queerness. It felt exciting, necessary, sexy, and, well, queer within the context that was more and more speaking about austerity, tightening belts, and questioning excess. Queer was excessive and promised as somewhere over a rainbow. But—it seemed to me—such excess and promises were for different ends. Queer sought to do justice to difference and to the lives of those who did not or refused to fit in normal ideas and paradigms. I was optimistic (perhaps naïve, a recurring feeling I experience) at this time in the midst of a theoretical terrain that preferred shame, negativity, and the antisocial (e.g., Bersani, 1995; Edelman, 2004; Love, 2009). I was enthralled with this negative archive that strangely fit with the feelings of the time. So, I read and wrote and read and revised. And I positioned myself within my context as one of the token queer scholars. I wanted to push an avowedly queer project (not necessarily knowing what that actually meant) that did not fear controversy (at least on the outside) or hide sex behind closed doors (unless one is doing so during office hours). It was fun and fascinating; some may have thought it frivolous.

And I must realize there existed a certain privilege of being able to do such "frivolous" work. I had a fellowship that provided me with five years of funding so I did not have to search for or justify my work. The institution supported my "queering," making me complicit in the re-institutionalization of queers. I was guaranteed "work" and funds to pay for living—not extravagantly of course, but well enough. I did not have to fight to engage in and do queer work. Queer paid. And aside from the initial queer-phobic advice from a professor, colleagues, faculty, and friends intellectually supported me. My work "queering" academia then was not laced with struggles for recognition or struggles that seemed endemic to my predecessors who paved the yellow bricks I skipped and sashayed on. I was "out and proud" and avowedly committed to such work, naively going about it and believing I had a right to do so since no one had told me differently (or I ignored them if they did). Naïveté may be quite useful in queer projects (Greteman, 2015).

As an adjunct professor now (contingently perhaps, *fingers crossed*), I sometimes wish I had taken that first year advice, helpfully queer-phobic as it may have been, and done research differently. Such a wish often leads me to fabulous fantasies of making a difference and having more material security, just like the stereotype of white gay men perpetuated in the media. And more important, such fantasies help(ed) me momentarily avoid feelings of failure. There may be a queer art of failure, as elucidated by Halberstam (2011), but feeling failure in the face of the impersonal institution is not the most fun or uplifting. Yet, the search for a tenure-track job itself may expose the strange and exhausting realities of queering academia. Am I queerer as an adjunct doing this work since my material realities are less secure than colleagues that have tenure-track jobs or are already tenured doing queer work? I am, by definition, more at risk. If so, what happens if my relationship to academia becomes less contingent? Do I also become less queer?

And is this what "becoming" means? Or in becoming "tenure track" is my queer moment over and I undone? I am not sure of how to respond to such questions and will perhaps only find surety after-the-fact—momentarily.

A MOMENT TO CONCLUDE

Experiences are as diverse as queers, so the work of queering represented here in various moments may appear more or less, or perhaps not at all, queer depending on you, the reader, and the context from which you are reading. The grass is often said to be greener on the other side, but perhaps once one gets there, one realizes it is just as brown; or more fabulous than can be imagined. Perhaps queering is taking the risk to find out and taking what comes.

NOTE

1. To hell with good intentions.

REFERENCES

Ahmed, S. (2012). *On being included: Racism and diversity in institutional life.* Durham, NC: Duke University Press.

Barber, S. M., & Clark, D. L. (2002). This piercing bouquet: An interview with Eve Kosofsky Sedgwick with Stephen M. Barber and David L. Clark. In *Regarding Sedgwick: Essays on queer culture and critical theory.* New York: Routledge.

Bersani, L. (1987). Is the rectum a grave? *October, 43*, 197–222.

Bersani, L. (1995). *Homos.* Cambridge, MA: Harvard University Press.

Bruckner, P. (2010). *The tyranny of guilt: An essay on western masochism.* Princeton, NJ: Princeton University Press.

Butler, J. (1997). *The psychic life of power.* Palo Alto, CA: Stanford University Press.

Butler, J. (2004). *Undoing gender.* New York: Routledge.

Butler, J., & Athanasiou, A. (2014). *Dispossession: The performative in the political.* New York: Polity.

Edelman, L. (2004). *No future: Queer theory and the death drive.* Durham, NC: Duke University Press.

Ferguson, R. (2012). *The reorder of things: The university and its pedagogies of minority difference.* Minneapolis, MN: University of Minnesota Press.

Ford, R. (2005). *Racial culture: A critique.* Princeton, NJ: Princeton University Press.

Foucault, M. (1997). Friendship as a way of life. In P. Rabinow (Ed.), *The essential works of Foucault, 1954–1984: Vol. 1, Ethics: Subjectivity and truth* (R. Hurley, Trans.; pp. 135–140). New York: The New Press.

Greteman, A. J. (2015). On being naïve: A queer aesthete in art education. *Journal of Social Theory in Art Education, 35*, 98–107.

Halberstam, J. (2011). *The queer art of failure*. Durham, NC: Duke University Press.
Halperin, D., & Traub, V. (2010). *Gay shame*. Chicago: University of Chicago Press.
Love, H. (2009). *Feeling backwards*. Cambridge, MA: Harvard University Press.
Sedgwick, E. K. (1993). *Tendencies*. Durham, NC: Duke University Press.
Sedgwick, E. K. (1997). *Novel gazing: Queer readings in fiction*. Durham, NC: Duke University Press.
Snediker, M. D. (2009). *Queer optimism: Lyric personhood and other felicitous persuasions*. Minneapolis: University of Minnesota Press.
Spade, D. (2011). *Normal life: Administrative violence, critical trans politics, and the limits of law*. Boston: South End.

CHAPTER TWO

Queer Paranoia: Worrying About and Through a Queer Dissertation Study

SUMMER PENNELL

When I began planning my dissertation, I was always thinking of scholars in the field of queer education. From examining texts on queer pedagogy, and listening to presentations at education conferences, I have noticed the tendency and "the danger of organizing our work along a queer spectrum, where the 'more queer' is privileged … over the 'less queer' … visible work in classrooms" (DePalma, 2010, p. 55). Despite queer theory's disdain of hierarchies, sometimes they are present in the field as scholars judge whose work is worthy. I was worried that my work in a middle school classroom would fall into the less queer category. Would my study demonstrate I was worthy of inclusion in this group of scholars? Would it be queer enough for them? Had I been misinterpreting queer theory and queer pedagogy, and would I be looked down upon when I presented my work at conferences?

I was paranoid, and this paranoia continued throughout the execution and analysis of my study, and it is still present as I write this memoir. Will this chapter prove my greatest academic fears of being unworthy of inclusion? While I was writing my dissertation and looking over my field notes, I noticed I was conducting a "paranoid reading" (Sedgwick, 2003) of my own study. As Miller (1988) wrote, quoted by Sedgwick, "Even the blandest (or bluffest) 'scholarly work' fears getting into trouble" (p. 131). In this memoir, I will share my paranoid reading of my doctoral dissertation work.

MATH FOR A CAUSE

Before I discuss my paranoia about my dissertation, I will briefly describe the study. Currently, I am a doctoral candidate in education at UNC-Chapel Hill. I completed my dissertation study in the fall of 2014 at a private middle school in a southern U.S. state. Along with my research partner, I collaborated with a classroom teacher (Morgan[1]) to create a text-heavy math class we called *Math for a Cause* that focused on social justice. One of the guiding theoretical frameworks was queer pedagogy, based on work by Britzman (1995) and DePalma, among others. Because collaboration was part of the process, I used a methodological combination of Participatory Action Research (PAR) (Kemmis & McTaggart, 2005) and postcritical ethnography (Noblit, Flores, & Murillo, 2004) and constantly reflected on the course while collecting data.

In the math course, we conducted three units centered on a social justice issue. My co-researcher and I chose the first topic, the killing of Michael Brown by a police officer in Ferguson, Missouri, because it was current. For the second unit, the students chose between (1) environmental issues, (2) healthcare, (3) LGBTQ rights, and (4) education. For the third unit, everyone focused on the issue of same-sex marriage. In the first two units, students began by reading a news article on the topic and completing a critical analysis of the text, such as looking for power structures and evidence of the author's or the subjects' beliefs. From this article and analysis, the students brainstormed a mathematical inquiry. For example, in the LGBTQ rights group in the second unit, they first read an article on Christian opposition to same-sex marriage. For their math problem, they wanted to find out the percentage of Christian churches that support gay marriage, by using data from a welcoming church's website, and compare this to the percentage of Christian churches that oppose gay marriage listed on another website. This would allow the students to get a fuller picture of what Christian groups believed. In the last unit we asked students to create a presentation that would showcase their mathematical investigations in relation to same-sex marriage. Some students looked at the increase of support of same-sex marriage over time using polling data, and another group attempted to find a statistical connection between suicide and states that allowed or did not allow same-sex marriage.

In my enthusiasm to try enacting queer pedagogy's tenets of breaking down boundaries and structures and our co-teacher's belief that the students could handle this freedom, we asked students to write their own math problems with very little scaffolding in place. As you may imagine, this caused a lot of confusion for the students. We asked them to examine difficult topics and then asked them to create their own math problems, which they had never done, and that required them to do their own independent research and data mining. As the course progressed we added more scaffolds as needed. Students gained valuable experience in problem creating and solving and began to see that math was much more flexible than they previously thought. Whereas before they thought of math as worksheets and correct answers, they came to see math as a creative process that they could contribute to in the same way they could create their own texts.

A PARANOID READING OF SAME-SEX MARRIAGE

It was the end-of-term focus on same-sex marriage that made me the most paranoid about my study. There are many good reasons marriage is a controversial topic in queer communities. Some reasons include that it is patriarchal and heteronormative; it takes focus away from youth safety and other queer issues; it benefits cisgender people and those on the gender binary; it prioritizes monogamy, and mainstream LGB organizations raise money and bring attention to marriage at the detriment of the needs of diverse queer communities. I once used it as a quick example in a manuscript, and reviewers responded that I should take it out because of its controversy. Therefore, during my study, I worried that I was selling out by condoning a focus on same-sex marriage in the course. My paranoia was anticipatory, in that I was projecting my worry onto future scholarly encounters, anticipating the bad news of ill-received presentations and manuscripts from my colleagues. The idea of paranoia as anticipatory points out its temporality, its "unidirectionally future-oriented vigilance that burrows both backward and forward … paranoia requires that bad news be always already known" (Sedgwick, p. 130). A paranoid person anticipates the bad news that will come and is always waiting for it to be confirmed.

This worry and paranoia about same-sex marriage showed up in my field notes and reflections. During the second unit, when one group was reading about Christians' oppositions to same-sex marriage, I wrote:

> I am very interested to see how the gay marriage one goes—it was clear that at least Ashley thought the Christian arguments were ludicrous, and I'm sure the other 2 do as well or they wouldn't have picked it. Sum Dood [students chose their own pseudonyms] is in [the Gay-Straight Alliance] so that probably has an influence on his choice. Wonder if there will be room for queering, when I go around and talk to the groups. At least we're already learning a lot, I'll just have to keep reminding myself that when things continue to be messy. (reflection, September 24, 2014)

Here, it is evident I am trying to talk myself out of my own paranoia. I wanted to ensure that I was looking to answer my research question regarding queer pedagogy—Is there evidence of queering (both in the curriculum and in student work and conversations), as seen by: questioning norms, limits, ignorance, and reading practices, (Britzman) and the queering of everyday moments (DePalma)—and looking to view queering as a verb. I hoped that by asking students questions that challenged their thinking, personal knowledge, and belief boundaries, the study would be "successfully" queered.

To further my justification, this focus on same-sex marriage was timely. Due to circuit court decisions in the fall, same-sex marriage became legal in our state while the class was unfolding. The school was founded on Quaker beliefs of inclusion, and because of this many queer parents sent their children to this school. The middle and high schools had active GSAs and regularly participated in local queer events including marching in the Pride parade. When same-sex marriage became legal, the school used their already-scheduled dance as a celebration. As such, it was a topic the students were already excited about and discussing and so it seemed a natural inclusion in our curriculum. However, my paranoid internal critic was taking the form of imagined queer scholars who were combative and unforgiving, and I anticipated future academic humiliation and shame. I imagined the queer police showing up in the classroom and berating me for not engaging the students in a discussion critiquing the institution of marriage, pointing out that marriage is oppressive, or asking them what issues they thought were equally or more important to queer communities than marriage. This paranoia is evident in a field note from that time:

> Morgan and I had already discussed doing something with LGBT rights [for the last unit], as that's something a majority of the class is interested in. With recent developments on marriage equality, this seems like a perfect topic. There are already many short articles I've seen that we could use, and existing charts, graphs, and maps that will work to give them some data, at least initially. Also, since it is developing right now, it will hopefully be exciting to be working on something that is unfolding currently. We could even ask [the GSA] advisor if she has talked about this in the club meetings and has any ideas. We could introduce the topic on a Tuesday [the class was held weekly on Tuesday and Thursday], and demonstrate a math problem creation and solving from this topic. As far as "queer" goes, this is a heavily debated topic and one that many queer activists see as heteronormative. But, it is what the kids are interested in and it's something that is accessible to them, which to me is more important than trying to make everything radical or the queerest of the queer. (field note, October 7, 2014)

Looking back, it is telling of my anticipatory views and concern for legitimacy that in my own field notes and reflections I was addressing imagined queer critics. Sedgwick addresses this aspect of paranoia when she describes it as a theory of negative affects. This means that "the only sense in which [the paranoid] may strive for positive affect at all is for the shield which it promises against humiliation" (Tomkins, 1963, pp. 458–459, as cited in Sedgwick, p. 136). By indulging in paranoia and anticipating the worst, the subject believes he or she can save him- or herself from future moments of humiliation. My writing was defensive as

I justified my choices to those internal critics and explained why it was acceptable to talk about an un-queer topic in a class based on queer pedagogy. I do still think it was important to talk about same-sex marriage with the students, though now I can be amused at myself as well as paranoid.

Yet despite these wild dreams of censure, I did not engage in those critical conversations with students. I felt I would be breaking their hearts if I told them some queer people do not believe in marriage at all. After talking with Morgan midterm, my co-researcher and I found out that some parents and students were complaining about the emotional heaviness of the course, and we all decided to focus on something positive to end the class on a good note. We wanted to show the students that social justice activism can lead to positive change. Thus, after several weeks of discussing heavy topics for which there were no simple solutions, I wanted to let the students celebrate a moment of triumph, however controversial and limited, for local queer communities. Frankly, I wanted a moment of rest and celebration myself. While the students had become increasingly comfortable with math and social problems without solutions, I wanted them to have this small solution to finish our class.

There were a few times where I engaged in more critical conversations with students about queer issues. Once, during the second unit, the group working on healthcare decided to focus on LGBT people and found survey data about trans* peoples' healthcare experiences. They were surprised and saddened by the discrimination trans* people described and also confused as to how it happened. I engaged them in conversation where we talked about the subtle and not so subtle ways that doctors might discriminate against trans* people, and I shared stories I had read or heard. Another time, when we asked the students to conduct calculations based on polling data,

> I asked if they knew what [the state] includes in their non-discrimination law. They named all the usual inclusions, and I told them they were correct except that [the state] doesn't protect for sexual orientation, gender identity, or gender expression. [My co-researcher] asked how gender was defined, and I said as male and female, as there no protection for trans people. … Then Sum Dood asked what do trans people have on their licenses, and I explained that it was their legal sex, but if you have a gender-affirming surgery … then you can bring a note from your doctor and get it changed.[2] But if you're in the middle, or don't want to specify, that's not an option. I'm glad that they're thinking of these things. I also explained how some people may not want to change it, and used the example of a trans man still needing "female" medical care, and needing their license to say F so that it would be covered [by insurance]. I also said I've heard of people just getting a new license and checking the different box and that going through, and how maybe sometimes it depends on who you see at the office and how carefully they're checking everything. I'm always glad when I get to discuss these things as they come up, and am glad they ask these questions. (field note, October 28, 2014)

This conversation was not "the queerest of the queer" perhaps, but it did give the students a better understanding of trans* peoples' experiences. From talking with the students, I knew that they had fairly clear understandings of lesbian, gay, and bisexual identities but did not know much about transgender identities or people who did not fall on the gender binary. We did not talk about these identities as categories and how they can be pulled apart, as the students were not ready. They needed a basic understanding before they could have a queered understanding, which is something I was realizing as the course progressed. It was this queering of daily moments (DePalma) that made me feel more confident and less paranoid that I was upholding at least some of the queer ideals I value.

CONCLUSION

It is not surprising that a graduate student would feel paranoid about her dissertation. It is a burden felt by many graduate students as they work to prove themselves worthy of inclusion in academia generally and their fields particularly. Some of this paranoia is justified and even encouraged, as advisors and mentors constantly push their students to question their methods and analyses and strengthen their scholarly rigor. However, I think my own paranoia was increased because of the queer nature of my project and my field. When Sedgwick wrote about a paranoid reading practice, she was referring in part to a phenomenon present in antihomophobic work. Drawing from psychoanalytic studies, she points out that paranoia that comes from a repression of homosexual desire teaches us more about the systemic oppression of homophobia and heterosexism than homosexuality itself. Further, she asserts that because of this ongoing connection between paranoia and homosexuality "it may have been structurally inevitable that the reading practices that became most available and fruitful in antihomophobic work would often in turn have been paranoid ones" (p. 127). Whether one is repressing one's own sexuality or not, in this analysis antihomophobic activists must always engage with the paranoid. According to Sedgwick's logic, queer scholars and activists cannot escape this paranoia in our own work.

Near the end of my study, I had the fortunate experience of talking about my work with a top scholar in queer theory and education. When I told her that I was using her tenets in a classroom she was quick to point out that they were never meant to be practices and were instead intended to interrogate pedagogy. I laughed at myself, and told her that I knew that but wanted to try them anyway. I also asked what she thought of talking about same-sex marriage with the students, and if that was counter-productive to the goals of queer pedagogy. She was dismissive of my worries, calling the opposition to same-sex marriage a concern of the younger generation and emphasizing that older generations of queer people had fought hard for that right. I have heard similar counter-arguments to queer marriage opposition before, that older generations of queer activists feel younger generations take their work for granted, perhaps because today's youth have more examples of queer people in mainstream media (Kunkle, 2015). This conversation helped lower my paranoia and reminded me that there is not one monolithic opinion in queer scholarship. Indeed, such a thing would be very un-queer.

As my research study was ending and I discussed my worries and shared data with my advisor, I gained more clarity on the queer nature of my work. Though the paranoia remained, by seeing the gains in abstract thought made by the students, my worrying lessened and imagined critics grew quieter. After the last day of class, I wrote this analytic reflection:

> The queering is not just an examination of their [student's] ignorance, but also the boundaries I had (through my research questions so closely aligned to the literature) of the study. Having [students] conceptualize of math in a new way, not just of social justice or its uses, was something beyond our expectations that opens up a lot of possibility for growth and change. I was so focused on seeing if their work matched the criteria of critical literacy and critical math that I may have missed this other phenomenon that doesn't fit into those narrowly-defined categories, had we not asked the students to reflect on their own experience. (reflection, November 14, 2014).

As I noted, my own queer paranoia was initially blinding me to the data and the richness of student experience. While at first I was looking for evidence that closely aligned or countered with the literature of my various theoretical frameworks, what I found was something in between. Thus, rather than remaining vigilant about looking for evidence of tenets of queer pedagogy from the literature, I opened my eyes to tenets emerging from my own data. Such a transformation in thought is likely true of most dissertation studies and I had to let go of my queer paranoia to go through this change. While my paranoia-induced imagined critics are still present, they are not as loud now. I hope they remain subdued enough to continue to encourage my internal reflection but do not paralyze me with paranoia, as I work toward finishing my dissertation and continue in my academic career.

NOTES

1. All names are pseudonyms.
2. After researching this later, I learned that you first must change your birth certificate, then bring this to the licensing office. Citation omitted so the location will remain anonymous.

REFERENCES

Britzman, D. (1995). Is there a queer pedagogy? Or stop reading straight. *Educational Theory, 45*(2), 151–165.

DePalma, R. (2010). The no outsiders project: In search of queer primary pedagogies. *Transformations: The Journal of Inclusive Scholarship & Pedagogy, 21*(2), 47–58.

Kemmis, S., & McTaggart, R. (2005). Communicative action and the public sphere. N. K. Denzin & Y. S. Lincoln (Eds.), *The Sage handbook of qualitative research* (3rd ed., pp. 559–603). Thousand Oaks, CA: Sage.

Kunkle, F. (2015, June 26). Older LGBT people say Supreme Court decision on gay marriage long overdue. *The Washington Post.* Retrieved from http://www.washingtonpost.com/local/social-issues/older-lgbt-people-say-supreme-court-decision-on-gay-marriage-long-overdue/2015/06/26/50cfbbd8-1c4d-11e5-bd7f-4611a60dd8e5_story.html

Miller, D. A. (1988). *The novel and the police.* Oakland: University of California Press.

Noblit, G. W., Flores, S. Y., & Murillo, E. G. (2004). *Postcritical ethnography: Reinscribing critique.* Cresskill, NJ: Hampton.

Sedgwick, E. K. (2003). *Touching feeling: Affect, pedagogy, performativity.* Durham, NC: Duke University Press.

Tomkins, S. (1963). *Affect imagery consciousness: Vol. 2, The negative affects.* New York: Springer.

CHAPTER THREE

Reconciling the Personal and Professional: Coming Out From the Classroom Closet

RYAN BURNS AND JANET D. JOHNSON

In this chapter, we (Ryan, a high school English teacher, and Janet, a teacher educator) dialogue about Ryan's experiences as a gay man teaching for social justice. Ryan was in Janet's first class of teacher candidates at Rhode Island College and has taught since 2007. Seeking personal and professional safety based on his sexual and political identities, Ryan has taught in four different school districts. Janet has continued her advocacy work for teachers and students at RIC, inviting Ryan and other teachers to participate in various research and professional development endeavors.

Over the years, our roles have shifted from professor (Janet) and student (Ryan) to college supervisor and cooperating teacher, to colleagues, and, finally, to friends. In this piece, we explore two critical incidents that illustrate the complexities Ryan has faced during his teaching journey and how conversations with Janet helped theorize those experiences. We chose the term "LGBT" instead of queer because Ryan identifies as gay. We are aware that this is a political as well as personal choice, but we believe it is important to stay true to his language.

WHO WE ARE

I (Ryan) am a White gay male who grew up with my sister in a single-mother household in an urban ring community. While I was not out at the time, I often associated with peers in high school who were socially, racially, and otherwise marginalized. I purposely chose to sit next to one of the few openly gay students. Although my courage and voice were underdeveloped, I could not ignore the abuse he faced. Still, I was not prepared to identify as gay. It was not until my undergraduate years as an English and Secondary Education major that I found my personal and professional voice, and more important, learned to use that voice.

I (Janet) am a White, heterosexual, middle class female who felt no sense of belonging growing up in a conservative Midwestern suburb. I had little exposure to any marginalized cultures but unconsciously sought them out because the expectations of my own were so stultifying. It was not until I became a teacher at an alternative high school that I learned about difference, compassion, and acceptance from my disenfranchised students. This led to graduate school and an academic understanding of critical theory and literacy, including teaching and advocating for social justice.

This chapter emanates from a research project that I (Janet) began eight years ago on the identities, beliefs, pedagogies, and tensions of English teachers committed to social justice. This group presented at local and national conferences, but I became concerned that I was doing research on, rather than with, the teachers. My interviews with Ryan led us to thinking about, together and separately, what it means to be a gay teacher (Ryan) and a teacher of teachers who identify as LGBT, openly or not (Janet).

Teaching in the era of accountability is risky business (Cochran-Smith & Lytle, 2009), and for teachers who identify as LGBT, the dangers are both personal and professional. Ryan's mother was one of the first to point out the risk he was taking, fearing that he would be victimized in ways she could feel if not necessarily name. Connell explores "a fundamental incompatibility between the demands of current LGBT politics, which center on the ethos of gay pride, and the norms of teaching professionalism, which expect teachers (gay and lesbian teachers in particular) to be cautious about their personal—and sexual—lives" (2015, p. 3). It is work to stay closeted, and it is work to come out.

I (Ryan) found it increasingly difficult to reconcile my personal and professional life. In an attempt to protect my personhood and my livelihood, I stifled and smothered myself; I became an inauthentic individual, an inauthentic teacher. I ask students to be "real"; I needed to do the same. Even as I was out to family and friends, I kept my sexuality private in my professional life until later in my career, which we describe below.

As Ryan's practicum professor, I (Janet) was naive when it came to the political nature of my candidates' sexual identities and how they might impact their professional lives and pedagogies. I struggled to know when and where to position myself, not wanting to assume that my support was needed but also wanting to be clearly available and open.

"I CRANKED UP THE SOCIAL JUSTICE DIAL A LITTLE BIT"

After a year at an urban school where his sexual identity and social justice teaching were not remarked upon, Ryan took a position at a suburban school. He immediately recognized the students' sense of White privilege and, thus, felt urgency in teaching them about racism, classism, sexism, and heterosexism within the prescribed curriculum.

The principal's response was swift and shocking: "Ryan, this stuff doesn't even belong in a high school health curriculum." I felt vulnerable. I felt my face burning red with anger. And yet, I sat in my chair and listened. "I would like to think that we do not need to be addressing this issue in class," he continued. But we do, I answered confidently in my head. His voice became a faint buzz in the background as I stared past him out the window. I kept telling myself that his narrow perspective was not a personal attack on me. My attempts, however, were unsuccessful. It was deeply personal.

Here is how it happened: My students and I had been analyzing Dante's *The Inferno*. We framed our work around essential questions such as, "What types of journeys do individuals go on and why?" and "What is the 'dark wood' in your life?" These questions brought the students deeper into the world of the text because of their personal natures. During class discussion, a student mentioned coming out and the darkness we as individuals have to go through in order to come to a place of light in our lives. I was both completely taken aback and excited by this contribution to the conversation. Students were willing to go there with me.

I used this moment in our classroom exchange as a springboard to the short story "Am I Blue?" and pushed the topic further by distributing a handful of questions from the Heterosexual Questionnaire. My goal was to highlight the point the student was making about issues of necessary journeys and darkness. I wanted students to think about their reactions to the questions without answering them, and how these reactions might connect to the unit's essential questions and *The Inferno*.

At that moment though, sitting in the principal's office, I saw that the school functioned as a system of power, surging with heteronormativity and ensuring the survival of the status quo. Yet, despite my temptation to be radical and vocal, I backed down. It was not a battle I could win. As a third year, untenured teacher, I was acutely aware of my vulnerable status. I was not out; even so, and like it or not, my sexuality was front and center.

Ryan told me (Janet) about the incident with his principal when I interviewed him for a research project on agentive teachers. He realized he had misread the system, saying, "Oh crap, this is a job. I'm not in college any more. You know, I can't just do this stuff." These feelings of professional vulnerability led him to "switch gears completely" as he "went … totally literal … multiple choice." This impacted his sense of identity as a social justice educator. "I felt like I shut down completely … I felt like my demeanor changed." This realization was deeply unsettling. "It is a part of you, not just 'I do social justice,'" Ryan explained.

Ryan also felt vulnerable in that, by teaching a story with a homosexual protagonist, his own sexuality might be exposed. During this time, he took the position of allowing students and colleagues to make up their minds about his sexuality, leaving them to question "Is he or isn't he?" Ryan, by nature a private person, was mindful of what Connell calls "the clashing expectations of [gay] pride and professionalism" (2015, p. 5).

As I (Ryan) reflect over the past eight years as a high school English educator, I would go back to that anxiety-filled moment when I was in the principal's office. I would ask him the pointed questions I am asking myself now and show him a snapshot of the future. Bullying is not an option. Suicide is not an option. How can we talk about issues that matter if we cannot name them?

But how could I find ways to work within and against the very system that privileges some and marginalizes others? Was a commitment to critical pedagogy and social justice worth the risk? How could I protect my personal and professional identity and integrity?

Throughout my time from high school to college to teaching, I found myself exploring old and discovering new layers of who I was as a teacher and as a person. And while I was relatively safe in my personal life, having been out as a gay man for almost five years, my professional life did not feel as safe. This negotiation of identity/identities was still new to me as a beginning teacher.

"I'M REALLY LIVING WHAT I BELIEVE IN"

After three years at Washington High School, the position was cut due to budget constraints. During the summer of 2011, Ryan obtained a new position in a more affluent suburban community.

When school started, I quickly learned that East Windsor was a safe place for me personally. The school had a thriving Gay-Straight Alliance (GSA) and the advisor was the English Department chair. Students, including a significant number of ally members, frequented the GSA meetings to participate in local and national events sponsored by GLSEN, including Trans Remembrance Day and working on the National AIDS quilt with AIDS Care Ocean State.

These events at the high school were juxtaposed with national news reports of LGBT teen suicides. I wondered about my personal safety as an adult faculty member. Could I grow in this school and community as an out educator? As I developed relationships with my English Department colleagues and others in the building, I saw and heard many references to marital partners: stories during lunch, pictures on the teacher desk, and weekend plans. I found myself quiet during these moments because I still was unsure of how I would be perceived or supported as a gay man, even though I was single at the time.

That winter, in January 2012, a friend mentioned that a local magazine had a special edition each February for singles in the southern New England area. Ten nominated participants would be selected as Providence's "Super Singles" for 2012. There would be a photo shoot for publication in the magazine and website as well as a celebration mixer. Despite my availability and eligibility as a single gay twenty-something, I was less than keen on the idea. I finally gave in. What harm would there be? What was the likelihood of being selected? I was shocked to receive an email from the editor expressing her congratulations for my selection as one of the ten "Super Singles."

I decided to participate and was initially not overly concerned with the impact this might have on my professional career. That anxiety would settle in later when I had to provide personal information and anecdotes about myself in order for the editor to construct a profile on me; I remember feeling tense in the days that followed. How accurate would the profile be if I didn't mention the fact that I was attracted to men? I struggled. I reflected. I couldn't get out of my own head. I reached out to friends, some gay and some straight. My sister, also an English educator, gave me perspective and grounded me. She reminded me of my students, past and present. She reminded me that I could be a role model for those students who need to see positive and healthy representations of out men and women. "Ryan," she said, "it's off with your head or off with your f*cking head." She was right. What of my students? What of those bullied youth who took their lives because they didn't feel safe or supported? As a soon to be 30-year-old man, what did I have to lose? That's all it took for me to be truthful about my sexuality in the profile.

Soon after the publication was released, I waited. The sky didn't fall. My school didn't go up in flames. I was in the clear.

Several weeks later, my department chair approached me and offered her support and congratulations. I was mortified and relieved at the same time. She mentioned that some students found the website while Googling me. A former lawyer and a person with gay family members, she brought the matter to the attention of the building administration in order to ensure that I was protected. I knew then that I had an ally. At that moment, I had come out for the second time in my life to open hearts and minds.

This was a sea change for him. Ryan told Janet,

> I'm really living what I believe in and teach more than what I did before because this was never out there, I was never out there. So … when I talk about identity now or when I talk about power, it's like a new meaning has been brought on.

For Ryan, teaching for social justice now went beyond the abstract and theoretical to the personal. He felt better able to support students who identified as LGBT because they knew he was living what he was teaching. "They know that I'm still Mr. Burns. It humanizes [homosexuality] in many ways."

Even as he was feeling safe in his sexual identity, his identity as a social justice educator was called into question by the same department chair who supported his coming out. The English curriculum was based on the canon, and many teachers taught from what Freire (1997) called the banking model, in which teachers were the experts and students the novices. Ryan was critiqued for his discussion-oriented classes and did not feel safe teaching critical material. As a result, he sought and found a more compatible district.

"THERE'S A CERTAIN AMOUNT OF RESPONSIBILITY"

Ryan's experience demonstrates the complexity that LGBT teachers face, especially when they are critically oriented. The "heterosexual bribe" (Sumara & Davis, 1999, p. 192) becomes a professional bribe. Evans (2002) describes two main threads in the current teaching discourse: that of a role model and that of professionalism. In both cases, the range of what is acceptable is limited, and the tensions between the "good teacher" discourse and the LGBT discourse are places of negotiation. Ryan's navigation of these discourses changed according to his comfort level with the school context and pedagogical goals.

Ryan has not gone back to the explicit critical teaching that put him in the principal's office many years ago. This choice is due not only to a sense of professional vulnerability but also to a different perspective on what it means to be a social justice educator. He has become increasingly comfortable with the tension between his laid-back personality and the expectations of gay pride and social justice education, both of which privilege a louder, more robust stance. Mary Rose O'Reilley calls this "the struggle all of us go through between the norms of our discipline and the demands of who we are" (1998, p. 32). In this case, the norms of gay pride are incompatible with the norms of teacher professionalism (Connell). The norms of current social justice teaching practices are at odds with his desire to provide a different kind of action agenda (Brass, 2014).

Because Ryan wants his students to "dig their own paths," his teaching has become less explicitly critical. He told Janet, "I'm aware of the agenda but don't need to be on the soapbox … [I let] the students guide [me] to where they need to be." Thus, he moved from explicit social justice teaching to teaching traditionally and now is in a learner-centered place where he asks students to question their assumptions. Being gay and teaching for social justice do not have to mean confrontation: "If I'm doing the thinking, doing, and talking, then that's a problem." BUT "there is a certain amount of responsibility that comes with it." Thus, he acknowledges a dissonance—one with which he will continue to wrestle. As O'Reilley puts it, teachers can "respect a person's ability to reenter his or her own life and reconfigure and transform it" (p. 32). He has moved from the soapbox to creating space for his students. Teaching for social justice, gay or not, does not have to look one way.

As a teacher educator, I (Janet) know there are multiple ways to be critical, and while my own stance is to confront inequity head-on, I am also aware that teachers work within systems where they have limited agency. In contrast, I have the relative safety of tenure and academic freedom. As Rose writes, "'Critical' does not mean pronouncing guilty verdicts so much as opening space for different kinds of judgment. … Its aim is not to predetermine judgment but to make judgment possible" (1996, p. 122, cited in Brass, 2014). These judgments take place within complex systems and dominant discourses, and teachers like Ryan need to feel a sense of safety as they navigate these spaces personally, professionally, and pedagogically.

In addition to supporting candidates' varied stances toward social justice, I want to more deliberately and explicitly support LGBT candidates and teachers. My candidates and I already use multiple critical lenses (Appleman, 2009) to read literature and plan lessons. We question dominant discourses of schooling and how students are positioned in specific ways by physical structures and language. We discuss the emotional work of teaching and relationships with students and others.

However, I (Janet) can more explicitly take a queer perspective. In addition to identifying myself as an ally, I can provide texts with LGBT themes and characters and critique texts in general by asking how the audience is constructed. Evans also suggests having candidates identify heteronormative discourses in their field placements. In doing all of these things, ambivalence and curiosity may arise as to how sexual identities are part of discourse, even in schools where sexuality, in theory, is absent but is in fact very much present.

It is easy for me (Ryan) to now recognize how I have often compartmentalized my life: separating personal and professional for my own safety as a novice teacher in 2007. The longer I taught, though, the harder it was to stay silent. I had to walk the walk and talk the talk. It took almost ten years of reflection and growth to pinpoint how and where my sexuality as a gay man intersected with other aspects of my life, namely my professional identity and career as an English educator. I am now more aware of the connection between my life outside of school and my life in school. For years, I negotiated my sexuality through silence in order to divert attention from myself. Making otherwise private and personal pieces of oneself public and available takes courage, especially within the current context of public education where the dominant discourse works to have educators like me removed from practice. As soon I came out, I became vulnerable. I am at peace with that vulnerability now.

Schools are conservative, heteronormative places. Teachers who identify as other, whether in their teaching beliefs or in their sexuality, are at risk. Connell notes that even as being gay is becoming more accepted, even celebrated, there is also still significant antigay harassment and discrimination. The awareness of his professional vulnerability has led Ryan to disrupt heteronormative narratives in some ways and not in others. His experiences convey the nonprescriptive nature of how LGBT teachers negotiate their identities and professional paths. Janet's bearing witness to Ryan's journey has developed her awareness and commitment to being an ally to LGBT candidates and teachers.

REFERENCES

Appleman, D. (2009) *Teaching literary theory to adolescents* (2nd ed.). Urbana, IL: NCTE.

Brass, J. (2014). Activist teacher education, Foucault, and the case of two English teachers. *English Education,* 46(3), 216–246.

Cochran-Smith, M., & Lytle, S. (2009). *Inquiry as stance: Practitioner research for the next generation.* New York: Teachers College Press.

Connell, C. (2015). *School's out: Gay and lesbian teachers in the classroom.* Oakland: University of California Press.

Evans, K. (2002). *Negotiating the self: Identity, sexuality, and emotion in learning to teach.* New York: Routledge.

Freire, P. (1997). *Pedagogy of the oppressed.* New York: Continuum.

O'Reilley, M. R. (1998). *Radical presence.* Portsmouth, NH: Boynton/Cook.

Rose, N. (1996). Power and subjectivity: Critical history and psychology. In C. F. Graumann & K. J. Gergen (Eds.), *Historical dimensions of psychological discourse* (pp. 103–124). Cambridge: Cambridge University Press.

Sumara, D., & Davis, B. (1999). Interrupting heteronormativity: Toward a queer curriculum theory. *Curriculum Inquiry,* 29(2), 191–208.

Part 2:
Queered Tensions: Beyond the Academy

CHAPTER FOUR

Remaining Stubbornly Faithful: What Queering Academia Does to Queer Teacher-Scholars

SARA STALEY AND BETHY LEONARDI

> I just made a t-shirt that says, "Feelings are not the enemy." I guess that's what [my work is] about—just being expressive with your feelings and the ways that we're culturally expected to closet our emotions.
>
> —ANDREA GIBSON

As queer teacher-scholars, we often turn to Gibson's work because of the masterful ways in which the poet unleashes feelings and lets them spill all over the place. (For those unfamiliar, Gibson is a queer poet-activist whose work explores trauma, gender, sexuality, white privilege, war, love, and feelings.) So as we considered where to begin, Gibson's theme that "feelings are not the enemy" seemed fitting. The research that informs this chapter is part of a larger project in which we set out to explore: What does queering academia do to queer teacher-scholars? Specifically, we engaged narrative inquiry to mine our experiences navigating the margins of institutional life in academia while advancing queer liberation in education spaces. Currently, our collaborative work focuses on supporting educational communities to create safer schools that affirm queer identities and preparing educators with knowledge, skills, and habits of heart and mind necessary for disrupting heteronormativity. Cultivating university-school partnerships has been critical to that queer endeavor. By "queering academia," then, we mean to emphasize that the object of this inquiry is our own lived experiences doing queer/ing work as queer people, and also that the institutional contexts we navigate, namely K–12 schools and the academy, are profoundly shaped by historical silence around gender and sexual diversity (Bryan, 2012; Meyer, 2010), heterosexism, and homophobia.

We were motivated to pursue this inquiry because there was something distinctly visceral that characterized our experiences doing queer/ing work, and we were closeting those emotional provocations. Further, those provocations seemed importantly shaped by the ways our queer identities have been directly implicated by the work. Building on the premise that feelings are not the enemy, we argue that the role of emotion in scholarly engagement that aims toward activism and anti-oppression constitutes a critical site of inquiry. Toward that end, we have taken the affective dimensions of our experiences as our starting point and brought the personal and political to bear on a narrative analysis of what queering academia *feels* like. Central to our framework is Ann Cvetkovich's (2003, 2012) queer approach to understanding trauma, which frames depression not as a medical condition to be pathologized, but as a socially constructed phenomenon with cultural, historical, and political roots.

In this chapter, we share what we found by tracing strands of heartbreak, self-perceived failure, and despair, as well as moments of hopeful possibility embedded in our narratives. We begin by elaborating the theoretical perspectives that informed our approach.

A QUEER PERSPECTIVE ON TRAUMA, NEGATIVE EMOTIONS, AND POLITICAL DEPRESSION

We wish to clarify that we use *queer* to signify antinormative sexual and gender identities that resist fixed classification and to situate our theoretical assumptions that gender and sexuality are fluid, expansive, constructed, and performative (Butler, 1990; Jagose, 1996; Pinar, 1998; Sedgwick, 1990), and subjects and subjectivities are contingent, unstable, and "perpetually becoming" (Browne & Nash, 2010, p. 1). Heeding Kumashiro's (2001) caution that *queer* can also erase (p. 4) gender and racial differences, we acknowledge that our self-identifications as queer teacher-scholars obscure that we are also white women and that our genders and race have powerfully shaped what queering academia feels like.

Bringing those queer perspectives to bear, our approach was informed by Cvetkovich's framework of trauma and political depression. Cvetkovich (2003) frames trauma as:

> a social and cultural discourse that emerges in response to the demands of grappling with the psychic consequences of historical events. Defined culturally rather than clinically, trauma becomes … a central category for looking at the intersections of emotional and social processes along with the intersections of history and memory. (p. 18)

From this perspective, catastrophic events remain obvious sites of trauma, but trauma is also recognized in its more mundane variations because, as Cvetkovich asserts, it is felt and experienced in ordinary moments of everyday life. Shaped by queer perspectives (e.g., Berlant, 2011; Boler, 1999; Butler, 1997, 2006; Sedgwick, 2003) and the feminist mantra that the personal is political, this approach to understanding trauma forges connections across everyday experiences of pain, including personal accounts of depression—or "feeling bad" (Cvetkovich, 2003, p. 3)—and the broader landscape of social, political, and historical ills (e.g., racism, homophobia, war). Cvetkovich (2012) argues that negative feelings such as despair, inertia, anxiety, and exhaustion, manifested in everyday life and often clinically diagnosed as depression, can be produced by complicated social problems and political disappointments. Central to that argument is the concept of *political depression*, or "the sense that customary forms of political response, including direct action and critical analysis, are no longer working either to change the world or to make us feel better" (p. 1). Bringing a political analysis to bear on depression involves finding community and public forums for expressing negative feelings that, as Cvetkovich notes, can "feel so debilitating, so far from hopefulness about the future and activism" (p. 2), in the service of generating new ways of thinking about hope, social transformation, and agency. It is in those spaces that cultivating hope becomes possible.

Cvetkovich provides us an analytic framework for exploring connections between our own moments of "feeling bad" and broader social, cultural, and historical contexts of silence, heterosexism, and homophobia. This queer perspective enables us to depathologize our own negative feelings and frame them not as liabilities but as resources for analysis and political action. Additionally, it enables us to forge connections across the personal and political, public and private, hope and despair, theory and affect, and to resist constructing those categories as reductive binaries. Finally, leveraging political depression has prompted us to ask of the emotionality of our experiences where it is possible to foster a hopefulness that "remains stubbornly faithful for no good reason" (Cvetkovich, 2012, p. 135).

METHODOLOGY

Narrative Inquiry: To address our research question, we engaged narrative inquiry as research method (Connelly & Clandinin, 1990). As a social phenomenon, narrative provides a way of characterizing human experience; as an analytic tool, narrative provides a way of studying that experience. Narrative inquiry frames everyday experience as a "source of important knowledge and understanding" (Clandinin & Rosiek, 2007, p. 42). Moreover, it carries a history of "listening to previously silenced voices" (Chase, 2005, p. 655).

Research Context: For Bethy, doing queer/ing work began in the fall of 2010, while she was still completing doctoral coursework; for Sara, it began in the fall of 2012, as she foregrounded queer issues while teaching a secondary language arts methods course. That year also marked the beginning of our collaborative efforts doing queer/ing work, which have involved acting as guest speakers in numerous undergraduate- and graduate-level classes; supporting faculty to take up queer topics in their courses; hosting campus-based institutes of professional learning for in-service teachers; and partnering with local districts to provide professional development for educators and district leadership. To date, we've worked with nearly 2,000 educators.

Data Collection and Analysis: Many of the experiences described above were connected to processes of conducting qualitative research, so we had an archive of written reflections, field notes, and teaching journals on which to draw for the purposes of exploring our research question. Because narrative inquiry frames human experience as always partial, "as lived in the midst, [and] as always unfolding over time, in diverse social contexts and places" (Caine, Estefan, & Clandinin, 2013, p. 575), we treated some of that writing generated prior to the launch of this study as important data sources. Additionally, for four months, each of us kept a journal in which we wrote in the genre of narrative with an eye to our organizing question. The content of those entries was informed by the everyday goings-on of our lives doing queer/ing work and by our review of narrative writing generated as part of previous research efforts. For example, Bethy reviewed journal entries and field notes collected as part of her dissertation, and Sara reviewed writing generated during a semester-long study of a teaching experience. In total, Bethy produced 33 entries (30 pages) and Sara, 17 entries (64 pages).

In our initial passes through those data, we noticed the presence of negative emotions—what Cvetkovich might call moments of "feeling bad." We also noticed that our narratives constructed the experience of doing queer/ing work as intensely personal, and yet intimately connected to something bigger than ourselves. We leveraged *political depression* as a tool to analyze connections between our negative feelings and that "something bigger than"—that is, the social, cultural, historical, and institutional contexts in which those feelings were embodied—and to mine our experiences for hopeful possibility. In our secondary passes, we asked: Where do our moments of "feeling bad" emerge, and under what circumstances? Where do our narratives point to moments of hopeful possibility? From those secondary passes, we constructed three themes: "emotional tolls," "sacrificing integrity," and "queerness as saving grace." We define and elaborate those themes below.

FINDINGS

Our analysis suggests that in doing queer/ing work as queer teacher-scholars, there were *emotional tolls*. That theme represents the embodied, viscerally experienced nature of feeling bad. Because emotionality was central to our research question and analytic lenses, that theme is inextricably linked to the other two. Therefore, in our discussion of the other themes, we underscore the emotional tolls of the work. Our analysis also constructed links between moments of feeling bad and acts of surrendering, refusing, or denying an integral part of ourselves, including our queer identities or a heartfelt emotional expression such as uncertainty, self-doubt, anger, and heartbreak, for fear of losing our audiences. These instances of *sacrificing integrity* often sat in relationship with desires to advance larger goals of equity and anti-oppression. Finally, we identified *queerness as saving grace*, which captures how hopeful possibility appeared thematically in the data—that is, moments in which queerness was, at once, a source of our emotional pain, strength, and comfort. This theme also points to how we locate our teacher-scholar selves in the struggle for queer liberation.

We employ narrative in our presentation of findings below. To contextualize the nature of *sacrificing integrity*, Sara draws from analysis of her entries; to contextualize *queerness as saving grace*, Bethy draws from hers.

SACRIFICING INTEGRITY

Graduate school marked a pivotal transition in my life: coming out as queer. Waking up to queerness initiated a self-conscious realization of how negotiable it had been in my teaching and research. Once "awake," I (Sara) began foregrounding queer issues in my work. It was the only way to find integrity. Tracing the emotional rhythms across my narratives, there were painful pulsations around my experience, putting that commitment to work in the methods course I was teaching. I kept a journal that semester, and reviewing its entries, the salience of feeling bad is striking. After receiving students' end-of-semester feedback, I wrote that I felt "like a failure" because several students reported not "learn[ing] enough 'methods'. … A few more pointed to the focus on LGBTQ material and inclusivity as 'disappointing' and coming at the expense of 'real' methods content" (June 25, 2013). One student wrote, "Talk about beating a dead horse." I took it personally.

Two years later, as part of this project, I reflected on why that semester incited in me such raw feelings of heartbreak. "The implications around my identity were different," I wrote, mostly because of "the gay thing," but also because of the anxiety surrounding the decision I made not to share my queer identity with my students. "Would they say that this was my 'agenda' and reject my invitations to learn about … advocate for and affirm queer youth?" I wondered. Recalling what it felt like to frame the course's queer emphasis, I wrote:

> I remember the warmth rise to my cheeks, hoping no one would call my bluff—ask me what my connection to these issues was, call me out for not being in my integrity as I implored the group to trust and accompany me as we charted this new terrain. … In writing this, I see a glaring contradiction. How could I have kept my identity and the impetus for my decision to foreground [queer issues] undercover while at the same time asking my students to do such vulnerable, discomforting work? How could I ask them to lean in when I could not? … In writing this, I also see that perhaps my biggest fear and critic was myself. But, moving through that semester was challenging. I remember sitting with the sinking feeling … that my students were wondering, *Why are we still talking about this gay stuff?* … I wonder why I didn't open up a conversation … around my hunches. I could have leveraged that conflict. … It's hard to have that kind of insight when you're taking up issues of equity and justice that implicate your own identity such that you (think you) have to cover who you are in order to advance the larger goal—or, at least that's what your novice-self thinks you have to do in order to make it through. (July 13, 2015)

In this example, "sacrificing integrity" was instantiated in the decision I made not to come out to my students—not to be forthcoming about what my personal stake was in reorganizing the methods curriculum, and to be compromised by the fear of being tagged as a graduate student with an "agenda." I'm certain there was some internalized homophobia at play that also prevented me from leading with integrity in that semester. Cvetkovich (2012) writes, "To feel that your work doesn't matter is to feel dead inside" (p. 18). To feel like you have to *deny* an integral part of your selfhood is to feel dead inside.

QUEERNESS AS SAVING GRACE

Throughout my narratives, I (Bethy) recognized that everyday instantiations of "feeling bad" have a past; they are connected to the histories and work of queer people who came before me. In the ways that the work hangs on my body, I carry that past. But the feelings also have a future. It's as if queer history and the future of queerness intersect in my daily experiences, because in some way, I feel like this work has the potential to change "the way things are," and that's where hope lands. These feelings are difficult to describe; they often surfaced in heartbreaking moments. During my dissertation study, examples were when Michael, an out, gay eighth grader went to school after weeks of refusing to go; when he tried to hurt himself; when kids teased him; and when he shared that he loved school and he had friends. In my narrative reflections, there is attention not only to Michael navigating school and self, but also to the collective struggle that comes with being othered and the need to "remain stubbornly faithful" (Cvetkovich, 2012, p. 135) to hopeful possibility. Those moments produce a certain grief *for those instances*—but also for the future of queerness, and for its rich and tragic past. In them, there is a delicate balance between how angry I am, how badly I feel, and how passionately I breathe because of that nexus. I share an example from June 2013:

> I read my first LGBT history book on the bus as I travelled … through Louisiana and Texas. I covered it with a cover from an old book … so no one would see it. I devoured it. There's something in the stories of people whose histories twist and turn, bump into the spaces where progress has yet to come … I read that book multiple times and cried each time—because of the deep sadness I felt for the ways the world throws people away, but also for the pride I felt being part of those people, being one of them. They grew me up—and their stories grew inside of me. … Those brave and angry and violently, loving souls. I am so indebted to them. I felt them on that bus in 1993, in my gut, my throat. … There is something to learning your history, to knowing where you come from—and as queer people we really don't know that history enough. … It's a tremendous and often silent struggle—so much love, and so much community, and so much loss … the subtleties, the sidesteps, the silences, the expectations to keep the peace, not be too out, not be out at all, for the sake of other people's comfort, their peace; that's the history in my bones. I can't unfeel that. There is a certain ache in the souls of people who have spent their lives trying to win.

Our framework has nudged us to ask where hope is possible. Throughout my reflections, hope was possible in moments where queerness hung heavily on my body, but also where it appeared as my saving grace, and where I felt part of something bigger than myself in the heaviness. Cvetkovich argues that negative emotions can be resources for political action, especially when shared in community. Throughout my data, this idea resonated. Remaining hopeful was directly tied to the collective ache of the past and future of queerness. There was a clear connection between the debt we owe to generations of queer folks who came before us and to the future of queer liberation; there was hope in that for me.

CONCLUSIONS

By exploring our felt experiences queering academia, we have used this forum as a public space in which to be expressive with our feelings in the service of building community, generating hope, and healing. But queer reflections like ours, rippled by emotionality, aren't often welcome in academic forums. Deliberately reflecting on what queering academia has felt like has deepened our understanding of how integral our moments of feeling bad have been to the nature of doing queer/ing work as queer people, and why we continue to do it in spite of emotional tolls. As our narratives suggest, emotional ripples were present throughout and surely shaped our subjectivities, so what are we to do with them if not write about them? We hope this inquiry has demonstrated the possibilities of embracing queer frameworks, like Cvetkovich's, and of inquiring into emotionality, or at least, giving it space to breathe in the work itself.

REFERENCES

Behar, R. (1996). *The vulnerable observer: Anthropology that breaks your heart.* Boston: Beacon.
Berlant, L. (2011). *Cruel optimism.* Durham, NC: Duke University Press.
Boler, M. (1999). *Feeling power: Emotions and education.* New York: Routledge.
Browne, K., & Nash, C. J. (2010). *Queer methods and methodologies: Intersecting queer theories and social science research.* Surrey, UK: Ashgate.
Bryan, J. (2012). *From the dress-up corner to the senior prom: Navigating gender and sexuality diversity in preK–12 schools.* Lanham, MD: Rowman & Littlefield Education.
Butler, J. (1990). *Gender trouble: Feminism and the subversion of identity.* New York: Routledge.
Butler, J. (1997). *The psychic life of power: Theories in subjection.* Stanford, CA: Stanford University Press.
Butler, J. (2006). *Precarious life: The powers of mourning and violence.* London: Verso.
Caine, V., Estefan, A., & Clandinin, D. J. (2013). A return to methodological commitment: Reflections on narrative inquiry. *Scandinavian Journal of Educational Research, 57*(6), 574–586.
Chase, S. E. (2005). Narrative inquiry: Multiple lenses, approaches, voices. In N. K. Denzin & Y. S. Lincoln (Eds.), *The handbook of qualitative research* (3rd ed., pp. 651–679). Thousand Oaks, CA: Sage.
Clandinin, J. D., & Rosiek, J. (2007). Mapping a landscape of narrative inquiry: Borderland, spaces and tensions. In D. Clandinin (Ed.), *Handbook of narrative inquiry: Mapping a methodology* (pp. 35–75). Thousand Oaks, CA: Sage.
Connelly, M. F., & Clandinin, J. D. (1990). Stories of experience and narrative inquiry. *Educational Researcher, 19*(5), 2–14.
Cvetkovich, A. (2003). *An archive of feelings: Trauma, sexuality, and lesbian public cultures.* Durham, NC: Duke University Press.
Cvetkovich, A. (2007). Public feelings. *South Atlantic Quarterly, 106*(3), 459–468.
Cvetkovich, A. (2012). *Depression: A public feeling.* Durham, NC: Duke University Press.
Gilbert, K. (2001). Introduction: Why are we interested in emotions? In K. R. Gilbert (Ed.), *The emotional nature of qualitative research* (pp. 3–15). Boca Raton, FL: CRC.
Jaggar, A. M. (1996). Love and knowledge: Emotion in feminist epistemology. In A. Garry & M. Pearsall (Eds.), *Women, knowledge, and reality: Explorations in feminist philosophy* (2nd ed., pp. 166–190). New York: Routledge.
Jagose, A. (1996). *Queer theory: An introduction.* New York: New York University Press.
Kumashiro, K. K. (2001). "Posts" perspectives on anti-oppressive education in social studies, English, mathematics, and science classrooms. *Educational Researcher, 30*(3), 3–12.
Leonardi, B. (2014). *Tilling the soil for LGBTQ inclusive policies: A case study of one school's attempt to bring policy into practice.* Unpublished doctoral dissertation, University of Colorado, Boulder.
Meyer, E. J. (2010). *Gender and sexual diversity in schools.* London: Springer.
Pinar, W. F. (Ed.). (1998). *Queer theory in education.* Mahwah, NJ: Lawrence Erlbaum.
Rager, K. B. (2005). Self-care and the qualitative researcher: When collecting data can break your heart. *Educational Researcher, 34*(4), 23–27.

Sedgwick, E. (1990). *Epistemology of the closet.* Berkeley, CA: University of California Press.

Sedgwick, E. (2003). *Touching feeling: Affect, pedagogy, performativity.* Durham, NC: Duke University Press.

Tillmann-Healy, L. M., & Kiesinger, C. E. (2001). Mirrors: Seeing each other and ourselves through fieldwork. In K. R. Gilbert (Ed.), *The emotional nature of qualitative research* (pp. 81–108). Boca Raton, FL: CRC.

CHAPTER FIVE

Inside. Out. Queer Time in Midcareer

MICHAEL BORGSTROM

During a recent bout of spring cleaning, I found myself rummaging through a box of souvenirs, grammar school artwork, assorted photographs, birthday cards, and the like—all relics of different times and places. Tucked within one of these piles was a typewritten note my eight-year-old self wrote to Parker Stevenson, the actor who portrayed Frank Hardy, the elder of the two Hardy boys, on the late-1970s television series *The Hardy Boys Mysteries*. Ostensibly a fan letter, it more nearly resembles a mash note. It reads in its entirety: "Dear Mr. Stevenson: How are you? My name is Michael. I really like you on the Hardy Boys. You are great, and you have good hair. Sincerely, Mike." On the bottom of the page, several spaces below the text, is the typewritten word "Transcript," followed by another caption: "Sent 5/3/78. Original on calligraphy. Parchment (yellow)."

Although I have no recollection of writing this note, its composition serves as a remarkably apt snapshot of a younger incarnation of myself. The tone is carefully polite, the sentiment appreciative yet measured, with only a sprinkling of adjectives and adverbs intended to communicate a not-too-fascinated interest. Even though I took care to compliment Mr. Stevenson's hair, the note's straightforward style (with its fussy punctuation and resolute lack of exclamation marks) is determinedly nonchalant, a juxtaposition encapsulated in the uneasy toggle between its formal introduction ("Michael") and strained attempt at a relaxed closing ("Mike"). This semi-public assertion of male-male appreciation, if not attraction, is complemented by the letter's rather nonnormative form. The word "transcript" at the end of the letter is a note to myself, a record that I sent the original correspondence on May 3, 1978. At the time, I was meticulous about transcribing copies of handwritten letters (with their dates) for my "files." The note, apparently, was penned in calligraphy on yellow parchment, and these details, too, jibe precisely with interests that absorbed me at that early age. I practiced calligraphy for hours on end after taking a class at a local community center, and parchment, to my mind, was simply the most appropriate material upon which to write with a calligraphic hand.

It is a very queer letter. Yet the queerness it records is not personally anticipatory. For while its sentiments would seem to invite a backward-looking knowing wink (young Michael/Mike simply doesn't understand what he's saying yet), the note itself is neither proto-homosexual (an appreciation for good hair does not equate with desire) nor proto-gay (parchment and calligraphy are no more the marks of a dandified sensibility than were that decade's admiration of platform shoes and bell-bottoms). Here, then, neither theme nor taste indexes queerness, especially since the elder Hardy Boy likely received scads of similar notes from young admirers. Still, in the archive that constitutes my pre-adolescent files, the letter does mark itself as unusual in terms of style and approach, attributes that reverberate across many years in many different contexts. In particular, the letter's odd, tentative gesture toward personal connection—withholding as much information as it shares in its attempt to effect that bond—records a dynamic that has informed key moments in my experiences within higher education. It is poignantly reminiscent before the fact, as it were.

Such queer resonance rests, in large part, in the letter's attitude toward time itself. For in contrast to similarly appreciative notes I wrote to other celebrities of the era (Lynda Carter, Charo, and Bonnie Franklin), my correspondence with Parker Stevenson omits two key details: the date and my age. My typical stylistic pattern was to place the date as a header, introduce myself ("My name is Michael"), and then include what I assumed was significant personal information ("I am eight years old"). Given the rigid precision of my youthful record- and file-keeping, it is difficult not to read the stylistic deviations of this particular letter, then, as explicit authorial choices. Indeed, while it is impossible to pinpoint the precise motives that prompted the note's composition, its withholding of such information suggests that it is up to something slightly different than the memos I wrote to other idols. What that something is, however, is not immediately clear.

One explanation, of course, is that the note documents an attempt to present myself as an age-appropriate candidate for Parker Stevenson's companionship. Because I was raised in the San Francisco Bay Area, I had the benefit, by virtue of location, of being exposed to a comparatively wide range of self-expressions (and diverse couplings), so it is not unlikely that I was aware of male-male desire at this early age. It is also the only letter I wrote to a male celebrity. Still, absent any direct proclamation of attraction, the letter's seeming queerness cannot easily serve as proof of incipient "identity." Indeed, even if a frank declaration of affection had made its way into the note, such a statement would serve less as an indication of a not-yet-known self than it would as a mere record of personal interest as it was expressed on May 3, 1978. Desire, after all, moves in capricious, even fickle, ways and, thus, it seems injudicious to assign too hastily a stable erotic identity with a given object choice at any particular moment (as true for eight-year-olds as it is for anyone). For similar reasons, I am also reluctant to read the letter's lack of outspoken attraction as indicative of any attempt at "closeting" my young self; the note's terseness, its lack of indirection, make it difficult to presume that secrecy or shame inform its composition. It simply introduces a speaker, says what it wants to say, and concludes.

And yet that missing information—details included with such regularity so as to be a tic in other letters—strikes me, now, as an ineluctably (albeit personally) queer gesture, one whose effects reverberate by way of a particular kind of temporal disruption. Although the transcript records a precise attention to chronological time (May 3, 1978), it holds personal time (my age) in abeyance; in so doing, it chronicles its immediate moment but casts past and future as indeterminate, unfixed, suspended. Regardless of motive, then, the letter's stylistic choices emphasize an implicit distinction between temporal sequence (a date) and history (a narrative in which the significance of a particular date accrues meaning). Through its positioning of a subject at a particular time but disconnected from a particular history, the transcript thus disrupts a naturalized understanding that time and history are always neatly aligned, or even that they must matter to one another at all.[1] Although it is true that I wrote to Parker Stevenson on May 3, 1978, the letter does not necessarily represent an early indication of same-sex desire as calibrated within chronological narratives of maturation or development, the key temporal pivot of which is often identified as "coming out." It only reveals that on this date I thought it was important to share my thoughts on Parker Stevenson's hair with him. To be sure, such sharing was in all likelihood a manifestation of some form of attraction, but without specific information about who I am in time, sexuality only exists in this note as a sensation, not as a burgeoning identity.

In this respect, the letter's queerest feature emerges in its disaggregation of history, time, and self. For while it might appear that I am attributing a bit too much meaning to only six lines, the note represents a quite familiar sense of being out of sync, of living aslant to chronological sequence. Queer theorist Elizabeth Freeman (2010) identifies this dynamic as characteristic of a particularly queer treatment of time, one that exists in contradistinction to what she describes as a more pervasive "chrononormativity": the processes by which people are "bound into socially meaningful embodiment through temporal regulation," and which depend upon naturalized "teleological schemes of events or strategies for living such as marriage, accumulation of health and wealth for the future, reproduction, childrearing, and death and its attendant rituals" (pp. 3 & 4).[2] In normative temporal frameworks, personal history is only comprehensible within steady chronological progression. A queer approach to time, by contrast, disrupts sequential organization through an ability to imagine, as Freeman puts it, "other possibilities for living in relation to indeterminately past, present, and future others: that is, of living historically" (p. xxii).

This sense of living outside of expected chronologies, of experiencing time and history as uncoupled from one another, has bubbled up with uncanny frequency for me at moments in which abiding by normative temporal sequence seems less an option than an obligation. Such feelings surface, certainly, in response to social expectations to engage the "strategies for living" that Freeman cites (e.g., reproduction, childrearing). But perhaps in no other context have I felt quite as acutely the effects of a personally messy and discontinuous temporality than I do in academia. Over the course of my career, a keen impression of being out of step, of never quite belonging, has productively influenced my scholarship and informed a range of related professional experiences: as a participant on various taskforces devoted to diversity within academia; as director of an interdisciplinary queer research consortium; and as a founding faculty member of the first LGBT major in California, created in the wake of Proposition 8 (which banned same-sex marriage in the state). This sense of estrangement, however, also has distinctly personal ramifications, particularly at moments when the expectations of the profession chafe against my background as a first-generation college student from a working-class family. Often, such experiences point to a rupture between personal history and normative chronology as my feelings of queerness within academia unfold and refold against themselves, recursive histories wrinkling against normative temporal sequence to form a sort of personal origami. In this way, the dynamic of being inside history but outside time (a sensation recorded in my letter to Parker Stevenson) notes not a past condition but rather one that is ongoing.

Several scholars detail similar attempts to describe queer experience in terms that complicate traditional chronologies, noting the various ways that nonnormativity might usefully be understood, for example, as "anachronism"; as a form of "growing sideways"; as an "untimely" encounter; as "feeling backward"; or as a "haunting."[3] It seems hardly surprising that such theories resonate for queer academics, in particular, since a queer critique of normative sequence (and a subsequent embrace of other temporal possibilities) speaks in compelling ways to the logics of progression that frequently characterize academic culture itself. Academia's rigorous adherence to definitions of time-to-degree, to schedules for publication, and to cycles of review, for example, intersects with other markers of academic time that have deeply personal ramifications (such as promotion, tenure, and sabbatical). Membership in the academy is predicated on a willingness to abide by these timelines, to accede to a normative chronological sequencing in order to build an academic career. And such membership, as the saying goes, has its privileges (such as promotion, tenure, and sabbatical). Yet within these temporal constraints there is exceedingly little room for false starts, for interruption, for surprise—all queerly inflected hallmarks of intellectual inquiry and scholarly production. A hiccup in the sequence can derail an academic career; a seemingly minor glitch can reverberate for decades. Thus, even within an environment that valorizes difference and encourages innovation, the chronological mandates of the academy—with its forceful emphasis on progressive movement—can feel relentlessly antiqueer in orientation.

Yet at the same time, academia itself is often wildly queer in practice, since fundamental to its structure is an ironic privileging of delay and regression, of thwarted development and suspended progress. Even the most focused of graduate students, for instance, is required to postpone the start of a career through at least five (and often more) years of postbaccalaureate study, all the while knowing that even though such sequencing ensures that a career cannot begin too early, it also cannot begin too late. In similarly queer fashion, the job market (and, if one is fortunate, a position on the tenure track) forces upon candidates a keen sense of infantilization, a continual rebirthing of oneself as uninitiated, as junior, as subordinate. Even the apparent realization of success in this context (a job) reverberates for many in queerly self-perplexing ways, threading through the excruciatingly private but ultimately quite common fear that one will be "outed" as an intellectual fraud, an academic sham. In this respect, the cyclical, repetitive motion of progression and recession that characterizes academic culture recalls, in some ways, those ideological narratives that identify queerness itself as form of arrested development. Indeed, because advancement in academia is often predicated on deferral, on a prolonging of "phases" of professional adolescence, to build a career in the field can feel like a decidedly queer endeavor.

Or so it has seemed to me. When taken as a whole, the path to my current location at midcareer is riddled with a series of temporal disjunctions that index fundamental discrepancies between the personal and the professional, between my own queer experiences (of sexuality, of class) and the normative expectations of academia. As the first (and only) person in my family to go to college, for example, a kind of free-floating disorientation structured my foremost experiences with higher education, a condition I now see as directly informed by class-based difference. At the time, though, I understood such perplexity as a personal flaw, indicative of a learning curve I simply needed to master on my own. This early sense of being out of sync with academic culture thus represented a reversal of the isolationist narrative often attached to nonnormative sexuality ("there is no one like me in the world") since with no mentors to provide guidance, and without even the understanding that I might need guidance, I had no models with whom I might compare my experience. A similar irony structured my first introductions to academic discussions of queerness and queer culture; I was bewildered by what seemed to me an exaggerated emphasis on the discrete and isolable as hallmarks of a sophisticated approach to nonnormative sexuality. These perspectives ran counter to my own belief that such difference instead required crucial forms of collectivity, a conviction formed by an understanding of queerness as a type of class-based belonging vis-à-vis the cultural devastation of the HIV/AIDS epidemic and the economic policies that abetted such annihilation. In this early academic context, then, I was intellectually out of step to the same degree that I was socially out of place.

I now see such examples of interrelated difference—how class might be experienced in terms of queerness, and how queerness might be experienced in terms of class—as symptomatic of a temporal misalignment between academia's notions of professional development and the recursive histories that inevitably shape a life. The urgency I felt to begin graduate school, for instance, was interrupted by a fiscal caution that stemmed directly from my class background. I deferred admission to universities I very much wanted to attend due to an instinctive anathema to potential debt, reapplying only to programs that would grant me full tuition (since a doctoral degree in English was a risky enough proposition, let alone a specialization in queer studies). Later, a similar temporal delay informed my experiences on the job market. After earning my degree, I secured a very fine position on the tenure track as a specialist in queer theory and culture, but the university that offered the job could not provide the health benefits for my (same-sex) partner that would make relocation feasible. A position in queer studies, at least in this context, could not accommodate the life of an actual queer person. While the irony of the situation was not lost on anyone involved, including my graduate advisors, I was counseled to accept the job, no matter the personal cost. Here again, though, a pragmatism born out of a braided class- and sexuality-based difference interrupted the forward march of professional progression: what if my partner fell ill? Or was in an accident? How would we afford to live? How would we survive? (Ultimately, I declined the offer.[4])

Over the years, this sense of living out of sync with the normative chronologies of academic culture has popped up with enough frequency to become at least reassuringly familiar, if never entirely pleasurable. And the point at which I find myself now, at midcareer, strikes me as perhaps the queerest time of all. Although future promotions beckon and new professional opportunities await, the temporal paths by which such prospects might be realized are much less clearly defined than they were pre-tenure. To be sure, professional expectations tied to regular cycles of review will still occur, but a strict sense of chronological order no longer presses with quite the same urgency. Indeed, progression itself seems more an option than an obligation, an act of election rather than a series of accommodations. Such open-endedness can prove oddly discomfiting, particularly after many years of acclimating to and abiding by the academy's comparatively austere normative timelines. And while I am hesitant to overemphasize the peculiar challenges of this situation (since anxieties over feelings of professional suspension vis-à-vis tenure are quite different, for instance, from those stemming from contingent employment), it is not surprising that a significant amount of critical attention has been devoted to the curious position of the post-tenure scholar, an academic location that some commentators associate with an emotional state known as "midcareer melancholy."[5] Indeed, absent a clear, chronological trajectory for progression, several uncertainties emerge at this stage of a career: How shall I shape my academic life? What do I want it to look like? How might I move next within this world? These are important questions. And they are queer questions, at least insofar as they capture a queerish sense of asynchrony and of being in-between.

Important, though, they also represent academic variations on the diverse opportunities for living that queerness itself has always provided. "How" can be surprisingly liberating. "What" can open up horizons of possibility. To be sure, disorientation is endemic to this site of professional deferral, especially since such suspension can feel like a temporal imposition. But to approach the world chronologically aslant need not mean an abdication of choice or a renunciation of agency. Instead, such dislocation might be understood as a provocation (even, generously, as an invitation): to potential, to resourcefulness, to originality. As such, the queer time of midcareer is also a time of reckoning, since it asks that close attention be paid to the ways that professional careers and personal histories are often messily entangled. These reckonings, perhaps especially if one is queer, can be as difficult as they are edifying. But they remind us that normative approaches to academic work (and, indeed, to a life itself) are neither mandatory nor inevitable. And they remind us, too, that the tidy partitions that seem to structure our lives—whether captured in a mash note or chronicled in a memoir—are often much more permeable than they might otherwise first appear.

NOTES

1. As Jordan Stein (2013) points out, "As a modality of narrative, history surely can obey the logic of temporal sequence, but it can also accommodate other kinds of temporalities. … With only a few exceptions, time is organized by consecutive sequence; but history is not necessarily so" (p. 857).
2. For a useful discussion of a comparable dynamic, see Dana Luciano's (2007) analysis of what she terms "chronobiopolitics," or the "sexual arrangement of the time of life" (p. 9).
3. See, respectively, the works by Rohy (2009); Stockton (2009); Coviello (2013); Love (2007); and McGarry (2008).
4. As Freeman (2010) puts this issue: "Failures or refusals to inhabit middle- and upper-middle-class habitus appear as, precisely, asynchrony, or time out of joint. And as denizens of times out

of joint, queers *are* a subjugated class … even as many of us occupy other positions of power including the economic" (p. 19).

5. See, for instance, the articles by Misra & Lundquist (2015); Pomeranz (2013); and Potter (2013).

REFERENCES

Coviello, P. (2013). *Tomorrow's parties: Sex and the untimely in nineteenth-century America*. New York: New York University Press.

Freeman, E. (2010). *Time binds: Queer temporalities, queer histories*. Durham, NC: Duke University Press.

Love, H. (2007). *Feeling backward: Loss and the politics of queer history*. Cambridge, MA: Harvard University Press.

Luciano, D. (2007). *Arranging grief: Sacred time and the body in nineteenth-century America*. New York: New York University Press.

McGarry, M. (2008). *Ghosts of futures past: Spiritualism and the cultural politics of nineteenth-century America*. Berkeley: University of California Press.

Misra, J., & Lundquist, J. (2015, May 29). Midcareer melancholy. *Inside Higher Ed*. Retrieved from https://www.insidehighered.com/advice/2015/05/29/essay-frustrations-associate-professors#.VWijoeaHYCk.facebook

Pomeranz, K. (2013, September). The next big thing: Supporting the second book. *Perspectives on History*. Retrieved from http://www.historians.org/publications-and-directories/perspectives-on-history/september-2013/the-next-big-thing-supporting-the-second-book

Potter, C. (2013, September 28). The associate professor blues. *The Chronicle of Higher Education*. Retrieved from http://chronicle.com/blognetwork/tenuredradical/2013/09/the-associate-professor-blues/

Rohy, V. (2009). *Anachronism and its others: Sexuality, race, temporality*. Albany, NY: SUNY Press.

Stein, J. A. (2013). American literary history and queer temporalities. *American Literary History, 25*(4), 855–869.

Stockton, K. B. (2009). *The queer child, or growing sideways in the twentieth century*. Durham, NC: Duke University Press.

CHAPTER SIX

How I Met Foucault: An Intellectual Career in, Around, and Near Queer Theory

KRISTEN A. RENN

1.

"Over the weekend we got goldfish. We named one Foucault and the other Derrida. But Derrida already died. So we're thinking Foucault's 'I'm not *really* pomo' critique of modernism may have a better future in theoretical circles."

"I'm sorry, but I have no idea what you're talking about. Who are Derrida and Foucault and what's pomo?"

That was how I first met Foucault—in a conversation with two undergrads at Brown in the early 1990s. I was working as a student affairs administrator—with one-third of my job dedicated to being the Liaison for Gay and Lesbian Issues, whatever "issues" those might be. Like many early folks in the professional niche that evolved into the contemporary area of lesbian, gay, bisexual, transgender, and queer (LGBTQ) campus resources, I came to the work after a series of well-publicized homophobic incidents precipitated a campus climate study and formation of a taskforce on gay and lesbian "concerns." At least the term *issues* was a step forward from *concerns.*

I studied psychology and music history as an undergrad and educational leadership as a master's student and never ran into poststructuralism, postmodernism, Michel, or Jacques along the way. The inscrutable semiotics majors at Brown—with their black turtlenecks and hipster eyeglasses—spoke of things postmodern, but in the pre-web days I never made my way to the library to try to find out what they meant. Brown's faculty at the time featured a number of important gay, lesbian, queer, and postmodern scholars (Lisa Duggan, Edmund White, and David Savran, among others), but my interactions with them were limited to campus climate committees or other administrative work. So it was two undergrad staff working with me on lesbian and gay issues who introduced me to Foucault and postmodernism.

I shudder now to think of the opportunities for intellectual exploration I squandered, but at the time my career goals were in administrative leadership, not academic scholarship. Working toward improved campus climate and cultivating the talent of queer Ivy Leaguers seemed to be contribution enough to the future of queer social and intellectual movements. And to be sure, I encountered young people who would go on to play leadership roles in national LGBT marches on Washington, queer media and film, politics, progressive nonprofits, and even queer educational research. I learned from them about postmodern theory, queer people of color activism, and the experiences of transgender youth—at least trans* youth in elite higher education institutions.

I did enough reading on lesbian and gay studies, feminist theory, and queer theory to know that they did not necessarily get along well. I also determined, after a few attempts at bringing queer theory into professional conversations that while postmodernism may be in part a product of the university, the university itself remains solidly modernist. Higher education in the United States—and many other nations—is built on a foundation of individualist, white, colonial, masculinist notions of meritocracy and cis-heteropatriarchy. Higher education has survived in the past few decades on a steady diet of neoliberal ideology that posits it as a private, rather than public, good. Attempts at queering administrative practice did not go well at Brown, an institution whose early history was entwined with the New England slave trade (Brown University Steering Committee on Slavery and Justice, 2006), and which was approaching its 250th birthday. Deconstruct *that* it seemed to say to my attempts to bring theory to practice.

2.

When I started my PhD at Boston College a few years after the goldfish incident, I met Foucault again, in my role as student. This meeting was deeper, richer, more complicated, more French. Not yet a friend, or even more than an acquaintance (perhaps a friend-of-friends), Foucault represented a chance to catch up on the theory I missed while working full-time between my master's and PhD. I expected to write a dissertation on lesbian, gay, and bisexual college students. I focused my early coursework in this direction and wrote several papers on queer topics. I continued working half-time at Brown and found that I understood my queer students' conversations about theory much more easily; I also found that administrative life conformed exactly to the norming and disciplining processes that Foucault named. Now I was aware of my complicity in the process. As the official "dean of queer students" I was fully co-opted and co-opting. But, I reminded myself, only half time, as I was also a full-time student.

Foucault's panopticon came to life the year I was the graduate student co-director of the gay and lesbian student organization at Boston College. The group, not officially recognized at the Jesuit university, held a drag show in December. The conservative student paper sent an undercover photographer to the event and by the next morning had faxed to the trustees what they claimed was pictorial evidence of gay students mocking the church (among other allegations of wrong doing, a student used a drag name that was a clear—and mildly suggestive—send-up of the university president). But covert surveillance was matched in this case by intentional self-surveillance, in the form of a videotape of the entire evening. In what would turn out to be a stroke of good luck, if not expert videography, the LGB student group had recorded the event. As the winter wore on and the dean of students—who, in another context was my professional colleague—investigated the gay and lesbian student group, I watched the wobbly video with administrators and faculty, a handful of sympathetic Jesuit priests among them. I appreciated the actual and theoretical irony inherent in the administrative disciplining of gay students at a Catholic university, as well as the students' conscious and self-conscious deployment of identity and my opportunity to playfully deconstruct administrative power.

"Listen, Bob," I said to the dean I had known for several years in student affairs professional circles. "You're the dean of students, so I know you have to do the investigation. But come on, we both know there's nothing here that's going to stick—we could never make this stick at Brown, either." I never again, however, questioned the power of surveillance and the need for disciplining forces to enact their roles. Foucault was really on to something, I thought, about this demonstration of theory in educational administrative practice.

3.

Seventeen years into my career as a faculty member I still worry that I do not do queer theory the right way, that I am not pomo enough, that I cannot keep up with the scholars in the black turtlenecks and hipster glasses. I have made part of my reputation on my work about LGBT and queer college students, but the reality is I am not really a queer theorist. I read it and can write about it, but my own epistemological preference leans a bit more critical, perhaps even postpositivist, than what I understand a truly postmodern perspective can sustain. A few years ago,

I came to terms with the likelihood that I am a theorist who is queer, who writes about queer subjects, subjectivities, and theory, but who is not a queer theorist per se. But then I met Foucault again.

I have the privilege to be a guest in intellectual circles with some of the brightest scholars working in educational research these days: a handful of trans* and genderqueer academics who are setting the field on fire, the way that the Brown undergrads with whom I worked did in their chosen careers. Through the work of T. J. Jourian, Z Nicolazzo, Erich Pitcher, and Dafina-Lazarus Stewart, among others, I have reengaged with the possibilities of deconstructing intellectual, political, and organizational constructs. In particular, Erich's study of trans* academics and the study's foundation in Critical Trans Politics (CTP) brought me into the writing of Dean Spade (2011, 2015), among others, and face to face again with Foucault, Derrida, and their ilk. But this time I am not a student affairs administrator or a graduate student. I am fully implicated as a professor, as an education researcher, in disciplining and norming processes that affect what Spade (2015), building from Critical Race Theory, women of color feminism, and Foucault's notion of the "apparatuses of security" (see Foucault, 2009), calls the "distribution of life chances" (p. 15). No goldfish, no drag show videos. Just face to face with the reality that I have reached a career stage and place (tenured full professor at a public research university) where a decision *not* to mobilize for change to the cis-heteropatriarchal structure of higher education is an endorsement of it and capitulation to enjoying the privileges it offers to an educated, white, economically secure, cisgender lesbian woman.

TURNING THE CTP LENS INWARD

With due appreciation for the work of Spade and other trans* academics, and with caution regarding appropriation of CTP by a cisgender white lesbian professor, I want to explore the ways that a CTP lens can illuminate my past and current positions in the academy. In particular, I want to explore how the varying positions of power and subjugation I experienced on my path from "dean of queer students" at Brown to professor of education at Michigan State University shaped and were shaped by my identities and by my professional work. In doing so, I take up the spirit of Spade's (2011) proposition that CTP "questions its own effectiveness, engaging in constant reflection and self-evaluation" (p. 19) and is "about practices and process rather than a point of arrival, resisting hierarchies of truth and reality and instead naming and refusing state violence" (pp. 19–20). By questioning three moments in my career as an educator, reflecting and self-evaluating, I intend to concentrate on practices and processes to examine my role in challenging, sometimes interrupting, but also in overlooking, ignoring, and perpetuating antitrans* and antiqueer violence through intersections with the neoliberal higher education systems in which I have embedded myself since my early career at Brown in 1989.

Brown University (www.brown.edu) is a small private university with a strong focus on undergraduate education. The seventh college to open in the British colonies in North America, it is one of eight elite Ivy League universities, albeit not as wealthy as Harvard, Yale, or Princeton and not as involved in graduate and professional education as the University of Pennsylvania, Columbia, or Cornell. In 1971 Brown fully absorbed its coordinate women's college, Pembroke, from which had graduated pioneers of 19th- and early 20th-century women's higher education. By the time I arrived as a young administrator, Brown was a "hot" college with a highly selective admissions rate (around 10%). Known for a liberal student body, it attracted the offspring of famous folks (e.g., President John F. Kennedy and Jacqueline Onassis, Jane Fonda, Diana Ross, Steven Spielberg) and less celebrated but deeply influential public figures and business people (Senator John Kerry, billionaire "buyout king" Henry Kravis). The aura of power and privilege for students and alum who were white, wealthy, and/or otherwise majoritized was palpable, especially at times such as the three-day commencement-and-reunion weekend when generations of Brunonians gathered on College Hill. To be sure, by the early 1990s there were substantial populations of students who did not fit this mold. Racial and social class tensions were in evidence, and queer students from any background faced bias, harassment, and occasional violence.

Into this mix I arrived as a young student affairs administrator, learning to find my voice as an advocate for students while also being an institutional agent. My white skin and Mount Holyoke[1] degree afforded me some credibility and privilege, though there was often a moment of confusion on the part of a student or colleague when they asked what year I had graduated (implied: from Brown) and I told them 1986, from Mount Holyoke. I experienced their willingness to treat me as "one of them"—or nearly one of them—with ambivalence, a feeling of "thanks for letting me staff your clubhouse, if not be in the club itself."

I experienced my acceptance among administrators as a cisgender out lesbian the same way: you accept me, but I am not really one of you. I have never looked or acted the part of conventional feminine cisgender girl or woman. An outspoken tomboy as a youth, I grew into the somewhat androgynous gender presentation typical among white girls in certain New England suburbs: somewhat sporty, a bit preppy, rarely overtly femme, practical haircut, unfussy personal upkeep and clothing. All in all, I fit the "old girls" style of female Ivy League administrators, though I deployed a few style choices—such as hair cut very short for the time, certain jewelry and clothes—to mark myself as "not heterosexual."

Taking a critical approach, I have to ask if I conformed in this way in order to gain and assert privilege in the professional setting, or if I found a professional setting that fit my personal style. A CTP perspective suggests that my cisgender identity and white privilege interacted with social class to provide a set of life chances (e.g., going to Mount Holyoke) that then provided additional life chances (working at Brown) that further compounded these privileges.

Once a Seven Sisters or Ivy League institution, even if not one of the most prestigious, is on one's resume, the accompanying privilege embeds into one's career path, offering additional security and beneficial life chances. Certainly my Mount Holyoke and Brown experiences were assets when I applied to the PhD program at Boston College. Raised Catholic and retaining cultural elements of that experience, I benefitted from religious, race, and social class privilege at BC. As a doctoral student on a primarily undergraduate campus, I had opportunities that my undergraduate friends did not. I felt complete freedom to study queer topics in my courses and to participate in the LGB (at the time, no T) student organization. Until the drag show incident, these privileges buffered me from the homophobia and cis-heterosexism that undergrads—and perhaps graduate students in less liberal academic programs—experienced regularly and systemically.

In the drag show kerfuffle my professional identity (a dean at Brown) brought additional privileges to interactions with the BC administration. My academic career was not on the line in any case, but having confidence as a professional peer—and at a more prestigious institution, no less—of the deans handling the situation afforded me additional confidence to push the case, mentor the undergraduates as activists, and seek out faculty allies. I was conscious of this privilege and worked it unabashedly, raising the question of when, if ever, it is acceptable to use one's privileges to counter oppression in one's own self-interest. As an ally, certainly, one is called to use privilege to act against others' oppression; but when it is for oneself, is it the same?

A Spadeian or Foucauldian analysis might suggest that any use of privilege plays into the overall system of uneven distribution of power and life chances. Does leaning into securities based on privileged domains negate the effect of activism for change in other, less secure domains? Perhaps not in the immediate, but surely in the larger context.

So what is a white, cis, lesbian, tenured full professor to do? I can't throw off the outcomes of salubrious life chances that have been afforded to me through accumulated privilege, nor would that necessarily serve the field of education and my students particularly well. My periodic reengagements with queer and now also trans* theory are a starting point for reflection that may lead to intellectual and, more important, concrete approaches to addressing "administrative norms or regularities [that] create structured insecurity and (mal)distribute life chances across populations" (Spade, 2015, p. 9). As I always have, I work in—and also study—higher education, a system that focuses, deflects, and directs life chances in nonrandom ways that purport to be based on merit but that never have been. I am keenly aware of (some of) the privileges afforded me in a neoliberal academy that I embraced as an undergraduate, a young professional, and an academic. I am occasionally made aware of the restrictions placed on me as a lesbian cisgender woman, but in many regards the achievements of my academic career have been in getting a seat at the table, in spite of the restrictions that felt more constraining when I was striving toward administrative leadership and then entering the tenure track. And yet I know that a "seat at the table" for me and people like me is not the point; changing the table or, more radically, getting rid of the table is where higher education needs to go.

Where I draw inspiration these days is from the work of Erich, T. J., Dafina-Lazarus, Z, and other scholars who have known longer than I that the point is about getting rid of the table. They already know that a seat at the table is not enough and work as intellectuals and activists against the reality that "trans resistance is emerging in a context of neoliberal politics where the choice to struggle for nothing more than incorporation into the neoliberal order is the most obvious option" (Spade, 2015, p. 18). When they introduce me to Spade and other trans* scholars, or when they put Foucault back in front of me, they show me that taking seriously the tenets of a Critical Trans Politics framework provides a new dimension to thinking about queer topics in higher education. This new dimension, in turn, prompts reflexivity that is essential to my scholarly (r)evolution. It takes me back through my academic biography to notice where various privileges opened unseen doors and accumulated to accelerate achievement of a fairly conventional career, a career built in large part on researching queer topics (the safety of which to pursue was also made possible by those same privileges).

The challenges I embrace for the next period of my career—when I sit, arguably, at the pinnacle of the hierarchy for an education professor at a land grant university (where the concepts "pinnacle of the hierarchy" and "education professor at a land grant university" form an oxymoron in many folks' minds)—are to turn my attention to addressing a wider frame of cis-heterosexism in my own work and to looking for ways to eliminate structures within higher education that continue inequitably to distribute life chances. It is clear that policies and practices that treat people equally do not lead to equity; even if they did, that equity would be a victory of neoliberal ideology in academe. Of course, implementing policies and practices that fully embrace the lived realities and identities of all people in (and seeking to enter) higher education is the right thing to do. But as Spade (2011, 2015) argues so clearly, it is insufficient.

Here I circle back to understand anew the meaning of the goldfish, the drag show, and my colleagues' good work. It is clear to me that whatever intellectual advances I make related to queer "issues," there is a common thread: my privilege has put me in a position to benefit from the intellectual advances of others, usually in subject positions less privileged than I. I am indebted to them as I work to understand the implications and obligations of this circumstance, to explore my accountability to them, and to work both within and against the system of higher education in which I have chosen—and been allowed—to embed myself.

NOTE

1. Mount Holyoke is a small, private liberal arts college. It is among the oldest U.S. women's colleges and is a member of the Seven Sisters. In 2014 it clarified its admissions policy to reflect the reality of changing notions of gender in society and on its campus. Mount Holyoke accepts applications from cisgender women and all trans* or genderqueer individuals, regardless of sex assigned at birth. Only cisgender, cissexual males are excluded (see https://www.mtholyoke.edu/policies/admission-transgender-students).

REFERENCES

Brown University Steering Committee on Slavery and Justice. (2006). *Slavery and justice*. Providence, RI: Brown University. Retrieved from http://www.brown.edu/Research/Slavery_Justice/documents/SlaveryAndJustice.pdf

Foucault, M. (2009). *Security, territory, population: Lectures at the Collège de France 1977–1978* (Vol. 4). (M. Senellart, Ed.; G. Burchell, Trans.). New York: Palgrave Macmillan.

Spade, D. (2011). *Normal life: Administrative violence, critical trans politics, and the limits of law*. Brooklyn, NY: South End.

Spade, D. (2015). *Normal life: Administrative violence, critical trans politics, and the limits of law* (Rev. & exp. ed.). Durham, NC: Duke University Press.

Part 3:
Queering Academic Spaces: Renarrating Lives

CHAPTER SEVEN

From Doctoral Student to Dr. Sweetie Darling: My Queer(ing) Journey in Academia

NELSON M. RODRIGUEZ

If my experience as a doctoral student at the Pennsylvania State University during the mid-1990s had much to do with encountering a broad constellation of critical ideas that would profoundly reshape how I see the world, then my experience as a professor, especially over the past 12 years, has been about how to piece together these ideas in ways that would sustain my queer work and identity in the academy. In this chapter, I reflect on the shifts in my institutional/intellectual location in academia, starting from being a doctoral student of critical pedagogy and cultural studies at the Pennsylvania State University. My memoir then moves to a primary focus on the past 12 years at The College of New Jersey (TCNJ), that is, on my movement from being a professor of education to my current position teaching mostly sexuality and queer studies courses within the context of a women's, gender, and sexuality studies department. Utilizing several courses I'm currently teaching, I consider what queering academia has meant during this period by making use of a number of concepts to think with, including affect/emotion, border crossing, criticality, and (queer) Eros. I don't theorize here each of these concepts; that will need to wait for another project. Instead, I sketch out how these concepts have informed what I do in terms of queering my approach to the teaching of a range of courses across the spectrum of educational, gender, and sexuality studies. In relation to scholarship and teaching, I then conclude my memoir with a discussion of the next phase of my work of queering academia.

A "QUEER" DETOUR THROUGH THE PENNSYLVANIA STATE UNIVERSITY

Throughout the mid- to late 1990s I pursued graduate study in State College, Pennsylvania, at Penn State. My program, in terms of coursework and dissertation topic, was broadly organized around the study of critical pedagogy and cultural studies. Pursuing a Ph.D., however, was not part of my original plan when I made the decision to attend graduate school. I was living in Miami, Florida, at the time and was teaching writing/composition courses as an adjunct at Miami Dade Community College (which now goes by the name Miami Dade College). I really enjoyed the work I was doing there, and my colleagues truly valued it. It was even intimated to me on several occasions that if I had had a master's degree I would have likely been hired into a full-time teaching position. My motivation, then, for pursuing an advanced degree was the hope that I could one day return to Miami Dade Community College and be hired full-time. Of course, this game plan did not come to pass.

I applied to Penn State's master's program in Curriculum and Instruction with a literacy studies focus. I also applied to the English Education program at Teachers College, Columbia University. I was accepted into both programs. I really had my heart set on attending Teachers College, but they didn't offer much in the way of financial assistance. Penn State, on the other hand, offered me significant financial assistance in the form of a full tuition waiver and stipend, so off to Penn State I went. I quickly fell into the hands of several critical theorists of education, including Joe Kincheloe (who became my dissertation advisor) and Henry Giroux. If memory serves me well, I think I met Joe by way of his partner, Shirley Steinberg, who I originally met early on in my program of studies in a doctoral seminar titled, Theory and Teaching of Composition, offered through Penn State's English Department. We sat next to one another on the first day of class. I sensed she knew I was a queer boy, and I remember thinking she might be a "fruit fly." We were both correct. Soon thereafter, Shirley introduced me to Joe who introduced me to Henry, and for the next several years I enrolled in their doctoral seminars. These included: Public Memory and Education, Power and Pedagogy, Pedagogy of Whiteness, Popular Culture and Critical Pedagogy, Postmodern Cognition, Cultural Studies Research, Historical Foundations of Critical Pedagogy, and Multiculturalism and Media. Rounding out my studies, I also took a number of seminars in the English Department, including Early American Literature (with Carla Mulford), Contemporary Literary Theory (with Jeffrey Nealon), and Introduction to Cultural Studies (with Evan Watkins). I also sat in a course taught by Sharon Crowley and another (I think on the topic of Deleuze and Foucault) taught by Richard Doyle.

Combined, these courses—and the readings and ideas I encountered in each—profoundly reshaped how I now make sense of and experience the world, especially in relation to the broad categories of power, identity, and social justice. I was introduced no doubt to the world of "criticality." That is, by way of these professors and their courses, I encountered the pedagogical, political, and theoretical conditions needed to border cross and grapple with a vast constellation of critical ideas, ideas perhaps best encompassed by the phrase "critical theories," and an overall experience that I would describe as queer(ing). It's difficult for me to imagine now not having the capacity to think critically in the way that I was trained while at Penn State. To be sure, the kind of critical encounter (and process of thinking) I've been describing has been absolutely central to my own transformation and survival both as a queer person and as a cultural worker in the academy. Eventually my critical education culminated at Penn State with researching and writing a dissertation on the topic of critical whiteness studies and teacher education. Among the many books and articles I read in whiteness studies, it was Ruth Frankenberg's (1993) critical ethnography, *White Women, Race Matters: The Social Construction of Whiteness*, that inspired the focus and direction of my dissertation. Coming out of this experience was also my first (1998) book publication, co-edited with Joe Kincheloe, Shirley Steinberg, and Ronald Chennault, titled *White Reign: Deploying Whiteness in America*. It's a bit ironic that as I write this memoir I have returned to the topic of critical whiteness studies by way of reading and discussing with my students Jane Ward's (2015) study, *Not Gay: Sex Between Straight White Men*, only now as a professor situated in a women's, gender, and sexuality department teaching courses primarily in queer studies.

THE COLLEGE OF NEW JERSEY, PHASE 1: SCHOOL OF EDUCATION

In the fall of 2004, I was hired into a tenure-track position at The College of New Jersey. At that time, I had been yearning to find a place in academia where I could do more critical work, particularly in my capacity as a professor of education. From 2000 to 2004 I lived in Boston, Massachusetts, teaching at Northeastern University. Overall it was a good experience, but I wasn't really doing the kind of critical work/teaching that I had been trained to do in graduate school. Hence, I looked for a new job, and found one: in educational foundations and research methodology at The College of New Jersey. I applied, interviewed, and was offered the position. As many in the business know, "educational foundations" can be understood as a phrase to describe "critical approaches to education," or at the least it can be conceptualized this way by some of us. (Such an approach, for instance, might examine questions of schooling and education by way of the lenses of sociology, history, philosophy, critical theory, etc.) For the most part, this conceptualization proved to be true in my case. Indeed, during my first several years in the School of Education at TCNJ, I taught a range of different undergraduate and graduate foundations courses, including: Schools and Communities; Historical and Political Context of Schools; Introduction to Educational Research; Social Problems and Education; and Cultural Foundations of Education. These courses provided me with the rationale I needed to work criticality into my curriculum and teaching. This included exposing students to scholarship in the areas of critical whiteness studies and/or in queer theory/studies (e.g., we read Pamela Perry's *Shades of White: White Kids and Racial Identities in High School*, 2002, and Mindy Blaise's *Playing It Straight: Uncovering Gender Discourses in the Early Childhood Classroom*, 2005). As time passed during my initial years at TCNJ, I started to feel that I needed to take up queer topics in a more sustained way in my courses. Gay, lesbian, and transgender issues were quickly becoming more front and center in public discourse, especially in light of the marriage equality movement that has sparked a global conversation and set of robust debates on "gay rights." Given this sociopolitical context, I also wanted to be able to take up queer studies, especially in my teaching, without always feeling the need to anchor such work solely within the context and concerns of schooling and education. I wanted to take up lesbian, gay, bisexual, transgender, and queer (LGBTQ) concerns with as many students, and across as many topics, as possible. In short, I sensed the importance of engaging in a critical praxis of "queering academia writ large."

THE COLLEGE OF NEW JERSEY, PHASE 2: SCHOOL OF HUMANITIES AND SOCIAL SCIENCES

While I don't remember exactly how it happened, in the fall of 2005 I was offered an opportunity to teach a course in critical masculinity studies during the spring 2006 term for TCNJ's Women's and Gender Studies Department. The course title was Men and Masculinities: Literary Perspectives. Teaching this course became a defining moment in my career at TCNJ, as it quickly led to further invitations to teach other gender studies courses. In addition, it became the catalyst that prompted major shifts in my institutional location, that is, from being positioned initially in a tenure-track line in the School of Education, to moving into a joint appointment scenario between the School of Education and the School of Humanities and Social Sciences (then called the School of Culture and Society), to my current position as fully appointed within the School of Humanities and Social Sciences within the Women's, Gender, and Sexuality Studies Department

(WGSS), where I am now tenured. These shifts, it should be noted, started to take place prior to receiving tenure, so the politics were a bit intense!

Even within WGSS, my teaching focus has shifted, from initially teaching courses mostly in gender and feminist studies to what I am doing now: teaching mostly sexuality and queer studies courses. Spanning the entire curriculum, from introductory courses to the capstone senior seminar, to date I have taught a total of 13 different WGSS courses: Senior Seminar: Methods and Theory (WGS 495); Topics in WGS: Critical Heterosexual Studies (WGS 470); Gender Equity in the Classroom (WGS 350); Transgender Studies (WGS 344); Queer Studies (WGS 343); LGBTQ Issues in K–12 Education (WGS 342); Feminist Theories (WGS 325); Men and Masculinities: Literary Perspectives (WGS 320); Politics of Sexuality (WGS 250); Introduction to Sexuality Studies (WGS 241); Introduction to Gay and Lesbian Studies (WGS 240); Gender and Popular Culture (WGS 220); and Women, Culture, and Society (WGS 200). When factoring in the education courses I mentioned previously, and add in a freshman seminar, I've taught a total of 19 different courses at TCNJ since 2004. I also created an abroad course, Queer Amsterdam, that I've yet to teach. It's only now in writing this memoir that I have paused to really think about how much work and energy it has taken to do all of this. I suppose it is the continued sense of urgency I feel to discuss all things LGBTQ with my students, especially at this historical moment, that keeps me inspired, that keeps me going.

Utilizing several of these courses, I would like to take a few moments to discuss how I enact queering my approach to teaching two introductory courses and several advanced seminars. As a related aside, it should be noted that the very presence of LGBT, sexuality, and queer studies constitutes in itself a queering of academia, especially when these courses are known about and populated by students from a wide spectrum of majors. But beyond visibility, I have begun over the last several years to reflect on how I queer my courses, reflecting on what queering means in these educational contexts. As I explain below, the vectors of queering often come through deploying and intersecting the concepts of affect/emotion, border crossing, criticality, and/or Eros.

In both of my introductory courses—Introduction to LGBT Studies and Introduction to Sexuality Studies—I have invited students to engage in significant forms of border crossing that tap into affective dimensions of learning. By border crossing, I mean the sustained process of crossing into "other knowledge domains" where encounters with new epistemologies can lead to ongoing transformations of the self. This notion is conveyed in the title, *Finding Out: An Introduction to LGBT Studies* (Gibson, Alexander, & Meem, 2014), the main text I've been using in my LGBT Studies course. In this course, many of the students have had little to no exposure to, say, U.S. LGBT histories. Encountering knowledge, for example, about the 1950s Lavender Scare or about the homophobic response on the part of the U.S. government to the 1980s AIDS crisis in gay urban communities can, and often does, create the conditions for students to reconstitute or shift their sense of self in light of such epistemological encounters that critical forms of border crossing instigate. In teaching about the AIDS crisis, I often enhance discussions by using documentaries and films (e.g., Epstein & Friedman, 1990, *Common Threads: Stories From the Quilt*; Weissman, 2011, *We Were Here*; and Murphy & Kramer, 2014, *The Normal Heart*) that require a great deal of "emotional work" that potentially queers students' identities by positioning them in a location of possible ongoing formation: that is, in a place where the relationship between the construction of knowledge, the development of critical consciousness, and identity formation is an ongoing one, ongoing during the course and hopefully beyond it.

In addition, I utilize Eros or the erotic as a way to queer my courses, in part because such deployments often position students (once again) to border cross into an understanding of and bearing witnessing to the immense spectrum of (queer) sexual practices. This in turn can generate a certain level of ongoing "identity work" as one responds affectively to the complexity of desire. In my Sexuality Studies course, for instance, we might watch the pilot episodes of *Queer as Folk* that depict the first simulated sex scene between two men in American television, exploring masturbation, rimming, and anal sex. Or produced more recently, we might view clips on the topic of BDSM practices by way of James Franco's (Voros, 2013) documentary, *Kink*. Or, we might read a range of scholarly articles and view any number of filmic texts on the Puppy Play scene that has become highly popular in places like San Francisco. In addition to the potential affective negotiations of identity that these various forms of border crossing engender, what makes this approach to teaching "queer" is that my students and I are in a public space—a classroom—discussing these topics. But here I draw from Haggerty and McGarry's (2015) reformulation of Gayle Rubin's (1993) declaration that "the time has come to think about sex" (p. 3) when reminding us that "the time to think about sex is always now" (p. 2), and to do so quite publicly, in light of the fact that sexuality continues unabated to be one of the most publicly political topics in circulation today on a global scale (e.g., see Altman & Symons, 2016; Plummer, 2015).

In my upper division courses, I also utilize the same concepts to create opportunities for students to border cross and "feel knowledge." In my Queer Studies seminar—a course in Queer Theory—students find themselves in a head-on collision with a theoretically robust anti-identitarianism set of discourses that deeply challenges them to rethink the very idea of "stability" across identifications related to biological sex, gender, and/or sexuality. In a course on "critical heterosexual studies," students encounter knowledge that highlights the social construction of heterosexuality as "performative," an "accomplishment," and what that potentially means in terms of identity formations in post-closeted culture (see Dean, 2014).

And in a course on LGBTQ issues in K–12 education, students grapple early on in the semester with an encounter with a compelling theoretical vocabulary on social justice education that could profoundly impact their ongoing identity work as future educators and/or parents (see Sensoy & DiAngelo, 2012).

QUEERING ACADEMIA: THE NEXT PHASE

As I embark on the next phase of my academic career, I feel well positioned to continue the work of queering academia. I continue to believe in the importance of sustaining a "visible dialogue" on all things LGBTQ in the academy. I see such a dialogue continuing to unfold in two ways: across scholarship and teaching. First, I remain committed to organizing, collaborating on, and publishing a broad range of scholarly projects situated at the intersection of queer studies and education. Generating ideas for new book projects is something I really enjoy doing. Ideas thankfully keep coming, and many times they emerge when I'm doing something else, for example when exercising! Some of these ideas/projects include organizing a collection of original essays on Michel Foucault's ideas on friendship and how they might be brought to bear on queer studies and education scholarship. I'm also planning a new volume showcasing a cross-section of work on the topic of "queer research methodologies in education." The production of a textbook on queer theory in education for the undergraduate market is also in the pipeline, as well as a reader on the same topic for graduate students. And finally, among many other projects, I'm excited to be currently organizing a volume that provides a cross-section of theoretical reflections on approaches to teaching LGBTQ studies within the field of education by way of drawing from one or more critical perspectives other than, or in addition to, LGBTQ studies—for example, affect studies, disability studies, critical race theory, critical science/environmental studies, critical theory, critical feminisms, among others.

I'm also thankful that I can help showcase the brilliant work of others by way of the two book series I currently co-edit—the *Queer Studies and Education* series (published with Palgrave Macmillan) and the *Routledge Critical Studies in Gender and Sexuality in Education* series. I'm also working on a new series with several other wonderful folks that will soon launch on the subject of queering teacher education.

In terms of teaching, I see a delightfully winding queer road ahead. I'm thankful I was able to recently organize, and receive approval for, a new minor in sexuality and queer studies. This new minor is quite timely and will serve well the students and faculty at TCNJ. Over the next two to three years, I also anticipate putting forward a proposal to create a new major in LGBTQ Studies. During this same period, I will be developing several additional new courses across a variety of topics, including global sexualities, media studies and sexualities, the contemporary gay male experience, kink 101, and critical methods in sexuality and queer studies. As LGBTQ social, cultural, and political issues continue to transform on a global scale any number of societal institutions, courses in sexuality and queer studies have become a significant way for generating a much-needed educational grounding in queer epistemologies in order for students to participate as politically engaged and informed citizens and intellectuals on the subject of LGBTQ as they move across space and time, both within the academy and well beyond.

MOVING FORWARD AS DR. SWEETIE DARLING ...

In the spring of 2012, I was voted to be TCNJ's faculty speaker at commencement. (Each year the graduating class votes on and invites a faculty member to speak at that year's commencement.) In May 2012 I stood in front of the graduating class and their family and friends, and introduced myself as "Dr. Sweetie Darling," a name I had pieced together from my longstanding admiration of Freddie Mercury's queer flamboyance coupled with my love of the BBC television sitcom, *Absolutely Fabulous*, a most-queer show for sure. After the commencement ceremony was over, a member of the Board of Trustees complimented me on creatively working Freddie Mercury and *Absolutely Fabulous* into the same speech. She also very much appreciated my name. Since then the name has stuck with my students. I look forward with queer exuberance to this next phase of queering academia in my capacity as Dr. Sweetie Darling.

REFERENCES

Altman, D., & Symons, J. (2016). *Queer wars: The new global polarization over gay rights.* Malden, MA: Polity.

Blaise, M. (2005). *Playing it straight: Uncovering gender discourses in the early childhood classroom.* New York: Routledge.

Cowen, R., & Lipman, D. (Creators). (2000). *Queer as folk.* [Series]. United States: Showtime Networks.

Dean, J. J. (2014). *Straights: Heterosexuality in post-closeted culture.* New York: New York University Press.

Epstein, R., & Friedman, J. (Directors). (1990). *Common threads: Stories from the quilt.* [Documentary]. United States: Telling Pictures.

Frankenberg, R. (1993). *White women, race matters: The social construction of whiteness.* Minneapolis: University of Minnesota Press.

Gibson, M. A., Alexander, J., & Meem, D. T. (Eds.). (2014). *Finding out: An introduction to LGBT studies.* Thousand Oaks, CA: Sage.

Haggerty, G. E., & McGarry, M. (Eds.). (2015). *A companion to lesbian, gay, bisexual, transgender, and queer studies*. Malden, MA: Wiley-Blackwell.

Kincheloe, J. L., Steinberg, S. R., Rodriguez, N. M., & Chennault, R. E. (Eds.). (1998). *White reign: Deploying whiteness in America*. New York: St. Martin's Griffin.

Murphy, R. (Director), & Kramer, L. (Writer). (2014). *The normal heart*. [Motion Picture]. United States: HBO Films.

Perry, P. (2002). *Shades of white: White kids and racial identities in high school*. Durham, NC: Duke University Press.

Plummer, K. (2015). *Cosmopolitan sexualities: Hope and the humanist imagination*. Malden, MA: Polity.

Rubin, G. (1993). Thinking sex: Notes for a radical theory of the politics of sexuality. In H. Abelove, M. A. Barale, & D. M. Halperin (Eds.), *The lesbian and gay studies reader* (pp. 3–44). New York: Routledge.

Sensoy, O., & DiAngelo, R. (2012). *Is everyone really equal? An introduction to key concepts in social justice education*. New York: Teachers College Press.

Voros, C. (Director). (2013). *Kink*. [Documentary]. United States: Rabbit Bandini Productions.

Ward, J. (2015). *Not gay: Sex between straight white men*. New York: New York University Press.

Weissman, D. (Producer & Director). (2011). *We were here*. [Documentary]. United States: Red Flag Releasing.

CHAPTER EIGHT

Working *With* and *Within*: *Weaving* Queer Spaces With Cycles of Resistance

JENNY KASSEN AND ALICIA LAPOINTE

INTRODUCTION

This narrative weaves together critical incidents of student-led (hetero/cis)normative[1] resistance at a Faculty of Education in Ontario, Canada. Through sharing our individual yet intersecting stories, we analyze the particularities of school-based events to make sense of our experiences as queer[2] under/graduate students. We highlight four elements within the cycles of resistance: visibility, antihomophobic/antitransphobic educational opportunities, impact/change, and reflection as we construct our "experience as story" (Connelly & Clandinin, 2006, p. 477). Our personal reflections provide a space to explore counternarratives to a Faculty of Education's cover story—sentiments and actions that embrace safety and inclusion rather than systemic deconstruction. Our work exposes the ragged fabric that is individualized accounts of homophobia and transphobia and reconstructs the threads to make visible systemic issues, such as (hetero/cis)normative pedagogies and practice (see Britzman, 1995; Linville, 2009). In sharing this narrative we attempt to unravel and rework privileged understandings of sexuality and gender, and stitch together how we worked *with* and *within* an institution's (hetero/cis) normative fabric to establish and nurture queer intellectual and physical spaces through cycles of resistance. Overall, it is the master narrative of safety and inclusion that we intended to unravel and refashion.

THEORETICAL FRAMEWORK

The queer theoretical insights of Britzman (1995, 1998) and Linville provide a lens for exploring sexual- and gender-based oppression as well as agency in schooling in terms of deconstructing hetero/cis normalcy and dismantling the impacts of heterosexual and cisgender privilege. From examining our under/graduate experiences with a queer frame, we are able to explore the important role student activism may play in addressing and combating the adverse effects of institutionalized homophobia, transphobia, and (hetero/cis)normativity in a higher education setting. Queer perspectives guide us in making sense of our lived experiences as minorities in terms of our identities and our positionality vis-à-vis the (hetero/cis) normative university milieu and help direct us to critical incidents where we were compelled to rethread our educational trajectory. Moreover, as we engaged in queer conversations we began to take action and plan initiatives that were designed to unravel the normative erasure of gender, sexual, and romantic minority (GSRM) content, perspectives, people, and history in everyday school life.

Drawing on the insights of Lindemann Nelson (1995), we reflect on the ways in which *counterstories*—narratives that "undo" a dominant narrative in order to "invite new interpretations and conclusions" (p. 23)—offer readings that resist (hetero/cis)normative "regimes of truth" (Sedgwick, 1990/2008, p. 8). We also employ Chase's (2005) and Downs's (2009) work as a means to "disrupt oppressive social processes" (Chase, p. 79). Overall, this narrative examines the ways in which individual counterstories come together to cultivate social change (Chase) and provide guidelines for future action (Lindemann Nelson).

METHODS

Narratives are constructed by analyzing stories (Frank, 2000) for meaning and significance (Xu & Connelly, 2010). Narratives not only detail lived experiences, but they capture feelings, thoughts, and interpretations of events (Chase) through the ways by which people communicate (Riley & Hawe, 2005); thus, narratives can help people make sense of the world around them (Bruner, 1994). Narrative work involves the story as the "method and phenomenon of study" (Pinnegar & Daynes, 2007, p. 5) and "comes out of a view of human experience in which humans, individually and socially, lead storied lives (Connelly & Clandinin, 2006, p. 477). As sexual minorities, we utilize story to challenge the status quo and analyze our experiences in particular moments in time (see Chase). Our tellings provide counternarratives to gender and sexuality (mis)understandings (see Barone, 2007). In sum, we seek to disrupt long-lived narratives—privileged forms of knowledge—that silence stories that are in need of telling.

DATA ANALYSIS

Critical analysis, a process of deconstructing and reconstructing personal experiences (see Clandinin & Connelly, 2000), was applied to examine our stories (see Pinnegar & Daynes). Admittedly, ideologies, assumptions, stereotypes, and personal characteristics are embedded in stories; thus, our analysis represents a partial version of reality (Spector-Mersel, 2010) that is influenced by particular people, places, and times (see Clandinin & Connelly, 2000). We utilize a weaving metaphor to offer a way into the data (Pinnegar & Daynes) and illustrate how we attempted to queer the education system. We confronted individual and institutional (hetero/cis)normative assumptions and actions by *weaving* new threads of understanding into the faculty's fabric with cycles of (hetero/cis)normative resistance.

WEAVINGS

Inspecting the Existing Fabric

We sit in the small office exchanging stories about our encounters with homophobia and (hetero/cis)normativity at the faculty. As we talk, an image emerges: the faculty as a tightly woven tapestry of safety and inclusion, years in its creation; in it, our experiences of, and resistance to, homophobia and (hetero/cis)normativity are dropped stitches: nearly imperceptible holes in the seemingly flawless cloth. Our experiences, independent of one another, overlap in several areas, and we wonder how many others have had similar experiences? How many dropped stitches are there, and how do we go about picking them up or mending the holes?

The faculty was not devoid of "diversity" initiatives; the prevailing discourse (Downs) wove a story of inclusion and safety with events, such as individual professional development days and specific lessons that focused on minority issues in our undergraduate programs. Like an appliqué—decorative needlework that sits on the surface of a larger piece—the staff-led initiatives stood out on the fabric of the faculty as ornaments—; evidence of inclusion, but not consistently integrated into the unfolding weave. As isolated events (see Britzman, 1995; Linville), they did little to disrupt tightly woven (hetero/cis)normativity that permeated the faculty the rest of the year. Although gender-based graduate courses were offered and queer perspectives were incorporated within classes in subsequent years, we felt decidedly on the fringe in relation to our peers who were not sensitive to the (hetero/cis)normativity that unfolded every day. When we met, our individual experiences came together as counterstories with which we could challenge (hetero/cis) normative assumptions and actions as we encountered them (Lindemann Nelson).

Being accused of pushing a gay agenda when discussing the erasure of GSRM content in curriculum, or negotiating queer identities within a Catholic educational context, previously left us feeling threadbare but could now be discussed as systemic issues. The new stitches that emerged through our conversations led us to take a closer look at the fabric we were a part of and to consider how we could extend our observations beyond our dialogue.

VISIBILITY

Gay-Straight Alliance Puzzle Activity

Twenty-three people sit in a circle at the Faculty of Education's first Gay-Straight Alliance (GSA) meeting. We have spent time individually designing large puzzle pieces that represent our hopes for the club. One by one, we put our pieces together, sharing our reasons for being there and our expectations. Each voice contributes color and texture to the slowly developing design that pulls together the dropped stitches. The new fabric grows stronger with each perspective. The puzzle remains unfinished on one side: there are extra pieces to accommodate the visions of new members as the group develops; this tapestry can stretch.

Although carefully planned out, the governing narrative of safe and inclusive education that lined the faculty was loose at the seams, and through these gaps (hetero/cis)normativity was able to slip through. This took the form of constant (hetero/cis)normative assumptions and frequent use of homophobic slurs within the faculty, among other manifestations. Forming a GSA countered current initiatives that did little to disrupt the Othering (see Kumashiro, 2002) that happened day to day and the isolation we experienced as a result. We felt that creating a space for queer people, voices, and thinking could pick up some of the dropped stitches by making GSRMs and their allies visible to each other, as well as to the larger community. We saw the GSA as a space where both undergraduate and graduate students could work together to identify areas of need and draw on each other's knowledge to patch these holes. In the first GSA meeting the puzzle activity revealed counterstories of limited sexual- and gender-based knowledge and a strong desire to learn.

Participants' voices created a netting with which they began mending areas of (hetero/cis)normativity. The collection of voices enabled internal visibility to extend to the larger faculty, as the intertwining of individual stories became the springboard for "collective problem solving" (Chase, p. 81). The puzzle—a visual representation of the group's counterstory—hung in the main hall, making the GSA visible to the rest of the faculty and inviting new members to join and engage with queer content. Over the course of the year the counterstories that emerged from the puzzle activity served to alter the fabric of the faculty. The now visible voices "offer[ed] a basis for group action that [could] have a lasting institutional effect" (Lindemann Nelson, p. 35). This was evident when GSA members designed and facilitated queer learning opportunities for their peers. These extracurricular explorations, which covered topics such as allyship and GSRM resource development, allowed club members to share their developing knowledge and encourage their peers to reflect on how they might queer their teaching practice.

ANTIHOMOPHOBIC/ANTITRANSPHOBIC EDUCATIONAL OPPORTUNITIES

The auditorium is crowded. Panelists take the stage and share their stories of GSRM issues in education. Teaching OUT, a student-led initiative, is the first of its kind at the faculty. It reaches beyond the edges of the school fabric and into the community in order to join a larger patchwork of community partners. Speaker and audience voices interlace as a dialogue emerges and the community pulls together strands of knowledge to contribute to a growing understanding of the issues that impact GSRMs in the field of education.

Both students and staff worked together to promote Teaching OUT as a means for marginal narratives to be heard (see Chase). Since knotted into the larger fabric of society are narratives that unilaterally position all GSRM people as victims, Teaching OUT sought to unravel dominant stories of marginalization by enlisting educational stakeholders to rework the twisted stitches. Stories of oppression were deconstructed and rethreaded, row by row, by engaging with GSRM content in ways that disrupted (hetero/cis)normalcy and resisted re-inscription of prevailing victim narratives (Downs). Through this process knots were untangled as counterstories of strength and resilience, and all textures and fibers offered new opportunities to recognize differences (Chase) by thinking the unthinkable (see Britzman, 1998). In addition, this event had at its core the objective of disaggregating the LGBTQ acronym by celebrating sexual and gender fluidity (Britzman, 1995, 1998) and "resist[ing] the tendency to homogenize difference" (Lindemann Nelson, p. 31). The expanded tapestry challenged the audience to rethink how GSRM people are storied in schools and the ways that we all implicitly contribute to (hetero/cis)normativity.

IMPACT/CHANGE

A circle of chairs is set up in the community room—a space reserved for guest speakers. The seating arrangement is intentional: in this circle everyone is a learner and contributor. Outside of the traditional static classroom, this space affords members enriched opportunities to relate to each other and participate in dialogue. Seven high school GSA members are the guest speakers today. They speak with authority as they answer questions posed by teacher candidates (TC): "What makes a good GSA advisor? How can we better support you?"

Lesbian, Gay, Bisexual, Trans, Two Spirit, Queer/Questioning (LGBT2Q) Issues in Education, a course created and taught by Alicia, was offered for the first time at the faculty in 2014. In its design, it worked *with* the grain of the Bachelor of Education program in terms of course conventions: as an elective it was available to all students, complete with all the expectations associated with an undergraduate level class. While it incorporated seamlessly into the structure of the program, the content and facilitation *within* the class worked against the grain to provide TCs with opportunities to rethink their conceptions of space and relationships as counternarratives. In order to establish a safer learning environment, the class co-constructed group guidelines that went beyond generic and assumed notions of safety and inclusion. TCs deliberately included themes of open-mindedness to others' stories and explicitly advocated for the use of GSRM-inclusive language in the classroom (e.g., not assuming people's gender and/or sexuality). In developing guidelines, students problematized preconceived and (hetero/cis)normative assumptions and acknowledged the importance of telling their own stories on their own terms. This agreement made it possible for the group to deconstruct dominant narratives of education, school, and the rules that govern them as "neutral" institutions (Lindemann Nelson) devoid of (hetero/cis) normative rules and regulations—the hidden curriculum. Explicitly voicing that sexual- and gender-based assumptions were unacceptable left no wiggle room for problematic language to slip through unchallenged. In fact, it exposed how much is taken for granted within the cover story of safety and inclusivity.

To disrupt the dominant narrative of teacher as knower and expert, youth were invited to speak to TCs. As experts of their own identities and experiences, the teacher-student relationship was queered insomuch that TCs learned *with* students (see Lapointe, 2015). Future teachers were "jolted into listening" (Chase, p. 80) as they came to appreciate the youths' depth of knowledge and understanding. Teacher advisors also accompanied the students and contributed to the discussion but were keenly aware that the space was designed to spotlight students' voices and stories. As the youth shared, TCs strung one question after another, realizing that knowledge construction is a reciprocal process. The impact of this experience was palpable as, with humility, TCs recognized that youths' counternarratives were teaching them lessons that were previously inaccessible. Overall, working *within* the natural flow of the weave enabled counternarratives, as evidenced though spatial and relational queering, to be threaded throughout the larger context of education (see Downs).

REFLECTION

It is quarter to six, almost time for GSA. Alicia questions the place of this club at the faculty. Membership, which has been in the 20s for the past two years, is now less than a handful of regularly attending individuals. The unspoken thoughts loop around each other: Are we doing enough? Do we need to be more active in the faculty or can we just meet as friends? Is the GSA a failure if only five people hang out? Do I still need the group? This is not what I thought GSA was going to be. Am I ok with this? Am I privileging education and advocacy over social support? Is this still something I want to make time for? Is this group even relevant now that there is a class that addresses GSRM issues? All these stories intertwine into one sentence: "I don't feel like going to GSA tonight; it will probably just be you and I anyways." Jenny answers, "It will probably just be you and I, but River may show up. If even one person comes it's worth it. It IS important."

We were excited to pick up where the previous year's GSA left off, expecting to provide internal and external educational patchwork *within* our community. The drastic change in attendance, however, shifted the club's focus to social support. Unprepared for this change, we found ourselves revisiting the needlework that crafted two "successful" years of work. We desperately tried to replicate the pattern as we failed to adjust to the club's new-found role; however, over time this tension loosened as we begin to examine our narratives that privileged education and activism over support. Had we stitched activism so firmly into place that we were now unable to see the importance of this new direction?

Our investment in maintaining an activist-centered GSA prevented us from seeing or hearing other stories that needed to be told. While new embroidery was developing we insisted on repeating known stitches. Through purposeful reflection we realized that new patterns enriched the faculty's fabric. Finer threads took the place of heavier, interwoven yarn of previous years, and an intricate pattern emerged: the club became a place for resisting isolation, engaging in intimate conversation, and developing more nuanced relationships. By releasing the taut netting, something different and subtle evolved organically, which inspired us to redefine our understanding of success. It challenged personal narratives that equated the value of the group with high membership and wide reach (Chase), while simultaneously resisting the expectation that the Other is responsible for educating the majority (Kumashiro). The weekly meetings dedicated time and space for our queer narratives to be shared, and these instances allowed us to better understand ourselves in relation to our context (Chase). Each filament of narrative spun by this small group was significant as they "embod[ied]—and [gave] us insight into—what is possible and intelligible within a specific context" (p. 79).

CONCLUSION

Each element is a row that builds on the other in cycles of resistance; visibility, antihomophobic/antitransphobic educational opportunities, impact/change, and reflection interlock to weave queer patterns. As we worked *with* and *within* we untangled the (hetero/cis)normative knots of our under/graduate experiences. The weaving continues to unfold as we speak back to dominant narratives (see Lindemann Nelson). We continue to attend to tensions in the weave, and work to incorporate counternarratives stitch by stitch, bringing about new understanding of how counternarratives can change the fabric, and the fabric can change us.

NOTES

1. Taken-for-granted attitudes and beliefs that position heterosexuality as "natural" and "normal." Taken-for-granted attitudes and beliefs that position cisgender (i.e., one's assigned sex at birth aligns with their gender identity) as "natural" and "normal."
2. Queer, in this context, is used to denote a nonnormative understanding and approach to teaching and learning. In terms of content, to "queer" means to envision that which is beyond traditional or "normal."

REFERENCES

Barone, T. (2007). A return to the gold standard? Questioning the future of narrative construction as educational research. *Qualitative Inquiry, 13*(4), 454–470.

Britzman, D. (1995). Is there a queer pedagogy? Or, stop reading straight. *Educational Theory, 45*(2), 151–165.

Britzman, D. (1998). *Lost subjects, contested objects: Towards a psychoanalytic inquiry of learning.* New York: State University of New York Press.

Bruner, J. S. (1994). Life as narrative. In A. H. Dyson & C. Genishi (Eds.), *The need for story: Cultural diversity in classroom and community* (pp. 28–37). Urbana, IL: National Council of Teachers of English.

Chase, S. E. (2005). Narrative inquiry: Multiple lenses, approaches, voices. In N. K. Denzin & Y. S. Lincoln (Eds.), *The Sage handbook of qualitative research* (3rd ed., pp. 57–94). Thousand Oaks, CA: Sage.

Clandinin, D. J., & Connelly, F. M. (2000). What do narrative inquirers do? In *Narrative inquiry: Experience and story in qualitative research* (pp. 48–62). San Francisco, CA: Jossey-Bass.

Connelly, F. M., & Clandinin, D. J. (1990). Stories of experience and narrative inquiry. *Educational Researcher, 19*(2), 1–14.

Connelly, F. M., & Clandinin, D. J. (2006). Narrative inquiry. In J. L. Green, G. Camilli, & P. Elmore (Eds.), *Handbook of complementary methods in education research* (3rd ed.) (pp. 477–487). Mahwah, NJ: Lawrence Erlbaum.

Downs, Y. (2009). Ethics and narrative research—a contradiction in terms? In *Narrative, memory and identities* (pp. 21–30). Huddersfield, UK: University of Huddersfield.

Frank, A. (2000). The standpoint of storyteller. *Qualitative Health Research, 10*(3), 354–365.

Kumashiro, K. (2002). *Troubling education: Queer activism and anti-oppressive pedagogy.* New York: RoutledgeFalmer.

Lapointe, A. (2015). Queering the social studies: Lessons to be learned from Canadian secondary school gay-straight alliances. *The Journal of Social Studies Research.* doi:10.1016/j.jssr.2015.07.004

Lindemann Nelson, H. (1995). Resistance and insubordination. *Hypatia, 10*(2), 23–40.

Linville, D. (2009). Queer theory and teen sexuality: Unclear lines. In J. Anyon (Ed.), *Theory and educational research: Toward critical social explanation*. New York: Routledge.

Pinnegar, S., & Daynes, G. D. (2007). Locating narrative inquiry historically. In D. J. Clandinin (Ed.), *Handbook of narrative inquiry: Mapping a methodology* (pp. 3–34). Thousand Oaks, CA: Sage.

Riley, T., & Hawe, P. (2005). Researching practice: The methodological case for narrative inquiry. *Theory & Practice, 20*(2), 226–236.

Sedgwick, E. K. (1990/2008). *Epistemology of the closet*. Berkeley & Los Angeles: University of California Press.

Spector-Mersel, G. (2010). Narrative research: Time for a paradigm. *Narrative Inquiry, 20*(1), 204–224.

Xu, S., & Connelly, M. (2010). Narrative inquiry for school based research. *Narrative Inquiry, 20*(2), 349–370.

CHAPTER NINE

Adopting a Queer Pedagogy as a Teaching Assistant

STEPHANIE ANNE SHELTON

"IF YOU'RE TEACHING QUEER STUFF, YOU'RE GETTING OFF TOPIC"

"If you could sign in so that we're able to verify your attendance, please." I scribbled my name in the blank, inwardly grumbling about this mandatory teaching assistant (TA) training. I waded through the lecture hall to pick up my training program and find a seat. Those sitting to my left were excitedly talking about teaching in the fall, discussing how nervous that they were to teach "for real." One popped her gum and volunteered, "I'm kinda scared, but I'm kinda excited too. I mean, I know how to teach. Everybody does, right? I took this same class when I was a freshman, so I know how it works." I rolled my eyes, resentment returning that I—after years of successful secondary and postsecondary teaching experience—had to sit beside Ms. Bubble Yum and her equally inexperienced friends and to endure whatever the training would entail.

The lights blinked to signal the program's start and then dimmed for the PowerPoint display. I sat through slide after slide detailing my responsibilities, the university's policies, and sample syllabi. The speaker then announced that the session would transition to discussing issues of equality, access, and diversity. "Find some people near you and discuss various situations involving diversity that might come up while you're teaching in your classrooms." I found myself absorbed into Bubble Yum's group. They listed off a variety of issues that were indeed important to consider: "We might have people who don't speak English well." "Yeah, and some students don't have a ton of money." "And, there are issues with race and ethnicity, and maybe religion, too." Suddenly there was silence. I realized that the others had stopped talking and were looking at me. Apparently they had gone around in a circle, and it was now my turn. I swallowed. "You know, two of my biggest concerns are serving queer students and addressing queer issues." Bubble Yum nodded vigorously. "Yes! I totally want to support my gay students." I shook my head. "Not just gay students. *Queer* students. Like, students who don't fit specific molds, or who break molds. And, I want to teach in a way that's queer, too." The person sitting to Bubble Yum's left looked pensive. He cleared his throat. "So, like, when you say 'queer,' I mean, that's gonna detract from what you're supposed to teach. We all get paid to teach something specific, right?" The others nodded. He continued, "So, um, if you're teaching queer stuff, you're getting off topic. I mean, I'd be getting off topic. I'm supposed to teach chemistry. I'm a chemistry guy."

THE LITERATURE ON TEACHING ASSISTANTS

The U.S. Department of Labor (2014) indicates that there are nearly 130,000 teaching assistants (TAs) working at American universities and colleges, roughly 10% of the entire postsecondary teaching force when one includes tenure-track and career-track faculty, as well as adjuncts and visiting professors. TAs, therefore, comprise a significant percentage of those teaching college courses, and they are sometimes responsible for more courses than faculty. Despite their presence and importance, there is little research on TAs' roles in education, even less research on TAs' pedagogical approaches, and almost no consideration of what it means for TAs to enact queer pedagogies.

The available literature primarily focuses either on the nature of TAs' responsibilities, such as how time gets divided between grading and teaching (e.g., Benassi & Fernald, 1993; Prieto, 2010; Sales, Comeau, Liddle, Perrone, Palmer, & Lynn, 2007; Sargent, Allen, Frahm, & Morris, 2009), or on how to best support TAs socially and emotionally (e.g., Rhodes, 1997; Weidert, Wendorf, Gurung, & Fitz, 2012). Fewer researchers specifically consider TAs in relation to pedagogy. Of those studies that are available, Stoeker, Schmidbauer, Mullin, and Young's (1993) evaluation is representative of the literature. They considered how TAs might support faculty who had adopted a critical pedagogy, assuming throughout that the instructional framework had come directly and solely from the faculty member. Based on existent research, one might assume that TAs do not have independent pedagogical approaches; that their methods and practices are determined by the faculty with whom they are paired or by the university training that they receive.

THE LITERATURE ON QUEER PEDAGOGIES

While there is not research that specifically discusses TAs' adoptions of, experiences with, or resistances to queer pedagogy, there is literature that considers the implications of queer instructional approaches both as an early career educator and at the postsecondary level. Both teacher educators Cosier and Sanders (2007) discussed their efforts to queer teacher preparation in their respective programs. Both had varying degrees of success and failure, but both were very aware of students' beliefs that the two professors were "imposing a homosexuality agenda on a class they [the students] saw as having little to do with queer concerns" (p. 25). Even during a playful activity intended to help students appreciate ways that images might queer notions of art or might be queer, the authors noted that "[n]o joy emerged from the exercise" (p. 26), and students were resentful of and shocked by the activity.

Krywanczyk (2007) discusses the unexpected struggles and successes of queering both the physical body and the curriculum as a first-year secondary teacher. Krywanczyk was determined to adopt "queer" as "a verb, not a noun" in teaching (p. 27). Despite some successes, including greater confidence in self-identity and gender expression, Krywanczyk's employers challenged "my activist endeavors" and indicated that they "would prefer a toned-down, less radical political methodology" (p. 27). At the postsecondary level, Stewart (2007) evaluated university landscapes in terms of how such spaces, along with their policies, course offerings, and administrations, supported or complicated queer identities and education practices. Though he found that a greater number of colleges and universities offered queer resources, courses, degree programs, and certificates than ever before, the fluid nature of queerness was in constant opposition to the often rigid structures of academic institutions; in short, "the struggle for its [queer academia's] very existence could ultimately be the cause of its self-destruction" because existing in higher education requires both "construct[ing] and maintain[ing] identity within academia" and navigating "categories that are 'exclusionary'" (p. 92). In other words, it is hard to fit something as fluid and flexible as queerness into an entity as fixed as higher education. The paltry body of literature on queer pedagogy and TAs reflects both the complexities of enacting a queer pedagogy in academia and both the resistances and the lack of support that those face who seek to do queer work.

AUTOETHNOGRAPHY AS A QUEER APPROACH

As I prepared to write this chapter, I struggled with how to write about queering teaching while staying within the traditional parameters of academic writing. I recognized that researched information would be essential, both to demonstrate the importance of TAs' experiences and to consider the implications of the near-nonexistent literature on TAs' pedagogical practices, particularly in relation to queer topics. Because there was so little literature from which I might draw, and because I wanted a way to communicate the complexities of queer pedagogy in a format that complemented queer work, I determined to hybridize autoethnographic elements and relevant literature, while focusing on queer pedagogy.

Autoethnography is a method that is constantly "in a state of flux and movement" (Jones, 2005, p. 764). Autoethnography "works to hold self and culture together" (p. 764), by making the author the "focus of the story, the one who tells and the one who experiences… . [The author] is the person at the intersection of the personal and the cultural" (Ellis, 2009, p. 13).

Autoethnography and queer topics connect well together to open "definitional boundaries" and to make "the politics of knowledge and experience central to what autoethnography is and does" (Jones & Adams, 2010, p. 199). The two work to "refuse received notions" of scholarship (p. 197) and to challenge norms as they relate to personal and to cultural understandings that involve gender and sexuality. Through autoethnography, I work to find the means of exploring how my own experiences might contribute to broader conversations about the ways that schools often silence queer discourse (Blackburn, 2012), and the possibilities of breaking those silences through queer pedagogy (Britzman, 1998).

"MAKE SURE THAT YOU HAVE YOUR PRIORITIES IN ORDER"

I sighed as another page floated to the floor. I had far too many sheets of paper and too few spaces on the table. I was working on my course syllabus, and I was stuck reflecting on what it meant to be queer, to teach queerly, and to queer my curriculum—all while meeting the expectations of my supervising teacher and the certification program for which I was a TA. I had various lists of potential activities and readings, but I did not feel like I was doing much more than integrating a few queer topics into a relatively standard curriculum. As an instructor of record, I had the luxury of crafting my own syllabus, but there were programmatic limitations, such as ensuring that the student teachers met each standard in their teaching portfolio and were prepared to submit unit plans before they began to teach independently.

The TA training on the previous day had been completely unhelpful in addressing queer issues in even the broadest sense. During the group discussion on my desire to support queer students and queer teaching, one of the veteran TAs from previous years had come over to facilitate what had clearly become a strong discussion between Bubble Yum, "Chemistry Guy," the others in the group, and me. Chemistry Guy had immediately tattled that I was "confusing a personal agenda with my responsibilities." I inwardly rolled my eyes, took a calming breath, and told the TA, who identified herself as "Rosa," "Look, I've been a teacher for years. You can address queer topics and still check everything officially required off of the to-do list. I don't know why there isn't more of a conversation on this issue, beyond just me in this group right here." The TA nodded as if she understood, paused, and then said, "Yeah, but teaching here is different. You have new responsibilities. That's what today's training is all about, you know. You have to make sure that you're following university guidelines and doing whatever it is that your college and department expect."

I outwardly rolled my eyes this time. "Do you think that teaching high school students or being an adjunct university instructor didn't bring specific responsibilities? If anything, there are fewer restrictions here." Rosa had started shaking her head "No" while I was talking; clearly she was only waiting for me to stop talking so that she could start. The moment I paused, she began, "Teaching high school and adjuncting aren't the same as being a TA. And, you need to accept that there are parts of who you are that are important and valuable that may just not fit completely into your classroom. You should speak with your supervisor about what's permissible or not, but you have to make sure that you have your priorities in order, and that you do the job that you were brought here to do."

QUEER PEDAGOGIES

To write about queer pedagogy as if there is a singular approach would be to un-queer queer teaching. The very nature of queerness is that it is always fluid, always multiple, always dynamic (Gamson, 2000; Hall, 2003). There are, however, consistent features to queer pedagogies that span disciplines, educators, and situations. To queer teaching is to problematize the ways that social structures such as classrooms normalize and enforce particular behaviors, such as being in a heterosexual relationship or being a female who behaves in a stereotypically feminine manner (Britzman). In doing so, queer pedagogies blur and challenge sociocultural boundaries (Whitlock, 2010). In adopting a queer pedagogy, teachers work to question how notions of normality are constructed and enforced, and they support their students' efforts to do the same.

One of the primary elements of a queer pedagogy is supporting learning spaces where those in privileged positions, such as students and teachers who are cisgendered or heterosexual, move their thinking and actions beyond tolerance; where those in subjugated positions, such as those who identify as or who are perceived as queer, are simply tolerated (Britzman). One measure of encouraging a classroom space in which people constantly examine both personal positions and socialization is through asking students and teachers to read beyond the self and to consider the many acculturated and conflicting elements of what one might initially consider to be a unified self. Britzman explains the importance of this approach:

> There are no innocent, normal, or unmediated readings … and representations draw upon [reading practices] to maintain a narrative or a self as normal, as deviant, as thinkable… . [I]dentities and the self knowledge that render them intelligible and unintelligible suggest more about the social effects of the political than they do about essential selves. (p. 226)

When students and teachers begin to appreciate the ways that external factors, such as political leanings and family values, directly shape who they are and how they respond to texts and discussions, they begin to appreciate ways to both queer those readings and themselves. Doing so supports making them more appreciative of others' queerness.

"THINKING ABOUT THIS STUFF JUST PISSES ME OFF"

Following Super-TA Rosa's insistence that I get my priorities in order and talk to my supervisor, I ascertained that—provided I was preparing the student teachers in my classroom for their field experiences and teacher portfolios—my department welcomed a queer pedagogy. My supervisor was unsure of what my approach meant, aside from the information in my syllabus, so she seated herself in the corner of my classroom at 8:00 a.m. on a Tuesday morning. I comprehended the make-or-break nature of the moment. If she understood what happened as successful and valuable, I would have a green light; if she determined that I, like others who have tried queer teaching approaches, was neglecting my true responsibilities to pursue a queer agenda, then Chemistry Guy, Bubble Yum, and the others would be right.

My students had had several days of program orientation and icebreakers, and most knew one another from other education courses. I was the only new variable for most of them. I reviewed my teaching agenda to get my thoughts in order and cleared my throat. "If all of you would check the class website, there's a short article that I want you to read. Either during or after your reading, make notes about personal reactions to the text. Just knee-jerk reactions. You won't necessarily have to share these publicly, so no filter necessary." Several students chuckled. One smiled and popped her knuckles in preparation. "I'm going to give you about five minutes total, so you won't finish, but that's okay. After we stop, I'll give you the next set of directions." I waited for them to begin reading about the Annoka-Hennepin school district's "neutrality policy" controversy, which had made national news after LGBTQ students had committed suicide due to the district's problematic responses to gender- and sexuality-based bullying ("Stop bullying: Speak up," 2011).

While they read, I watched their faces, hoping that their expressions would give me insight into their responses. One student's brow furrowed, and she scribbled furiously in the margins. Another hummed some nondescript tune while pecking at her laptop. Still another pulled at his hair while he rested his head on his palms. After five minutes, I told them, "Okay, stop." All 24 of them dutifully put their pens down or looked up from their keyboards. I knew that what followed was the tricky part. "I want you to look at what you've written as if you've never seen it before. As if you happened to read the same text as a stranger and then found that individual's reading notes." The one who had red palm prints on his forehead from his reading position looked confused. I continued, "What I want you to do is consider from where or from whom those reactions came from. For example, if I read this article and wrote, 'I'm shocked that the administration thought this policy would work in the first place,' then I have a lot of different factors to consider in that one sentence." I turned and quickly wrote the sentence on the dry erase board behind me. I felt slightly dizzy, and I was unsure if it was nerves or if it was the alcohol-heavy scent of the marker. As I turned, I held onto the marker tray.

I pointed to the word "shocked." "See this word 'shocked'? That word carries a lot of assumptions about schools, about students, about school leaders, even though it's just one word. Consider for a second: why might I be shocked? What ideas might I have learned, assumed, or observed about school spaces that that word would be the one that I would choose?" I waited an uncomfortable ten seconds until the student who had hummed during the reading offered, "I mean, I guess you think schools should be the opposite of this. That's why we get shocked, right? 'Cause things work the opposite of how we figure? So, whatever happened should've been the reverse for you to not be shocked." She cocked her head to the side and asked her peers, "Does that make sense?" Several nodded and another added, "Yeah. So, like, you figure schools do stuff to keep students safe. You know, rules that make sure kids aren't in danger, that they don't hurt themselves."

I nodded. "Okay. So, if those are assumptions that that word suggests that I made, then dig deeper. If I assume that administration should do the opposite of this, then I am also assuming that they had the authority to act differently. And, I'm assuming that students need protection and that schools need such policies in the first place. What do those assumptions suggest about my beliefs concerning schools?" A student that the program director had described as a "firecracker" raised her hand. "So, I'm gonna be real with y'all. Thinking about this stuff just pisses me off." Several students looked surprised, but most looked only wary. I was both. I proceeded cautiously. "Okay, so, what specifically upsets you about talking about this exercise? My word choice? My assumptions? The article's content? All of the above? None of the above?"

She shrugged. "I dunno. I mean, I guess I'm just now thinking about how we just put people in power, like these district people, and then we think, 'Oh, well if they have power, they'll do the right thing.' What kind of dumb-ass assumption is that? Because these people have authority, we just trust them to do what ought to be done? This neutrality policy thing—of course they passed it. It was a nice, safe, easy middle road for them. They didn't have to write any rules about queer kids, but they got to pretend that everyone was protected. And no one really questioned them until people died. I'm looking at stuff I wrote, and I have stuff like, 'OMG—fucking idiots thought this would work?!?' I mean, if I'm that mad, then I clearly expected different. I was obviously—what was that word? 'Acculturated?' Yeah. Acculturated into this nonsense of trusting these morons because they wear nice suits and have fancy titles. I'm only mad because stuff got bad. The policy was stupid the whole time, but I only realized it when people died." She smacked her forehead. "Unbelievable!"

She had given us the perfect opening to discuss power structures in complex ways. "Okay," I started, "I'm going to write up here 'people in power' and 'cultural assumptions about authority' based on what Isabell just said. I want all of you to pick one or two of the statements that you wrote as you read and consider what norms you took for granted either before, during, or after reading about this issue. Take a few minutes, and jot any additional thoughts." I waited for about five minutes, and then told them to share with those at their tables. I emphasized that they were merely sharing reactions and evaluations, not weighing the validity of or their agreements with others' points. The discussion buzzed. All were outraged that students had been hurt, but while some aligned with Isabell, others argued that they understood what the school district had intended.

After a few minutes, I felt confident that we were able to examine various power structures that directly and invisibly influenced school district administrators, teachers, students, and community members. I wanted to then shift the focus from the external to the internal. As Britzman puts it, I wanted my students to consider what factors permitted them and me to "maintain a narrative or a self as normal, as deviant, as thinkable" (p. 226). I interrupted the chatter surrounding their analyses of school power structures. "Okay, we're going to dig a bit deeper again. We've talked a lot about the school district, the teachers, the kids, the parents, and this policy. I want you to think about you now, in relation to those conversations. Presumably you all think that you're pretty normal." A few interrupted with laughter and one muttered "I don't know about that!" "So, at least normal enough for you to think that this program would willingly certify you to teach, right? What parts of your assumptions about schools help you to align with larger societal assumptions? What parts of your reactions put you in opposition to the majority of people? What parts help those sitting in this room with you to understand you as someone who could be a good teacher?" A few looked uncertain. "So, if we were to go back to my example of me being shocked—we already talked about my assumptions of the school board's power and of children needing protection. How do those aspects of my response help to align me with others?" I paused. A student cleared her throat and offered, "Well, I mean, school's about hierarchy, so you recognize the food chain, I guess. And, any decent teacher would presumably want kids to be safe."

I nodded. "Okay, so those things help me to fit with general understandings of what it means to be a teacher. What parts of my shock keep me from fitting into whatever you think of when you think of a standard teacher?" Isabell's hand shot up immediately. "Yeah, so that you would want any policy in place that might maybe protect queer kids—not necessarily a popular opinion in some places, right? I mean, it's probably why these morons passed it in the first place. They were trying to do the right thing without pissing somebody off. Even though I've just been mad this whole class period." Several laughed. I smiled. "So, using Isabell's offering as a beginning, I want you to begin to examine how your responses and your discussions of efforts to navigate school power structures, specifically in relation to the issue of these LGBTQ students, reflect ways that you fit or don't fit into what people think of when they think 'teacher.'"

As class closed, I gave my students the next steps of this analytical work. "I want all of you to do two things before you come back next week. First, I want you to share your written responses and thoughts with at least two other people, so that they can maybe see cultural assumptions that you might miss. That whole 'Can't see the forest for the trees kind of thing.' Second, because one of your portfolio standards is professional reflection and another is appreciation for diversity and social justice, I want you to think about how your individual responses from today contradict with and complement one another. For example, in my sentence about me being shocked, I simultaneously accepted the school district's authority and reacted strongly that LGBTQ students weren't protected. One part of that accepts what might be the status quo; one part of that might go against popular opinion. In other words, I want you to begin to recognize that who you are as a teacher is way more complicated than 'I want to help kids.' You are someone who will love, hate, agree, and resent all at one time. I want you to see how you constantly shift between those different parts of yourself but still manage to function as someone who seems cohesive to others."

As the students filed out, some complained that class had given them a headache and some shifted to topics related to upcoming classes. In the back corner, my supervisor waited until they had all filed out before asking, "So, I know that was an article about LGBTQ issues. I totally get how that related to the portfolios and standards. If you want to incorporate those topics, it's fine with me." I smiled to thank her and then explained, "The topic of the neutrality policy definitely made the discussion focus in on LGBTQ students, but queer pedagogy is way bigger than that. They're leaving here after one day, questioning school norms and power structures, and they're realizing that they're all fragmented and contradictory people who are constantly shaped by social and cultural expectations. *They* are queer; their *thinking* is queer." She nodded. "Good. I look forward to having some queer portfolios and teacher candidates. I'll be back to see them and you in action again. All of that made me think, too." As she walked out, I wondered if Bubble Yum and Chemistry Guy had been as relieved by their first day as a TA as I had been.

CONCLUSION

As I navigate higher education as a TA who self-identifies as queer and who actively incorporates queer topics and queer-ing work into my curriculum, I am constantly aware of the limitations that I face. I am not a faculty member who has even a limited level of protection from holding a Ph.D. or from having earned tenure. I am always fully accountable to my department, and I know that the constant competition for funding means that there are many other graduate students who are happy to fill my slot, even before I graduate. And losing my funding would mean losing my tuition waiver, my stipend, and my insurance.

TAs are an incredibly vulnerable group. TAs are also, however, incredibly powerful. We serve thousands of other students and hundreds of faculty, and we make up a significant portion of the postsecondary teaching ranks. Research on pedagogy does little to credit TAs with having pedagogical positions, and queer research has done little to include TAs at all. This chapter seeks to offer both a specific discussion of the value and complexity of a queer pedagogy and to demonstrate how queer education and education research might become with empowered TAs. Queer pedagogy "refuses normal practices and practices of normalcy" and imagines a "sociality unhinged from the dominant conceptual order" (Britzman, p. 227). Who better to do the unhinging than TAs—a group already navigating competing identities as student, researcher, teacher, and so forth while existing on the fringe of academic professionalism? To be a TA is arguably a constantly queer state, and such an in-flux identity could support queer pedagogy in a range of disciplines.

REFERENCES

Benassi, V., & Fernald, P. (1993). Preparing tomorrow's psychologists for careers in academe. *Teaching of Psychology, 20*(3), 149–155.

Blackburn, M. V. (2012). *Interrupting hate: Homophobia in schools and what literacy can do about it.* New York: Teachers College Press.
Britzman, D. (1998). Is there a queer pedagogy? Or, stop reading straight. In W. F. Pinar (Ed.), *Curriculum: Toward new identities* (pp. 211–227). New York: Garland.
Cosier, K., & Sanders, J. H., III. (2007). Queering art teacher education. *International Journal of Art & Design Education, 26*(1), 21–30.
Ellis, C. (2009). *Revision: Autoethnographic reflections on life and work.* Walnut Creek, CA: Left Coast.
Gamson, J. (2000). Sexualities, queer theory, and qualitative research. In N. K. Denzin & Y. S. Lincoln (Eds.), *Handbook of qualitative research* (2nd ed., pp. 347–365). Thousand Oaks, CA: Sage.
Hall, D. (2003). *Queer theories.* New York: Palgrave Macmillan.
Jones, S. H. (2005). Autoethnography: Making the personal political. In N. K. Denzin & Y. S. Lincoln (Eds.), *The Sage handbook of qualitative research* (3rd ed., pp. 763–791). Thousand Oaks, CA: Sage.
Jones, S. H., & Adams, T. E. (2010). Autoethnography is a queer method. In K. Browne & C. J. Nash (Eds.), *Queer methods and methodologies: Intersecting queer theories and social science research* (pp. 195–214). Burlington, VT: Ashgate.
Krywanczyk, L. (2007, Fall). Queering public school pedagogy as a first-year teacher. *Radical Teacher, 79*, 27–34.
Prieto, L. R. (2010, August). *Guiding the UTA experience: The modified integrated developmental model.* Paper presented at the annual American Psychological Association convention, San Diego, CA.
Rhodes, T. D. (1997). Graduate teaching assistant training: Examining issues of socialization and emotionally painful incidents in the classroom. *North Dakota Journal of Speech & Theatre, 10*(1), 52–63.
Sales, D., Comeau, D., Liddle, K., Perrone, L., Palmer, K., & Lynn, D. (2007). Preparing future faculty: An interdisciplinary undergraduate science course taught by graduate and postdoctoral teacher-scholars. *Journal of College Science Teaching, 36*(4), 24–30.
Sargent, L., Allen, B., Frahm, J., & Morris, G. (2009). Enhancing the experience of student teams in large classes: Training teaching assistants to be coaches. *Journal of Management Education, 33*(5), 526–552. doi: 10.1177/1052562909334092
Stewart, T. (2007). Vying for an unsustainable/inappropriate(d)/organic queer space in higher education. *Journal of Curriculum & Pedagogy, 4*(2), 89–95.
Stoecker, R., Schmidbauer, M., Mullin, J., & Young, M. (1993). Integrating writing and the teaching assistant to enhance critical pedagogy. *Teaching Sociology, 21*(4), 332–340.
Stop bullying: Speak up. (2011). Retrieved from http://www.cnn.com/SPECIALS/2011/bullying/
United States Department of Labor. (2014). *Occupational outlook handbook: Teacher assistants.* Retrieved from http://www.bls.gov/ooh/education-training-and-library/teacher-assistants.htm
United States Department of Labor. (2014). Occupational outlook handbook: Teacher assistants. Retrieved from http://www.bls.gov/ooh/education-training-and-library/teacher-assistants.htm
Weidert, J. M., Wendorf, A. R., Gurung, R. A. R., & Fitz, T. (2012). A survey of graduate and undergraduate teaching assistants. *College Teaching, 60*(3), 95–103.
Whitlock, R. U. (2010). Getting queer: Teacher education, gender studies, and the cross-disciplinary quest for queer pedagogies. *Issues in Teacher Education, 19*(2), 81–104.

CHAPTER TEN

Sanctioning Unsanctioned Texts: The True Story of a Gay Writer

MICHAEL WENK

In the TV show *Transparent* (Soloway, 2014), Jeffery Tambor plays Mort, a retired professor and father of three adult children who, late in life, begins to transition to a woman, Maura. We see flashbacks of Mort in the 1980s, searching a magazine rack at a bohemian bookstore for answers about his predicament (being constructed as a man). Mort is forced to seek answers outside the sanctioned literacies of the university setting. Inside a seedy bookstore, he finds information about his identity in "tawdry" magazines.

Like Mort, queer students understand the shortcomings of the "autonomous" approach to literacy (Street, 2003) found in schools, and on their own time, they turn to documentaries, sitcoms, young adult novels, blogs, public health websites, chatrooms, and YouTube channels—to name a few—as a means to explore and affirm their queer identities. With characteristics of interactivity and fluidity, out-of-school literacies bear little resemblance to the "formally imposed/officially sanctioned sequenced curriculum which is founded on texts as information sources" (Lankshear & Knobel, 2006, p. 6). Even so, queer youth could benefit from educators who could help to mediate texts and support students as they discover and try on identities.

When I was 13, I needed a teacher to show me possibilities for authoring a queer life. I needed a teacher to say, "This is a queer poet. This poetry is queer. Can you queer this poetry?" I needed a teacher to write alongside me, to tackle difficult topics and school assignments, like "What would happen if two men did get married?" I could have explored queer options, such as an opinion piece for a local paper or short poem for a coffeehouse audience. Instead, I was positioned to examine tepid topics and sketch safe (heterosexual) characters to inhabit my stories. As a result, my desire to become a writer—and my desires as a young gay man—found an outlet in furtive poems written in the sanctuary of my bedroom. Not having access to many of the electronic resources available to young people today, I reached out to a former teacher to serve as a critical witness (Dutro, 2010) to these poems.

*****

Don, the librarian at my junior high school, sat across from me at the shiny, plastic table, munching a McDonald's cheeseburger. I sat, munching a cheeseburger in silence, watching him. He reached for a french fry and flipped a page over, reading another of the 15 or so poems I had written neatly in ink on typewriter paper. I sipped my Coke, wondering if I should have turned over these documents to him. I felt the exuberance of a double agent, revealing strategic secrets that might help win the war, if they could be deciphered. I also felt my betrayal might lead to grave harm to innocent civilians. It was my first—and even to this day—my only audience for those poems.

"Wow, you've done a lot of writing, Mike," he finally said, looking up. "When did you write these poems?"

"Over the past few months, I guess."

"Hmmm … I like this one," he said, pushing a sheet of paper over to me. "You say, society destroys people like me. What do you mean by that: people like me?"

"Um, I don't know. People who think differently?"

He laughed. "Well, you definitely have a different way of thinking. Like when you wore a tinfoil hat around school to shield your head from gamma rays."

I smiled, but Don was still seeking clues. "Are you saying that you are different than everyone else?"

"Yes."

"How?"

I took a long sip on my Coke, thinking. Seconds passed. I grabbed a french fry and twisted it between my fingers. Don waited patiently, with just a hint of a smile. A McDonald's employee moved past the table, mopping in a prescribed sequence of strokes.

"I don't know," I finally said. "I don't feel like everybody else."

"In what way?"

A fence sitting metaphor truly is appropriate here, because how I answered would determine which way I would fall. The effect would be cataclysmic for a ninth grade boy in 1981.

In what way? In many ways. I was a poet. I was a wrestler. I enjoyed sitting in a deer blind at dusk—20 feet above the ground in the deep Michigan woods—listening for whitetails while watching chickadees dance on branches above me. I loved playing basketball in my friend's driveway. Slow dancing to Lionel Richie and Styx songs with Dawn and Barb and Brenda at junior high dances. Holed up in my room, listening to Tiger games on the radio, reading Robert Louis Stevenson books, wondering what would happen if a boy I liked found out.

If I was sitting in Don's seat, a vantage point on myself as a 14-year-old—and I have occupied that seat as a teacher many times in my career—I might have seen uncertainty and confusion in my eyes. I might have seen me sizing up the situation, following the cascading dominoes. I might have heard the flip of a switch and seen a well-lit room go completely dark. I might have heard the guile of an adolescent boy in this response:

"It's just a phase, right Don? I mean, I'm growing up. That's normal, right?"

"Yes, that's normal. But …"

"So I guess there's nothing to these poems but the hormonal rantings of a teenager."

Don laughed. He seemed like he wanted to pose another pointy question, but then realized the light was off. My soul had gone dark. "Did you listen to that Mahler tape yet?"

"Yes," I lied.

"What did you think?"

"It reminds me a lot of the hormonal rantings of a teenager." He laughed again, shaking his head.

"OK, we'd better go."

"Thanks for the cheeseburger, Don."

"Anytime."

*****

Early in life, in elementary school, I tried to make my deviant sexual desires invisible. My intuition about the world told me not to display effeminate traits in what I said, how I spoke, or how I moved. On TV I could see Jack Tripper (played by John Ritter) enact a silly parody of a gay man in *Three's Company* (Ross, 1977), and Anita Bryant crusading against homosexuality on the national news. In my own home, a rare resource about my sexuality was *The Ann Landers Encyclopedia A–Z* (Landers, 1978), which offered pro and con arguments about homosexuality. My awareness of the AIDS epidemic mirrored much of the rest of the nation: I was ignorant and fearful. I saw pictures of the dying and felt only aversion and confusion. At that time, I wasn't attuned to a single affirming Discourse regarding queer people.

And so I performed an identity I thought my teachers, my peers, and my family wanted for me. I acted straight, citing masculine markers in my performance. I desperately hoped my performance would allow me to pass as a "straight" person. For closeted gays and lesbians, passing is not just acting a certain way: it is also not acting a certain way. Irvine (2001) calls this "erasure," in which "an ideology simplifies the sociolinguistic field" (p. 33). For queer youth, erasure means wiping out effortless ways of speaking and/or gesturing to perform in a way that is culturally intelligible. In junior high school, for example, I could be bookish but I also had to play football.

In tenth grade, I remember walking to my first period class with my friend Jon, a senior who gave me a ride to school because I couldn't drive yet. We met up with his three friends—I'll call them Obnoxious, Loud, and Rude—and so I melted into the background while they carried on. They spotted Roger, a boy who had attended school with me since kindergarten, holding his books to his chest as he hurried down the hallway toward us. One of the guys called out, voice full of sunshine and lisping affectation: "Roger! Roger, honey! You are so GAY!" Raucous laughter as Roger passed by me, his face red and his head bowed. I remember thinking to myself, *Don't ever be that guy. Don't ever be gay.*

What guy did I want to be? I wanted to be a writer. Since first grade, I had been labeled as a writer by my teachers, but I think it had more to do with technical proficiency, or a lack of mechanical missteps that conserves red ink and allows teachers to skim to the end, where a few quick strokes can make an A, giving extra time to "correct" the more error-prone essays. What challenge had I offered to my teachers as readers? What fat and gristle did they have to chew and swallow and uncomfortably digest? And what challenge did they offer me? When I think back as far as kindergarten, I can't remember a specific teacher who taught me how to write, except my first grade teacher, who showed us how to make the letters of the alphabet. Maybe my memory is faulty, but my archive of school writing assignments shows little direction from teachers, especially in providing me with options to explore possible identities. Conspicuously absent from writing assignments—most any assignment, in fact—was sexuality. And so my confusion as a gay young man found an outlet in late night free verse rather than school-time acrostic.

Even though sexuality is a fact of school life, with school dances and same-sex physical education classes and novels and textbooks that feature the deeds of heterosexuals, few educators wish to address anything but a narrow, proscribed version of sexuality in their classrooms. Among educators, there is always a sense of relief that someone else will teach about more complicated, controversial topics regarding sexuality: a biology teacher or a health teacher, for example, might share the wonders of sperm and egg. In teaching about sexuality, the biology teacher or the health teacher is given special dispensation: according to Bourdieu (1993), "The whole social order is behind them" (p. 74). He continues: "Not anyone can assert anything, or else does so at his peril" (p. 74). If teachers are restricted from including sexuality in their curricula, where does that leave budding writers (budding deviants), in terms of exploring and constructing identities outside the "heterosexual matrix"? (Butler, 1990, p. 151)

As a young writer, I knew that asserting anything about my sexuality would be perilous. And so I stuck to safe topics. In a tribute to freedom for a third grade poster contest, I didn't recognize how the phrase "all men are created equal" from my reproduction of the Declaration of Independence might apply to burgeoning homosexuals like me. My research paper in tenth grade examined the life of J. R. R. Tolkien—dry detail followed by lifeless anecdote—instead of analyzing the Others that populated his books. A short story in twelfth grade emulated the plots of the spy novels I was reading. What might my story have looked like if I had been able to read *Will Grayson, Will Grayson* (Green & Levithan, 2010) instead? Literacy activities have historically lacked meaningful opportunities for queer youth to deconstruct their own or others' gender performance, to publicly challenge how others position them, or to participate in hopeful dialogue about gender and sexuality.

During my junior year of college, my writerly aspirations were completely snuffed out. On the second day of my advanced creative writing class, our professor held court about the mysteries of writing short stories and my classmates waved sheaths of paper and described the surreal plots that occupied their waking and sleeping moments. Somehow, among this crew, I knew I was doomed to be left behind like Melville's Pip, alone in the vast ocean, watching Stubb's boat disappear over the horizon.

As eager writers trickled out of class, my professor said, "Michael, may I have a word with you?" His wan smile told me this was a man I did not know, a man I could not fathom, who lived in a world I would never glimpse.

Gathering my notebook, I faced my professor, my teacher of writing.

"Michael, you are not enrolled in this class," he said.

"Oh, well, I have my schedule right here."

"Michael, the writing sample you submitted … it doesn't strike me as real. As you know, proficient writing samples are a prerequisite for entrance into this class. I have read yours, and they are not very good."

My face said everything; there was nothing to say. In flustered silence, I left the room, already forgotten by this great man of learning as I hurried down the hallway and out the huge doors of Angell Hall into the dim Michigan winter.

Sometimes, many years must pass before you finally hear what someone was trying to tell you. I now realize the professor was right. Undiplomatic. Cold, even. But right.

My writing wasn't real. I wasn't committing my truth to the page. Because in 1986, very little of what I said or wrote represented what I knew in my head and felt in my heart. In my short stories, I fabricated a version of the truth that didn't ring true. A straight world. Or at least, asexual. Nonthreatening. Uncontroversial. So devoid of desire that no authentic characters inhabited the short stories that I was supposed to workshop in the short story class I never took.

Am I still angry about the professor's pronouncement? Yes. Who was looking out for my queer soul when I wasn't able to care for it myself? Who was teaching me to write the truth? Sadly, no one in the English Department at Michigan. And so, my ambitions to write faded away like a shadow on a sunless January afternoon. Upon graduating from college, I no longer sought an identity as a writer.

*****

Instead, I became an English teacher. Early in my teaching career, I worked as a substitute teacher and a coach. I got a call to sub at my old high school. During second period American history, I stood in front of the class, hands on hips, and tried to explain the assignment to the students. A hand went up. Not a question about history, but instead, the 16-year-old girl said, "Teacher, when you have your hands on your hips, it makes you look gay." During my lengthy career as a teacher, I never again stood in front of students with my hands on my hips. In fact, I made a conscious effort to reform anything that might lead students to wonder if I was gay. I edited my speech, particularly paying attention to the lisp that I first attempted to amend with the help of a speech therapist when I was in elementary school. My version of masculine power in the classroom meant standing with folded arms and straight posture, speaking authoritatively, patrolling my classroom like a soldier, and reproducing my father's stern look of disapproval whenever a student strayed. By performing markers of masculinity and steering clear of anything that I thought might be perceived as queer, I contributed to heterosexual hegemony in my school, even to homophobia.

Nieto and Bode (2011) say that teachers are products of educational systems that have "a history of racism, exclusion, and debilitating pedagogy. As a consequence, their practices may reflect their experiences, and they may unwittingly perpetuate policies and approaches that are harmful to many of their students" (p. 23). Carried over from my own childhood, a cornerstone of my existence as a closeted gay teacher was to protect myself from being a target of my students' antigay sentiment or being ostracized by the community where I taught. In doing so, I fed into a culture that can be toxic to queer students.

For 16 years as an English teacher, I championed the outsider status of literary antiheroes like Ponyboy Curtis, Holden Caulfield, Lennie and George, Mark Mathabane, and Maya Angelou, which was my own subtle response to the steady stream of intolerance that all of us see in the world. What I had not done is champion the outsider status of queer students who sat right in front of me and who, like me, struggled with their sexualities and their identities and their place in a society that, even today, often regards them with overt hostility.

*****

At age 44, I enrolled in a PhD program at the University of Colorado, Boulder. As part of my doctoral dissertation, I conducted a study about how literacy curriculum might be more inclusive of queer students. My dissertation addressed the ways in which Discourses contribute to the construction and enactment of students' performances of sexuality and gender via school writing assignments. Utilizing a methodology known as *student voice research* (Fine, 2007; Rodriguez & Brown, 2009), I formed a Curriculum Design Team where teachers and high school students collaborated in the construction of writing assignments that offered opportunities to explore queer issues and identities. The study capitalized on the expertise and empathy of the two teachers as well as the queer sensibility of seven members of a high school Gay-Straight Alliance (GSA). Participants examined how non-normative identities were materialized or foreclosed in their school's curriculum and developed writing assignments that promoted visibility, exploration, critique, and affirmation of Discourses (Gee, 2010) that affect queer youth. Students in the study brought a queer sensibility to the meetings of the Curriculum Design Team, which impacted meeting dynamics as well as how teachers took up Discourses impacting queer youth. Participants concluded that schools can and must provide opportunities for exploration of performances of identity and critique of heteronormativity, so that queer and straight students alike not only are able to disrupt the powerful myth of normative sexuality but also safely explore, construct, and enact identities via reading and writing assignments.

Students in the study acknowledged a dearth of opportunities to study queer history, read about queer identities in literature, or produce queer-themed compositions, even in the present day. As a possible remedy, students collaborated with teachers to develop writing assignments that utilized choice to explore rights and identities as major themes in history and language arts, respectively. In generating ideas for writing assignments, students promoted the inclusion of unsanctioned school texts, such as documentaries, young adult novels, nonfiction texts, blogs, and TV shows, as alternatives to the literary canon and the ubiquitous history book. Students were not only able to deliver resources teachers had never heard of but also remind teachers of useful pedagogical practices. *Choice*, according to students in the study, fosters "creative freedom," while teacher modeling about the nature of writing assignments would make writing assignments "a lot more inclusive." *Modeling* was emphasized as an instructional practice for teachers to employ so that choice did not seem daunting and did not engender bigotry. Choice and modeling were positioned as tools a teacher could use to cultivate critical perspectives, a way to untether the school from powerful heteronormative Discourses while inspiring students to consider queer issues and identities in their writing assignments.

Findings from my study suggested that curricular discussions about sexuality and gender must extend beyond K–12 staff meetings, teacher education courses, and even K–12 and college classrooms, to include student voices in the construction (and not just enactment) of curriculum. In collaborating with students, rather than advocating for them, teachers open up the possibility for ongoing dialogue, especially as they find the ground shifting under them as Discourses about gender and sexuality continue to evolve. The roles taken by participants in this study troubled what it means for a teacher to be an ally, and further, called into question just who is an ally when students and teachers engage in ongoing, productive dialogue about sexuality and gender. When teachers create learning communities where diverse Discourses are generated, explored, and critiqued, students are able to step into agentive roles as literacy learners. Representations of queer folk, whether in *Three's Company* or *Glee*, become starting points for reading, writing, and discussion in democratic classrooms.

In the seven students who participated in my study, I found my teachers of writing. More than any writing teacher, they provided resources for me to explore, space that felt safe, and language for me to experiment with. Under their tutelage, I read *Luna* (Peters, 2004), a groundbreaking novel about a transgender teen. I visited blogs written by lesbians for lesbians about lesbians. As I met with students, with their background in GSA, I entered into more honest and much richer conversations about sexuality and gender than I ever had experienced. I felt safe exploring my own identities and the meanings of Discourses that had influenced me. And finally, as I transcribed our meetings, I put words to page that, for the first time in my life, revealed real and important insights about the identities I had struggled with as well as wished to become. Among those identities were *writer* and *gay man.*

Near the end of the study, I watched *We Were Here* (Weissman, 2011), because student participants recommended this documentary film as powerful testimony about the AIDS crisis in the United States. As I watched, I learned about a period of history that I lived through. As a young gay man, I was a witness to the AIDS crisis in this country, yet at that time I saw and heard nothing that truly mattered about the queer community. One of the primary Discourses of the film is how the AIDS crisis united members of the queer community and their allies. Words like *community*, *club*, *village*, *family*, and *home* were used to describe the relationships among queer people and their allies. This conception of community is a legacy that deeply resonated with the young people in my study when they viewed and discussed queer-themed films. It's one of the Discourses from the queer community that they fully embraced and that they passed along to me, a situation I find to be full of irony and hope.

REFERENCES

Bourdieu, P. (1993). *Language and symbolic power.* Cambridge, MA: Harvard University Press.

Butler, J. (1990). *Gender trouble: Feminism and the subversion of identity.* New York: Routledge.

Dutro, E. (2010). What "hard times" means: Mandated curricula, middle-class assumptions, and the lives of poor children. *Research in the Teaching of English, 44*, 255–291.

Fine, M. (2007). An epilogue, of sorts. In J. Cammarota & M. Fine (Eds.), *Revolutionizing education: Youth participatory action research* (pp. 213–234). New York: Routledge.

Gee, J. (2010). *An introduction to discourse analysis: Theory and method* (3rd ed.). New York: Routledge.

Green, J., & Levithan, D. (2010). *Will Grayson, Will Grayson.* London: Dutton Juvenile.

Irvine, J. (2001). "Style" as distinctiveness. In P. Eckert & J. Rickford (Eds.), *Style and sociolinguistic variation* (pp. 21–32). Cambridge: Cambridge University Press.

Landers, A. (1978). *The Ann Landers encyclopedia A to Z.* New York: Ballantine.

Lankshear, C., & Knobel, M. (2006). *New Literacies: Changing knowledge and classroom learning.* Buckingham: Open University Press.

Nieto, S., & Bode, P. (2011). *Affirming diversity: The sociopolitical context of multicultural education.* Boston: Pearson.

Peters, J. A. (2004). *Luna.* New York: Little, Brown Books for Young Readers.

Rodriguez, L., & Brown, T. (2009). From voice to agency: Guiding principles for participatory action research with youth. *New Directions for Youth Development, 123*, 19–34.

Ross, M. (Executive Producer). (1977). *Three's Company.* [Television series]. United States: NRW Productions/T.T.C. Productions.

Soloway, J. (Executive Producer). (2014). *Transparent.* [Television series]. United States: Amazon Studios.

Street, B. (2003). What's "new" in New Literacy Studies? Critical approaches to literacy in theory and practice. *Current Issues in Comparative Education, 5*(2), 77–91.

Weissman, D. (Producer & Director). (2011). *We were here.* [Documentary]. United States: Red Flag Releasing.

Part 4:
Misrecognition: From Invisibility Into Visibility

CHAPTER ELEVEN

(Un)becoming Trans*: Every Breath You Take and Every …

sj MILLER

move you make
every bond you break,
every step you take, I'll be watching you.
—STING (1983)

These lyrics, sung by Police in their album *Synchronicity* was not only on the Billboard Top 100 list for eight weeks in a row, but it also was named Song of the Year by *Billboard Magazine.* When interviewed about the song, Sting, the band's lead vocalist, said it was meant to be a love song imbued with nuances of surveillance and control. Well, I was 13 when the song came out and little did Sting know that his song was wrapping coils around my delicate and prepubescent body and encircling me "with trenches and barbed wire" (1985), a barbed wire that would both foreclose parts of my being and yet open up my life to a newness and unknown possibility. The trans*ness and untrans*ness I embodied, had always embodied, oozed out to the track of "Every Breath You Take," and through my prickled pores, the song became my (un)broken record that would continue to replay its haunting line,

Every breath you take and every move you make,
every bond you break,
every step you take,
I'll be watching you.

As I was becoming trans*,[1] I was (un)becoming trans* and with each move I made, each breath I took, and each bond forged, I was watched, while I became, and (un)became trans*.

This narrative highlights my unbecoming and coming to terms with my trans* identity and the path I would forge while surveilled and controlled by the constructs into which I was being socially and emotionally policed. This narrative unravels through several inter-stories that highlight pivotal moments for my (un)becoming a trans* academic.

MY TRANS* HISTORY

At one year old, I was a curious and precocious toddler, feeling my way through the world, putting everything in sight in my mouth, and grabbing spoons to use the family dog as a drum. I ran around *a lot*. In fact, I ran around so much, my family predicted I would become a phenomenal runner or some type of athlete. It was the early 1970s so my parents dressed me in gaudy suede jumpers with bling, pink socks, and clogs. Sort of a mismatch to the identity I'd begun to exhibit.

At two, my affinity for running had accelerated. Now, I ran after the dog, the neighbor, the birds, and right out of the door, into the yard, and even the street. My mom supported these adventurous pursuits, but my dad didn't think it was appropriate for me to behave this way and even asserted, "I don't want my daughter to be a tomboy." I was just being myself.

From ages three to five, I looked like a boy. My hair fro'd, my now tube socks hiked up to my knees, my cut-offs pretty hideous even for the 1970s, and my appearance, masculine. I liked to watch my dad pee standing up, and when alone, tried to emulate the behavior, but with limited success, and lots of splatter on the floor. I liked to watch my dad shaving, and when alone, would smear toothpaste on my face and trace it off with strokes of the toothbrush. I was far more successful with this task than with the attempts at urinating. I loved to ride my Huffy BMX bike around the neighborhood and bring food home to my mom and sister when my dad was late home from work. I stepped into a caregiving role quite naturally, because it was just what felt *right*.

I loved playing football topless in the streets like the other boys did and seemed to be living life in a way that just *seemed* right and normal. Then one day I ran into the house screaming, "I want to be a boy!" My parents did not understand these words, but actually maybe they did. In response, my dad began to gender me in passive-aggressive ways. For special events, he would wrestle me into dresses and heels, only for me to then throw my body into dog shit and roll around in it. Then my dad would beat me and dress me up again. Helpless and in tears, my mom watched passively as her only recourse. To different degrees, this family battle would play out for the next forty years.

At five years old, I entered school. I mostly had boys as friends and enacted behavior typical of other boys. I played sports during recess, sat with the boys at lunch, *tried* to pee in the boy's restroom, and only wanted to be in classroom groups with other boys. The only gender marker that revealed that I was a girl was my clothing and the colors, those that typically demarcate girl's identities. I didn't understand when the class was separated into groups based on gender and why I was put into the groups with other girls. After all, I felt like a boy, thought I was a boy, and was treated like a boy by other boys in school.

As I continued into my primary and secondary schooling years, gender was not on the radar in my teachers' classrooms. Music, dating, film, and athletics were the only aspects of my life, outside of my family, that gave me sources to understand my gender confusion. I was drawn to musicians for unconscious reasons. For me, the artists and bands included Morrissey (the Smiths), Adam Ant, David Byrne, Tracy Chapman, Boy George, Depeche Mode, the Talking Heads, Kate Bush, Pet Shop Boys, Erasure, Trio, Oingo Boingo, New Order, and Yaz, all who expressed challenges to the gender binary through both looks *and* lyrics. My favorite musician was and still is Robert Smith, lead singer of The Cure. Smith dressed in black, had disheveled hair, worse lipstick, and occasionally even dresses. Smith's lyrics were poetic, dark and forlorn but they brought meaning, order, and respite to me. I listened to everything produced by The Cure until it drowned out the negative thoughts about my internal gender struggle. The Cure *was* the cure.

Throughout high school, I dated males. I didn't understand my feelings but was drawn to boys as if I were one. Though I had many close female friends and was attracted to some of them, it was not from the identity of female; I was drawn to them as if I *were* male. So I continued to live my life, dated males, acquired friends along a continuum of genders and with queered identities—gay, lesbian, bisexual, and straight. All of this just felt *normal*. The unconscious urges to be with males, as a male, remained unremitting but I did not know how to talk about them. None of my teachers addressed gender or sexual identity in my classes. I read no texts with examples of others or myself that could possibly help me understand who I was and was (un)becoming. Even with friends and teachers I adored, I was lost at school.

I turned to film for reasons similar to music. Films assuaged a curiosity that gave visual recognition to different identities in the world. Without the language to support the unconscious emotionality I felt, films such as *The Unbearable Lightness of Being*, *The Rocky Horror Picture Show*, *I've Heard the Mermaids Singing*, and all films by Ivory Merchant Productions, became running stills that shaped and informed who I was (un)becoming. Many of the characters in the films, and the actors who illuminated them, gave a calm to a raging storm brewing inside me.

Soccer and swimming, two stabilizing factors for my identity development throughout secondary school, provided critical spaces and opportunities to release pain and confusion. Again, without language to know what I felt inside, those sports calmed the inner rage—at least temporarily. I was a better than average swimmer and often placed in the top five at meets in both freestyle and butterfly sprints. My natural talent, however, as a runner, was channeled into soccer, and I was a *star*. As a forward, I broke district and state records, led my team to compete at the state level, and became the first female All-American in New Mexico. Six top academic and Division 1 schools offered me scholarships. I choose Cal-Berkeley. With memories of my family, music, friends, teachers, school, and film, I left for college—it was 1988 and the line "Every breath you take and every move you make, every bond you break, every step you take, I'll be watching you," haunted me each and every step of the way. The future was unknown, and it would take me until age forty, twenty-two years later, to come to terms with my gender confusion.

RECOGNITION

The struggle for recognition is at the core of human identity. With social positioning as the presumed or "normative" condition, those whose gender identities fall outside of the binary tend to be misrecognized and misunderstood and suffer from what I call a *recognition gap*, much as I did in my childhood and adolescence. Misrecognition subverts the possibility to be made credible, legible, or to be read and/or truly understood. When one is misrecognized, it is altogether difficult to hold a positive self-image, knowing that others may hold a different or negative image (Harris-Perry, 2011). When the presumed normative condition is challenged, though, a corollary emerges; this presupposition suggests that at the base of the human condition, people are in search of positive recognition because it validates their humanity.

Looking back into *my* youth, there was no common language for society to help people understand gender confusion, or if there was it was not brought into my life—I refer to this as trans*erasure (Miller, forthcoming). This has left me little room to wonder why a core group of my peers in high school and even in college—many who felt similar to me—have only come to identify as trans* or gender creative[2] later in their lives. Though, as language and understanding around trans* and gender-creative identities have become part of the social fabric of society, youth have had more access to recent changes in healthcare and therapeutic services that support them in their processes of becoming and coming to terms with their true selves. These opportunities for visibility have galvanized a movement fortifying validation and generating opportunities for both personal and social recognition. Now, we see more trans* and gender-creative people portrayed positively in the media. With individuals such as Laverne Cox, Janet Mock, Chaz Bono, Aydian Dowling, Scott Turner Schofield, Ian Harvey, and Caitlyn Jenner, and TV shows such as *Transparent*, *Becoming Us*, *Orange Is the New Black*, *The Fosters,* and *All That Jazz*, just to name a few, we see a growing media presence. With an estimated 700,000 trans* people now living in the United States, there is even the Out Trans 100, an annual award given to individuals who demonstrate courage through their efforts to promote visibility in their professions and communities. But where we still fall short is in how to support pre-K–12 teachers about how to integrate and normalize instruction that affirms and recognizes trans* and gender-creative youth. These identities are nearly invisible in curriculum and in the Common Core Standards. Plain and simple, trans* and gender-creative recognition must become integrated into schools.

To understand the role of recognition for trans* and gender-creative youth in schools, I turn for inspiration to W. E. B. Du Bois, who, in *The Souls of Black Folk* (1903), wrote about the struggle for Black recognition and validation in the United States. In this book, Du Bois describes a double-consciousness, that sense of simultaneously holding up two images of the self, the internal and the external—while always trying to compose and reconcile one's identity. He concerns himself with how the disintegration of the two generates internal strife and confusion about a positive sense of self-worth, just as I shared in my story.

Similar to what Du Bois names as a source for internal strife, for youth who live outside of the gender binary and challenge traditionally entrenched forms of gender expression such as trans* and gender-creative youth, they too experience a double-consciousness. As they strive and yearn to be positively recognized by peers, teachers, and family members, they experience microaggressions, because of their systemic reinforcement, and are forced to placate others by representing themselves in incomplete or false ways that they believe will be seen as socially acceptable in order to survive a school day. Such false fronts or defensive strategies are emotionally and cognitively exhausting and difficult (Miller, Burns, & Johnson, 2013); otherwise known as *emotional labor* (Hochschild, 1983; Nadal, River, & Corpus, 2010; Nordmarken, 2012), trans* and gender-creative youth are thereby positioned by the school system to sustain a learned or detached tolerance to buffer the self against the countless microaggressions experienced throughout a typical school day.

Research from Gay, Lesbian, and Straight Education Network (GLSEN) (Kosciw, Greytak, & Diaz, 2008; Kosciw, Greytak, Diaz, & Bartkiewicz, 2010; Kosciw, Greytak, Palmer, & Boesen, 2014) reveals that at the secondary level, trans* youth have identities that are "made" vulnerable to incurring the highest rates among their peers of bullying, harassment, truancy, dropping out, mental health issues (Kosciw, Greytak, Diaz, & Bartkiewicz, 2010; Miller, Burns, & Johnson, 2013), and suicidal ideation (Ybarra, Mitchell, & Kosciw, 2014). Such deleterious realities beget a deeper and more systemic issue that unearths how underprepared teachers and schools are equipped to mediate learning that affirms and creates and then *sustains* classrooms of recognition and school spaces *for all* (Jennings, 2014; Quinn & Meiners, 2011).

When school climates support and privilege the normalization of heterosexist, cisgender, Eurocentric, uni-dimensional (i.e., non-intersectional) or gendernormative beliefs—even unconsciously—it forces students who fall outside of those dominant identifiers to focus on simple survival rather than on success and fulfillment in school (Miller, 2012; Miller & Gilligan, 2014). When school is not safe or affirming, or lacks a pedagogy of recognition, it leaves little to the imagination why trans* and gender creative are taking their lives faster than society can keep up with. As potential remedy to disrupt this double-consciousness and an erasure of such youth, a trans* pedagogy must become part and parcel within educational contexts. Such legitimacies then of the human spirit, when affirmed by and through a trans* pedagogy, invite trans* and gender creative youth to see their intra, inter, and social value mirrored and experience (a)gender[3] self-determination[4] and justice. My hope for the millennial generation of trans* and gender-creative youth is that they can start living the lives they were meant to have from an early age, be affirmed and recognized for who they are, and not wait a lifetime to find themselves. Educating (parents) teachers and school personnel across grade levels is an intervention and potential remedy.

TRANS*ING EDUCATION INTO THE FUTURE—THIS CANNOT WAIT: IN THE TRANS*/POST-TRANS*

As students develop (a)gender self-determination, their lived and embodied recognitions by self and other have immeasurable potential to be spatialized into contexts and the indeterminate. Over time, as more trans* and gender-creative youth impact spaces, opinions can change—they *must* change. Though change has been happening for decades, just less visibly, consider this—trans* and gender-creative youth will continue to age, some may marry, some will become parents, some grandparents, and even great-grandparents. Some may become laborers, professionals (e.g., teachers, professors, doctors, therapists, lawyers, dentists), CEOs and, yes, even politicians. Their presence (and across continents) will occur within myriad socioeconomic, cultural, ethnic, religious/nonreligious, spiritual, and linguistic spaces. They will comprise different national origins, (a)sexual orientations, (a)gender expressions, philosophies, genetic information, HIV status, veteran status, body sizes, heights, and mental and physical abilities. For those who support the psycho-social-emotional development of trans* and gender-creative youth, many of us already know and deeply believe that they are *no* different than any other being and are thereby entitled to the same inalienable rights and to be treated with dignity.

*****

So, what might a trans*/post-trans* schooling system look like, and how might that potentially change humanity? As trans* becomes part of the fabric of the schooling system and woven into the mainstream of society, we enter into a post-trans* space. A post-trans* space, though indeterminate, would demonstrate how contexts have become sustainable to hold and care for the commonplace normalization of the trans* and gender-creative body. In these myriad spaces (e.g., school, jobs, families, etc.) trans* and gender creativity would no longer incur macroaggressions nor marginalization, but for those who embody these glorious identities they would experience the same dignities entitled to any other human. In this post-trans* space, the possibility for the unknown and for new knowledges to continue to emerge would become part of social and interpersonal discourses. On a macro scale then, by accepting the unknown to its larger normalization, a post-trans space becomes accepted without redress. In post-trans* contexts, therefore, while people will always see difference, the prior systemic misrecognition dysphoria of trans* and gender creativity collapses.

If indeed this post-trans* space were realized, a space where trans*ness blends but doesn't blend in, and as trans* and gender-creative youth, and all people for that matter, experience these expanding contexts, humanity might not only see more trans*gentleness, they might see and experience more trans* and gender-creative justice. In the wake of such justice then, for schools, curricula would include trans* and gender-creative narratives, books of all genres and storylines, histories, political victories, trailblazers, photos and pictures, and media icons. Students would have ample options for names, (a)pronouns, and (a)gender. There would be no fear of bullying or harassment related to bathrooms, locker rooms, and physical education classes and, most important, school would no longer be about survival, it would be about success, thriving and fulfillment. For the once surveilled, the noise and emotional labor once tolerated finally fade away into the distance.

TODAY

At forty years old, and after drawing upon the courage from the youth of our world, I decided to medically transition from female *toward* male—as I name it. I am (a)pronouned and (a)gender. For most of my life, I could not look in the mirror because I hated what I saw—and experienced a double-consciousness. I *hated* having breasts, a vagina, and a body that produced estrogen. So, to remedy my inner rage and because I needed to walk from potential suicide for the third time, I started taking testosterone (T), the day after I received tenure. This medical transition was planned in collaboration with my therapist and was a very conscious decision. Within six weeks of starting T, I had a double mastectomy, and within six weeks of my mastectomy, I had a hysterectomy and oophorectomy.[5] A year later, I had a metoidioplasty,[6] scrotoplasty,[7] and pelvic release.[8] I will inject T weekly for the rest of my life so I can continue to appear male, and that is how I want to be read by the world. I am a transsexual[9] and have become comfortable and happy, finally, in my body. Now, after fully healing from these surgeries, I can look in the mirror and recognize the person I always felt I was on the inside. Now they are in synch with each other. The next step in this journey is how to be read and recognized by and in the world around me. That is still my process in becoming the human I always knew I was and am.

I am honored to be the first tenured trans* professor in English education and I know that my field and those related "[are] watching me." Though I do make missteps along the way, I take my role very seriously as a scholar-activist, writer, colleague, advocate, supporter to families and peers, and as mentor to dozens of up and coming trans* academics. I am often interviewed for dissertations, called upon by the press, and almost daily by friends in tears who don't know what to do for their kids or their friends' kids, or how to educate their kids' teachers about trans* issues. These myriad roles tell me that we are in desperate times for visible trans* academics, who, in teacher education can educate pre- and in-service teachers about how to support a rapidly growing number of trans* kids and the issues they are facing.

It has taken nearly a lifetime of inner struggle to understand myself and my (un)becoming and to understand my own internal and unconscious drive (Vinacke, 1960). Had teachers understood my gender confusion and introduced dialogue, development of safe spaces, and lessons with trans* narratives, it is likely I would have grown up with an affirmed and more stable sense of self. I still and will likely always struggle with a vulnerabilized self, with a frailty that cannot be reversed, and even fractured relationships. Had the world been more kind, compassionate, and prepared to meet my needs while I was growing up, it is likely that I would not still be playing catch up. If this were to now happen, the trans* and gender creative youth of the world needn't remain vulnerabilized anymore. They would not live a life coiled by "trenches and barbed wire," nor would they feel they would have to *(un)become* to *become*, or live with the noise of "every move you make … every bond you break, every step you take, I'll be watching you"; rather, they would just be free to be themselves in a world better prepared to embrace, accept, love, and recognize them from birth.

NOTES

1. I refer to trans*, a prefix or adjective used as an abbreviation of transgender, derived from the Greek word meaning "across from" or "on the other side of." Many consider trans* to be an inclusive and useful umbrella term. Trans (without the asterisk) is most often applied to trans men and trans women, and the asterisk is used more broadly to refer to all non-cisgender gender identities, such as agender, cross-dresser, bigender, genderfluid, gender**k, genderless, genderqueer, nonbinary, nongender, third gender, trans man, trans woman, transgender, transsexual and two-spirit.
2. Expressing gender in a way that demonstrates individual freedom of expression and does not conform to any gender.
3. I refer to (a)gender as a rejection of gender as a biological or social construct altogether and refusing to identify with gender. The lowercase (a) in parenthesis does not nullify gender, it is a way of combining the terms so both gender refusal and gender are collapsed into one word.
4. (A)gender self-determination is the inherent right to both occupy one's (a)gender and make choices to self-identify in a way that authenticates self-expression. It is also a type of self-granted or inherited permission that can help one refute or rise above social critique; it presumes choice and rejects an imposition to be defined or regulated; it presumes that humans are entitled to unsettle knowledge, which can generate new possibilities of legibility; and, it means that any representation of (a)gender deserves the same inalienable rights and the same dignities and protections as any other human. This de "factoness" grants individuals ways of intervening in and disrupting social and political processes because one's discourse and self-determined ways of being demonstrate placement as a viable stakeholder in society, revealing that no one personhood is of any more or less of value than any other.
5. The removal of the ovaries which means the body no longer produces estrogen.
6. The process of cutting the outer labia and fissuring it around the clitoris in order to create a neo-phallus.
7. The process of creating a scrotum by implanting testicles from the outer labia.
8. An incision made in order to reposition the surgically created phallus.
9. While not all trans* people have surgeries or take T, as there is no single trans* story, it was important for me. Trans* people are on a spectrum of identities just as are cisgender people.

REFERENCES

Du Bois, W. E. B. (1903). *Souls of black folk*. Chicago: A.C. McClurg.

Harris-Perry, M. (2011). *Sister citizen: Shame, stereotypes, and black women in America*. New Haven, CT: Yale University Press.

Hochschild, A. (1983). *The managed heart: The commercialization of human feeling*. Berkeley: University of California Press.

Jennings, T. (2014). Is the mere mention enough? Representation across five different venues of educator preparation. In L. Meyer & D. Carlson (Eds.), *Gender and sexualities in education: A reader* (pp. 400–412). New York: Peter Lang.

Kosciw, J., Greytak, E., & Diaz, E. (2008). *The 2007 national school climate survey: The experiences of lesbian, gay, bisexual and transgender youth in our nation's schools*. New York: GLSEN.

Kosciw, J., Greytak, E., Diaz, E., & Bartkiewicz, M. (2010). *The 2009 national school climate survey: The experiences of lesbian, gay, bisexual and transgender youth in our nation's schools.* New York: GLSEN.

Kosciw, J. G., Greytak, E. A., Palmer, N. A., & Boesen, M. J. (2014). *The 2013 national school climate survey: The experiences of lesbian, gay, bisexual and transgender youth in our nation's schools.* New York: GLSEN.

Miller, s. (2012). Mythology of the norm: Disrupting the culture of bullying in schools. *English Journal, 101*(6), 107–109.

Miller, s. (forthcoming). *Teaching, affirming, and recognizing trans and gender creative youth: A queer literacy framework.* New York: Palgrave Macmillan.

Miller, s., Burns, L., & Johnson, T. S. (2013). *Generation BULLIED 2.0: Prevention and intervention strategies for our most vulnerable students.* New York: Peter Lang.

Miller, s. & Gilligan, J. (2014). Heteronormative harassment: Queer bullying and gender non-conforming students. In D. Carlson & E. Meyer (Eds.), *Handbook of gender and sexualities in education* (pp. 217–229). New York: Peter Lang.

Nadal, K. L., River, D. P., & Corpus, M. J. H. (2010). Sexual orientation, and transgender microaggressions: Implications for mental health and counseling. In D. W. Sue (Ed.), *Microaggressions and marginality: Manifestation, dynamics, and impact* (pp. 217–240). Hoboken, NJ: Wiley.

Nordmarken, S. (2012). *Everyday transgender emotional inequality: Microaggressions, micropolitics, and minority emotional work.* Unpublished paper presented at The American Sociological Association Annual Meeting, Denver, CO.

Quinn, T., & Meiners, E. R. (2011). Teacher education, struggles for social justice, and the historical erasure of lesbian, gay, bisexual, transgender, and queer lives. In A. Ball & C. Tyson (Eds.), *Studying diversity in teacher education* (pp. 135–151). Lanham, MD: Rowman & Littlefield.

Sting. (1983). Every breath you take [Recorded by Police]. On *Synchronicity* [Record]. Quebec, Canada: A&M.

Sting. (1985). Fortress around your heart. On *Dream of the Blue Turtles* [Record]. Quebec, Canada: A&M.

Vinacke, W. E. (1960). The drive-modification theory of human motivation. *Journal of Genetic Psychology, 96*, 245–268.

Ybarra, M. L., Mitchell, K. J., & Kosciw, J. G. (2014). The relation between suicidal ideation and bullying victimization in a national sample of transgender and non-transgender adolescents. In P. Goldblum, D. Espelage, J. Chu, & B. Bognar (Eds.), *Youth suicide and bullying: Challenges and strategies for prevention and intervention* (pp. 134–147). New York: Oxford University Press.

CHAPTER TWELVE

Queering the Inquiry Body: Critical Science Teaching From the Margins

KERRITA K. MAYFIELD

> Disidentification is meant to be descriptive of the survival strategies the minority subject practices in order to negotiate a phobic majoritarian public sphere that continuously elides or punishes the existence of subjects who do not conform to the phantasm of normative citizenship.
>
> —Muñoz, 1999, p. 4

I did not intend to start with Muñoz. I started writing this chapter between Ferguson and "I can't breathe" and am editing it after the contested release of the full 30-minute video that shows 12-year-old Tamir Rice not only being shot within seconds of the police car's arrival, but also his 14-year-old sister being thrown to the ground, handcuffed, then put in the back of said police car when she runs toward his body—where she sits while it takes 13 minutes for him to be taken away in an ambulance for care. The curricular care of children is my business. I kept getting distracted by the consequences of harboring a visually different embodiment; being or being perceived as queer in normative spaces; of being perceived as not one of us in the former slave-holding heteropatriarchy that is our nation-state. The reality is that fancy talk cannot mute the majoritarian gaze and its consequences upon those deemed unwelcome in certain spaces.

And, thus, the schisms between training and embodied praxis, intellect and spirit, production and reflexivity are made real, and create a state where the intersections of identity are tension filled and disorienting, like a piece with two introductions. The original opening:

One of my favorite childhood books was *Discovering Science on Your Own*. Editor Paul Blackwood closes the introduction with this nugget about the value of independent scientific discovery. He notes, "Children see or hear or otherwise observe what happens in a very small part of the universe. In this way, they build understandings and concepts that help explain events in a larger universe—the goal of all scientists." Printed in 1963, every chapter, from "Astronomy" to "Sound" to "Living Things," contains corner-folded pages—experiments I replicated when I could cajole the materials from my mother. In this book, an active and engaged white male, named Billy in my head, appears 39 times. His compatriot, named Heidi because that seemed appropriate for a small white girl, appears only twice—once actively engaged in experimentation and once as a slack-armed figure standing to the side. Billy embodies science inquiry as we understand it, he is experimenting, observing, practicing, constructing a body of knowledge; when he is still, he is attentive to his implements of science. There are innumerable drawings of hands doing things, but let us assume they belong to the book's residents and thus competently white. Missing is any child who looked like me then: tall, dark brown, poufy 1970s kid afro, female. (Okay. That looks like me now.) As a science teacher and preservice teacher trainer I bring this book to my precareer teachers when the subject is the social formations of (science) inquiry. In part, to explore the ways our knowledge systems are formed in the cauldron of norming discourses. And to talk about the ways even simple texts form our understanding of the rules that we abide by in our pursuit of knowledge.

But what do these two openings—one professionally normed and the other visceral—have to do with queering processes of science inquiry? How do stories of neutral inquiry mediate queer embodiment? And last, what do these openings reveal about the ways our bodies queer curricular spaces and alter narratives of belonging and competence? These are prompts I will address in this chapter as well as explicating queering the science curriculum as a series of specific curricular engagements. But warning, as an educator, part of my queering praxis is promoting life in the ellipses; there are no neat and normed answers here.

EMBODYING QUEER COMPETENCE

Paul Blackwood was more right than he knew about the formative nature of knowledge when applied to larger contexts. As a person whose intersections trouble various hegemonies, there is a cellular level understanding that my presence in many spaces is a challenging counterpublic to stories of where my body is supposed to be and what truths are embodied within it (Muñoz, 1999). For queering educators, the project of curriculum disruption is both a statement of professional purpose and a declaration of liminal space occupation. Frankly, I pondered whether to verify my own intersecting (sexual) identities here as part of the memoir theme. What I arrived at was that as an irretrievably tall, curvy, unabashedly brown woman, with a lush, multicolored nimbus of natural hair, a voluminous laugh, an affinity for bright colors, whose Christianity seeps into my learning spaces in my declaration that "I will not cast my pearls before swine—so you guys need to do the reading!" I am already a body written upon by stories new and ancient to the Americas and its various educational and structural hegemonies. Part of my power in heteropatriarchal spaces is strategic narrative disclosure, in part because there are inevitable tensions between the visible and assumed stories of this body and what it represents. My very presence queers narratives of power.

There is no singular queer body or embodiment of optimal queerness. Even as a curious child who grew into a curious woman with a terminal degree in curriculum design alongside an undergraduate one in biology, alongside another in studio arts, and yet another in the teaching of science and technology, with more than a decade of teaching science to high schoolers, I have had moments where I wondered if science would be—should be—my story. I won my high school's science fair—twice! Yet, I flew under the radar with my senior biology thesis at a top-rated liberal arts college for which I am also a class agent, never had a student teacher like other science department colleagues in the high school I helped create, and still hear colleagues wonder aloud almost 10 years into this academic iteration whether I will be "a good researcher" when I transgress some institutional norm. What excites and sustains me is the hidden curriculum of the science book with which I opened this chapter, the idea that science curriculum is an egalitarian opportunity for welcoming all bodies and all bodies of knowledge into inquiry spaces (Mayfield, 2014).

McCutcheon (1988) describes the curriculum as "what students have an opportunity to learn under the auspices of schools" (p. 191). She notes further that the overt curriculum, which will receive sustained attention here, is "a formal, policy-level curriculum" (p. 191) enacted in classrooms by teachers. Curriculum is a curated sociocultural artifact that articulates and reifies hegemonic power structures. Yet, teaching is still deeply embodied craft—and if queering/querying perspectives are not there, possible futures are lost. Muñoz notes that such counterlogic could destabilize white supremacy, the state, and misogyny.

In the postmodern literature there are many articles about heteronormativity, homophobia, and heteropatriarchy in classroom spaces, and the content, students, and teachers within them (Blackburn, 2012; Halperin, 2003; Kumashiro, 2001; Pascoe, 2012; Smith, 2010). Yet queerness is treated in classroom spaces as a content or theoretical area for study (Halperin), category of identity (Jagose, 1996), a state of being in the context of school and youth spaces (Kumashiro), or in the context of school-based organizations like a Gay Straight Alliance (GSA Network, 2013), rather than a process for interrogating the constructions of curriculum as a living social enterprise. These narratives affix queer identity neatly in the hegemony of schooling but do not address the cultural production of teachers as creators of liberation spaces. Curriculum workers, thus, are also invisibilized or essentialized; in part, because embedded in the assumption of curriculum leadership is adherence to normed discourses of gender, gender performance, relationship arrangement, or educator positionality. The intersections of any teacher's identities are subsumed, reconstituted, compressed, hierarchized, or magnified by the academic processes of inquiry and the assumptions of leadership in, and ownership of, learning spaces. The intentional use of "teacher" references the careful work that goes into the craft of fully embodied instruction.

Over the last 25 years, researchers have explored the ways liminal bodies in hierarchical and socially legitimated structures (like school or academe) struggle within success. These women (Clance & Imes, 1978), racial minority graduate students (Cokley, McClain, Enciso & Martinez, 2013), or First Nations people in a counseling setting (Blue, Darou & Ruano, 2015) live with the tensions between institutional presence and disembodied dislocation *within* the structure. A queer embodied curriculum presents a corporeal challenge to the status quo of certain bodies having legitimated rights to occupy educational spaces and helm praxis.

Teaching is a performative act where the public demonstration of knowledge, truth, and expertise is embedded in effective teaching. This spectacle of knowing is akin to Muñoz's concept of queer performance, as the teacher/performer is "standing onstage alone, with or without props, bent on the project of opening up a world" (p. 1). The liminal body is consumed, paraded, and externally defined by the academic structures in which they work and can thus be constituted as a problem. The movement from imposter—one who feels as if his or her success in a liminal body comes from luck—to imposer—one who can bend the structures to their will—emerges but at a cost, as our embodied successes in learning spaces are counternarratives to the stories of who belongs there.

QUEERING AND QUERYING MYTHS OF NEUTRAL PRACTICE

Queerness itself has had many iterations since it rose in the early 1990s as a term used to define persons whose practices exploded beyond the gender, sexuality, and performance binaries present in many Westernized social systems (Halperin). The call to transgress against rigid identity categorization was used by liminal persons to describe a positionality, practice, or acts of resistance that reified the rights of the practitioner's presence in dominant constructs (Butler, 1993; Halperin; Jagose; Stein & Plummer, 1994). Intersectionality further and beautifully destabilizes the category as persons with multiple identities and privileges push at queer's boundaries and inclusions (Russell & Truong, 2001). Queer's classificatory power is partially derived from its reclamation of a derogatory term used to marginalize nonheteronormative forms of gender and sexuality performance and the people associated with these practices. But missing is the space where the marginal being examines the ways other bodies and bodies of performance alter the meaning of space occupation. Muñoz notes that this troubling of space occupation from being queer to doing queer "take[s] space in the social that has been colonized by the logics of white normativity and heteronormativity" (p. xii). As a neologism, queer theory creates liberation through the pairing of a countercultural term with the legitimate and academic currency of theorizing, inquiry, praxis, and publication. Some examples of heteropatriarchal and heteronormative hegemony would be the AIDS crises of the 1980s and 1990s in the United States (Shilts, 1987), the invisibility of genderqueer persons within the gay rights movement after Stonewall (Devor & Matt, 2004), and the perpetuation of identity politics as categories of social action (Jagose; Butler). Further, the unfixedness of queerness beyond simply gay, lesbian, bisexual, asexual, and pansexual, among other identities, creates an opportunity for a rich and varied set of explorations of the construction of normed knowledges present in formal learning environments. Subsequently, queer positionality(ies) within the academy became a political category meant to pervert (use intentional) the structures of sociopolitical and legitimate knowledge domination of classrooms. As I will discuss later, classrooms could be counternarrative spaces and still meet curricular demands.

The disproportionality of bodies between who is teaching and who is being taught is larger now than it ever has been, as 83.1% of classroom teachers are white in a nation that by 2019 is predicted to have minority youth be the norm majority in classroom spaces (Bass, 2012; National Center for Educational Statistics, 2008). My queering project is about interrogating content as an operationalization of postmodern inquiry, which in a reconsidered system may address the formation of science content knowledge and create stronger integration between science educator identity and sociocurricular realities.

QUEERING THE CURRICULA OF SCIENCE

As preK–12 schools are sites that reify social norms, conditions, and categories (Anyon, 1981), they are perfect places for exploring how a learner's lived experiences influence the content, content applications, and the contexts by which the language and meaning of ideas evolve. Moje, Ciechanowski, Kramer, Ellis, Carrillo, and Collazo (2004) use Moll's concept of Third Space to discuss that curricula, and subsequently schools, are hybrid designs where the learning space and its processes are a co-creation of the students, the teachers, and the content's particular form of delivery. In this system, when students' bodies of knowledge are incorporated within the curricular enterprise, they are empowered to bring their concomitant knowledge into the learning space and have those ways of knowing recognized in the legitimated place called school.

Yosso (2005) describes multiple forms of capital (i.e., navigational, linguistic, social) that act like hybridity and allow learners to introduce into classrooms their vast array of skills and attributes. The zeitgeist of American schools in postmodernity is one where schools reproduce critical aspects of the wider culture as an act of producing a specific kind of citizen (Kellner, 2003). The curriculum of K–16 schools has always been a sociocultural and globally aware artifact responsible for enacting the aspirations of the people and the never-ending project of nation building (Parkerson & Parkerson, 2001).

The queer project of K–16 curriculum development assumes that knowledge is neither neutral nor context-free and must be continually rooted in context. Problematically, in the standards-based era of neoconservative and assessment-driven politics, schools, teachers, and instructional spaces are squeezed ever tighter in their attempts to deliver egalitarian-oriented and student-responsive content to an increasingly global population of learners in a way that is mindful of the demands of state and federal assessment projects (Madeloni & Gorlewski, 2013). The curricula of schools are reflective of bodies who are under assault. But this is not news.

In spending time in secondary schools participating in classrooms, extracurricular activities, and school-sponsored events, Pascoe advocates an uncoupling of the male body from the embodiment of masculinity, while advocating the use of queer theory as a lens for analyzing how masculinity and femininity are performed in (secondary) school spaces. Students are treated as embodied subjects whose gender identities are embedded in their perceptions and practices. The next section offers a critical perspective on the project of curriculum design alongside an example of queered content change.

QUEERING SCIENCE CONTENT

While there is a persistent and increasingly urgent need for nimble school systems that can recognize the needs of an ever more diverse populace, I offer queering as an attempt to move beyond narratives of mere categorization into a process of more holistic curriculum construction. Curriculum leadership emerges from bodies laden with context, interactions, and stories. Unlike the linguistic change from denigration into power that queer denotes, queering as a curricular process does not seek to, in the words of Solórzano and Yosso (2002), reproduce majoritarian (and heterosexist) narratives of domination. Instead, queering is an engagement in criticality that deconstructs, interrogates, and reconstructs in the most postmodern sense what it means to use this particular form of nonhegemonic analysis to illuminate the constructions and maintenance of school-legitimated knowledge. Queering itself is an intentionally jarring process that aligns with what we know about learning cycles and the incorporation of new information overlaid upon existing schema: there is discord with any new information, a necessary scaffolding change, then resolution of the new with the old (Piaget cited in Woolfolk, 1987).

The critical reattachment of queer and queering to the process of curricular interrogation is the recognition of marginal discourses around hierarchy, discursiveness, liminality, and identity creation. Muñoz frames these acts of ideology as operating within apparati and their practices.

Halperin's critique of the queer movement as it was executed in graduate schools was that queer theory acted as a homogenizing force that delivered a sanitized form of inquiry that had veered away from queer theory motivated by an "impulse to transform what could count as knowledge, as well as by a determination to transform the practices by which knowledge functioned within the institution of the university" (p. 343). To harken back to the ways queering the curriculum reveal the heteropatriarchal influences of these reductionist content perspectives, I offer these examples from my work as a queering biology teacher.

Watson, Crick, and Wilkins have been largely given credit for being the first scientists to create a working model of the helical structure of the DNA molecule. They received a Nobel Prize in physiology or medicine in 1962. These gentlemen had attempted several models from their prior knowledge of the relative amounts of thymine, guanine, cytosine, and adenine in a nucleus. While their work rested upon the research of other scientists, they had a complex and persistent rival in Rosalind Franklin, an accomplished X-ray crystallographer and peer who was also pursuing the question of DNA's structure and who had openly criticized their structural failures. Franklin's expertise with creating X-ray images was also used in the war effort on studying the atomic structure of graphite and coal, among other pioneering work. Watson and Crick's response was to hire away a male peer (Wilkins) from her research lab with whom she did not work well, and Wilkins took some of her work with him: the famous Photo 51, which clearly indicated the heretofore misunderstood arrangement of DNA's components.

The conversation with learners in biology classrooms about the discovery of what makes us human is often framed by the great and neutral race for knowledge; an amalgam of the "natural" acts of competition, inquiry, and the inevitable and human quest to better understand their world. Further, any movement away from a strictly factual instead of interactional approach to science knowledge is seen as a threat to rigor. This narrative of scientific triumph is firmly embedded in a capitalist story of the meritorious nature of discovery while obscuring the heteropatriarchal acts that buttressed Watson, Wilkins, and Crick's beliefs about their rights to discovery granted by their position in the gender hierarchy, a gender hierarchy reinforced by their institutions of higher education.

The offering of biology class examples is an intentional attempt to rally against the normalization of what content is considered available for queering and to reject myths of curricular neutrality. As a generalist secondary teacher trainer, I regularly receive pushback from my undergraduates when asked to design content curriculum in an emancipatory, social justice, or multiculturally aware way. Often the complaint is that the curricular content of subject areas like biology, chemistry, or mathematics does not lend itself to more exploratory and discursive lenses of curriculum construction and content analysis. The students perceive the content to portend a specific perspective on multiculturalism (and their white failures within it) and demand a fixed perspective in order for curricular practice to be done well. Queering is a challenge to the binary (off/on, man/woman, center/margin, content/digression, aggressor/victim, good war/bad war) nature of knowledge and knowledge production as reified by preK–16 schools and their curricula.

But how does queering occur as a concrete curricular strategy of potential emancipation across disciplines? A queered approach would be to ask: "What other perspectives exist around this concept?" "Under what structures has this knowledge been propagated and to whose benefit?" "How is our witnessing of this form of knowledge production regulated by others and who might these regulators be?" "What is going on in this time period/world that has informed this idea?" "Who or what else has been influenced by this idea?" Queering as a process is not a panacea to the invisibility of certain bodies in the preK–16 curricula, but it offers illumination of liminal spaces and people, while presenting a content-centered intellectual challenge to the larger structures that underpin various forms of institutionally legitimated knowledge.

Andrea Smith, in a 2010 article about the intersections of queer theory and native students, explores the ways queering can be an exploration of Native American people and their sovereign positionalities to recenter a person or identity group within a larger dominant social narrative. When educational institutions borrow widely from postmodern theoretical offshoots like queer theory, critical race theory, and native critical theory to create processes of inquiry, there is movement toward focusing on a subject linked to its wider sociocultural and historical conditions.

Consider the work of Ernst Haeckel, often called the father of modern biology, as an example of furthering Smith's need for a form of queering that extends beyond subject/person/group-based inquiry. Ernst Haeckel is widely credited with developing the visual organization of species, called a phylogenic tree. His anatomical and scientific drawings were groundbreaking at a time when science texts had few images. His ideas about the origins of "man" were so significant he once simply pointed to a continent and declared it the place where the evidence about human origins would be found. (He was wrong.) An early supporter of Darwin's theories about the origins of species, Haeckel was born in 1834 at the beginning of the Victorian era and died during the rise of Modernism. His associations were many and were in some ways already queered: his work presented clear challenges to the current scientific orthodoxy, and he was a scientist, philosopher, and artist who moved past the boundaries of Modern thought. His work was bountiful, and scientists everywhere owe much to his methodological and scientific inquiries.

However, as an early proponent of Social Darwinism, a feeder ideology to eugenics,[1] Haeckel's work is intimately connected to popular misconceptions that abound in scientific racism and were codified by (white male) peers to support their beliefs about their place in the social hierarchy. The perversion of Darwin's ideas when applied to the problems of race, class, colonialism, and immigration was underwritten by a heteropatriarchal acceptance of the ways scientific inquiry underwrote imperialist hegemony. The categorization of humans in a hierarchy rationalized projects of domination across the globe, including every industrialized nation of the time. How these men viewed their discoveries, how those ideas were understood to impact the people and institutions around them, and the longevity of their science-supported (il)legitimacies do not exist in a vacuum. There are many such stories, from the Tuskegee syphilis study, its sister study in Guatemala in the 1980s, the use of slave cadavers in medical schools in Northern science classes, the Rockefellers' funding of Eugenics social societies, North Carolina's 2013 court-ordered payments to sterilized (black, poor, or non-neurotypical) women, to Henrietta Lacks's cervical cells that were used to establish experimental cell lines without her permission—liminal bodies have been used in scientific inquiry to underwrite their domination.

CONCLUSION

Clearly, queering as a method of inquiry and mode of analytical pushback against dominant constructions of legitimated curricular knowledge is not an easy process. We know that when students fail to see themselves in the curriculum and do not have curriculum connected to their multiple worlds, they tend to fail to achieve at school in its demands (Cummins, 2001; National Science Foundation, 2013). The issue and examples presented here are not critiques of heterosexual white men engaged with educational systems that benefit from such hierarchies; privilege itself is not a dichotomous off/on event and we all have it *and* oppression as our kyriarchal power shifts and various forms of capital are utilized (Schussler Fiorenza, 1992; Yosso).

As a matter of fact, this body is more used to being science's subject than its conductor, and that reality permeates my curriculum as a science teacher. And using that awareness to teach better is the project of curricular disidentification, to queer Muñoz's concept.

But how is queering as a process potentially emancipatory as I claimed prior? Unlike other uses of queer, meant to acknowledge and recenter marginalized persons, *queering* asks that the processes surrounding the materiality of knowledge production become central in the transmission of said information. Further, and most important, emancipation does not rely upon the presence and uplift of invisibilized groups, as with the additive curriculum; instead all students become aware of the ways they and their various identities are complicit in systems in knowledge production and oppression. Every student and their identities are also implicated in the holistic creation of emancipatory forms of inquiry. Every marginal body matters and has knowledge to contribute, and that fact makes it crucial to protect all children's potential and to hold their bodies/constructs/lives/stories sacred in a learning space. Educators, regardless of their embodiment, must acknowledge in the postmodern their role as propagators of curricula redolent of its time and space, as such curricular content can never neutrally exist in isolation from the world and its systems. Ways of knowing promulgated by curricula are simply snapshots of cultural, financial, local, and global zeitgeists. Curriculum queering is another process of rigorous inquiry about the world. Glibly, I would state that every educator/performer is just a little bit queer, but more important, every classroom's curriculum needs to have queering as a process.

NOTE

1. Eugenics uses scientific tools like (the incorrect) phrenology, legal state-sponsored sterilization, and charts of human characteristics linking colonized people to apes to assert the genetic superiority of people from the Western European diaspora. Eugenics has long been associated with the rise of Nazism, but many states in the United States also had sterilization policies against the "infirm," that is, liminal, citizens into the 1970s (Helms & Tomlinson, 2011; Kuhl, 1994; North Carolina Department of Administration, 2011).

REFERENCES

Acker, S. (1987). Feminist theory and the study of gender and education. *International Review of Education, 33*(4), 419–435.

Anyon, J. (1981). Schools as agencies of social legitimation. *Journal of Curriculum Theorizing, 3*(2), 86–103.

Bass, F. (2012, December 12). Census Bureau says minority youth to be majority by 2019. Retrieved from http://www.bloomberg.com/news/articles/2012-12-12/census-bureau-says-minority-youth-to-be-majority-by-2019

Blackburn, M. V. (2012). *Interrupting hate: Homophobia in schools and what literacy can do about it.* New York: Teachers College Press.

Blue, A. W., Darou, W. G., & Ruano, C. (2015). Through silence we speak: Approaches to counselling and psychotherapy with Canadian First Nation clients. *Online Readings in Psychology and Culture, 10*(3). http://dx.doi.org/10.9707/2307-0919.1095

Butler, J. (1993). *Bodies that matter: On the discursive limits of "sex."* New York: Routledge.

Clance, P. & Imes, S. A. (1978). The imposter phenomenon in high achieving women: Dynamics and therapeutic intervention. *Psychotherapy: Research, Theory & Practice, 15*(3), 241–247. http://dx.doi.org/10.1037/h0086006

Cokley, K., McClain, S., Enciso, A., Martinez, M. (2013). An examination of the impact of minority status stress and impostor feelings on the mental health of diverse ethnic minority college students. *Journal of Multicultural Counseling and Development, 41*(2), 82–95.

Cummins, J. (2001). Empowering minority students: A framework for intervention. *Harvard Educational Review, 71*(4), 656–675.

Devor, A., & Matt, N. (2004). ONE, Inc. and Reed Erickson: The uneasy collaboration of gay and trans activism, 1964–2003. *GLQ: A Journal of Lesbian and Gay Studies, 10*(2), 179–209.

Gay Straight Alliance Network. (2013). http://www.gsanetwork.org/

Halperin, D. M. (2003). The normalization of Queer Theory. *Journal of Homosexuality, 45*(2/3/4), 339–343. doi: 10.1300/J082v45n02_17

Helms, A. D., & Tomlinson, T. (September 26, 2011). Wallace Kuralt's era of sterilization. *The Charlotte Observer.* Retrieved from http://www.charlotteobserver.com/news/local/article9068186.html

Jagose, A. (1996). *Queer Theory.* Melbourne, Australia: University of Melbourne Press.

Kellner, D. (2003). Toward a critical theory of education. Retrieved January, 18, 2008, from https://pages.gseis.ucla.edu/faculty/kellner/essays/towardcriticaltheoryofed.pdf

Kuhl, S. (1994). *The Nazi connection: Eugenics, American racism, and German National Socialism.* Oxford: Oxford University Press.

Kumashiro, K. K. (2001). Queer students of color and antiracist, antiheterosexist education: Paradoxes of identity and activism. In K. K. Kumashiro (Ed.), *Troubling intersections of race and sexuality: Queer students of color and anti-oppressive education* (pp. 1–26). Lanham, MD: Rowman & Littlefield.

Madeloni, B., & Gorlewski, J. (2013, Summer). Wrong answer to the wrong question. *Rethinking Schools, 27*(4). Retrieved from http://www.rethinkingschools.org/archive/27_04/27_04_madeloni-gorlewski.shtml

Mayfield, K. K. (2014). Creating a critical genetics curriculum as a counternarrative to/in the urban imaginary. *Urban Education*, 1–30. doi: 10.1177/0042085914553672

McCutcheon, G. (1988). Curriculum and the work of teachers. In D. J. Flinders & S. J. Thornton (Eds.), *The curriculum studies reader* (pp. 188–197). New York: Routledge.

Mohanty, C. T. (2003). *Feminism without borders.* Durham, NC: Duke University Press.

Moje, E. R., Ciechanowski, K. M., Kramer, K., Ellis, L., Carrillo, R., & Collazo, T. (2004). Working toward third space in content area literacy: An examination of everyday funds of knowledge. *Reading Research Quarterly, 39*(1), 38–70.

Muñoz, J. E. (1999). *Disidentifications: Queers of color and the performance of politics.* Minneapolis: University of Minnesota Press.

National Center for Educational Statistics. (2008). Retrieved from https://nces.ed.gov/
National Science Foundation. (2013, February). *Women, minorities, and persons with disabilities in science and engineering*. Arlington, VA. NSF 13–304.
North Carolina Department of Administration. (2011). Office of Justice for Sterilization Victims. Retrieved from http://www.sterilizationvictims.nc.gov/
Parkerson, D., & Parkerson, J. A. (2001). *Transitions in American education: A social history of teaching* (2nd ed.). New York: Taylor & Francis.
Pascoe, C. J. (2012). *Dude you're a fag: Masculinity and sexuality in high school.* Berkeley: University of California Press.
Russell, S. T., & Truong, N. L. (2001). Adolescent sexual orientation, race and ethnicity, and school environments: A national study of sexual minority youth of color. In K. K. Kumashiro (Ed.), *Troubling intersections of race and sexuality: Queer students of color and anti-oppressive education* (pp. 113–130). Lanham, MD: Rowman & Littlefield.
Schussler Fiorenza, E. (1992). *But she said: Feminist practices of biblical interpretation.* Boston: Beacon.
Shilts, R. (1987). *And the band played on: Politics, people and the AIDS epidemic.* New York: St. Martin's.
Smith, A. (2010). Queer theory and native studies: The heteronormativity of settler colonialism. *GLQ: A Journal of Lesbian and Gay Studies, 16*(1–2), 41–68. doi: 10.1215/10642684-2009-012
Solórzarno, D., & Yosso, T. (2002). Critical race methodology: Counter-storytelling as an analytical framework for education research. *Qualitative Inquiry, 8*(1), 23–44.
Stein, A., & Plummer, K. (1994). "I can't even think straight!" Queer theory and the missing sexual revolution in sociology. *Sociological Theory, 12*(2), 178–187.
Woolfolk, A. E. (1987). *Educational psychology* (3rd ed.). Englewood Cliffs, NJ: Prentice-Hall.
Yosso, T. (2005). Whose culture has capital? A critical race theory discussion of community cultural wealth. *Race, Ethnicity and Education, 8*(1), 69–91.
Zola, I. K. (1993). Self, identity, and the naming question: Reflections on the language of disability, in perspectives on disability. *Social Science Medicine, 36*(2), 167–173.

CHAPTER THIRTEEN

Intersectional Warrior: Battling the Onslaught of Layered Microaggressions in the Academy

DARRELL CLEVELAND HUCKS

INTRODUCTION

Predominantly white institutions (PWI) of higher education across the country continue to struggle with building diversity at both the faculty and student levels. Many institutions put forth their respective commitment to diversifying their institutions via recruitment initiatives. The benefits of diverse learning environments have long been discussed in the higher education research literature (Hurtado, Milem, Clayton-Pedersen, and Allen, 1999; Milem and Hakuta, 2000; Hurtado, Alvarez, Guillermo-Wann, Cuellar, and Arellano, 2012). Still, the negative experiences encountered by non-white individuals or groups entering PWIs are being well documented (Cooper and Stevens, 2002; Turner, Gonzalez and Chock, 2004; Turner, Gonzalez and Wood, 2008). Unfortunately, when most people advocate for diversity they are advocating for skin-color or racial diversity. On the surface, this level of diversity would be the easiest to determine at-a-glance and the easiest to monitor with little authentic engagement.

However, we must then ask ourselves is a commitment to recruiting diverse individuals a passive process or a surface level diversity (SLD) endeavor? Or should it be an active process of engagement that goes well beyond the surface of skin color differences? If it is the later, then institutions need to move beyond the observing phase and explore the quality of their engagement with those who they identify as diverse.

Institutions need to prepare existing faculty to engage with diverse faculty beyond just noting differences in skin color—all too often that is the case. Historically, SLD subjects faculty and students of color to existing racist beliefs, stereotypical judgments and daily micro-aggressions which puts them into fight or flight mode. Many of them leave such emotionally draining unsafe academic environments. According to a recent article by Kerry Ann Rockquemore (2016), President of the National Center for Faculty Development and Diversity, institutions must move beyond recruitment and critically examine their retention processes and retention problems to promote long-term change. Given our collective history as people of color, still struggling with issues of global inequity and oppression, many researchers believe that faculty and students are already grappling with the presence of PTSD (Post Traumatic Stress Disorder) and Racial Battle Fatigue Syndrome (Fasching-Varner, Albert, Mitchell, and Allen, 2014). Dealing with the daily onslaught of micro-aggressions that often occur to faculty of color in racist and white privileged environments can take a major toll on their effectiveness and ability to function.

THE CHALLENGE OF SURFACE LEVEL DIVERSITY (SLD)

The challenges faced by traditionally white higher education institutions must be clearly identified and addressed regarding their quest to enhance diversity. SLD does not allow the complexity of diverse people's lives and experiences to find a safe harbor, and the institution to effectively embrace diverse faculty and students (Rockquemore, 2016). My own lived experiences as both a student attending predominantly white institutions and now as a faculty member at a predominantly white institution belies the complexity of my experiences on both levels. On surface level, my identity as a Black person of African decent is frequently responded to solely based on negative associations others have of my skin color. I identify as a Black male whose family roots can be traced to chattel slavery in the United States. Layer this with my gay sexual orientation and it then becomes a question of navigating the often intersectionally "troubled waters" of the academy at a PWI. My experiences and how I process them take into account my layered identity including my race and the other important aspects of who I am as a human being and an educator.

Intersectional Warrior

Navigating the intersectionality of race, gender, class, spirituality, and sexual orientation has been like playing an endless game of chess in my professional life. There are times of agency when I can move freely within the academic context without much credence to consequence (teaching and working on my own scholarship);

then there are times, actually most times, when I have to study the academic terrain and carefully plot my trajectory for moving forward as an African American male on the academic chessboard to tenure and continued success without feeling oppressed. I find myself, often seemingly, navigating alone—so each decision has to be carefully considered. The one clear aspect of the game that I am keenly aware of is that the challenges can be almost insurmountable and the supports may be few, if any at times. By no means is this a complaint—just the ever-present reality check of an academically successful African American male working at a predominantly white institution of higher learning.

For some of my academic colleagues I am, seemingly, a wonder—more someone to ponder than understand. Currently, as there are only a few academics of color teaching at my institution in different disciplines—the feeling of being in the minority is a constant. However, while my colleagues have visible numbers of people that they may identify with, I have numbers too, just inside my head, heart, and the field—the numbers of African Americans who are a part of a history that runs deep within my soul—my very being. My story is one that is shaped and inextricably woven to thousands, if not millions, of other stories that are not visible to the naked eye. When I enter the room, many will always see only one man, most are not aware of the "spiritual" legions that enter the room with me.

Growing up in a Baptist family that attended church regularly, I was taught and still believe that one is never alone—God and the ancestors are always with you, especially in times of struggle and strife. I was also taught that I stand on the shoulders of those who have come before me. My success is honoring their historic legacy; doing steadfast work and maintaining my integrity is how I pay my respects to them in return, and readying my shoulders for the ones who will need them for support in the future. In sharing my insights into my own educational story through the intersectionality of my race, gender, class, spirituality, and sexuality (Collins, 2015) and the theory of collective achievement (Hucks, 2014), I hope to challenge existing SLD in higher education. These theoretical frameworks will help contextualize the power dynamics at work in my narrative and social inequities that exist on a broader level.

Historically, African American males have found themselves occupying the lower levels regarding academic achievement and occupy a place in society that is frequently laced with negative perceptions. As a young African American male growing up in the Bronx, NY in the 1970's, I was unaware of how these negative societal perceptions was impacting my life and the lives of other African American males I grew up with in my neighborhood. It wasn't until I got much older that I became conscious of how "suspect" we often are viewed by society at large (Dance 2002; Ferguson 2001; Majors and Billson, 1992; Noguera, 2008).

By the time my family moved into a home in a predominantly white NJ neighborhood, I was well aware of these perceptions and the impact they could and would have on our lives. My parents, both born in the South, always encouraged me to do well in school and indeed, expected that I would. I loved to read, although by the time I was a teenager in the eighties I don't remember being in a school climate that encouraged us to do so. To the contrary, those African American males in my class always seemed to act like we didn't read anything—even if we did. Even though I was often in honors classes, my peers only discussed books in class and we never really discussed studying or homework outside of class. I remember being acutely aware in high school that we were already sorted into particular tracks; my friends and I were on the college bound track. Others were on the "just finish high school track", some were on the "bound to dropout early" track, and the rest were on the "bound for trouble" track. African American male students in the last group—often found cutting class, hanging out in bathrooms and hallways, or not in school at all—were already being treated like criminals and thugs by the teachers and the administrators (Howard, 2008; Jackson and Moore, 2006; Rowley and Bowman, 2009).

Reflecting on this situation now, I would wager that these were probably some very brilliant minds that were being disengaged regularly in my suburban high school. I was frequently bored in school, but because of the fear of getting in worse trouble from my parents I chose not to follow in my peers' truant footsteps—there would be no need for prison because my parents would have killed me. I did well in school, or got by, largely due to my family's expectations of me, and I wanted to go to college—my primary reason at the time was to escape the boredom of high school. My high school guidance counselor never encouraged me to apply to colleges—it was my parents and older sister who had engrained this college expectation into my brain.

Ironically, it was years later that preparing children for college became a personal priority as a teacher. After graduating college with a Bachelor's degree in communication, I began to work in advertising sales for a well-known alternative newspaper. I later returned to the fashion business and soon found myself volunteering to work for Literacy Partners of NY. This is when I began to want to make a contribution to my community by working with adult emergent readers and writers. My mindset at the time was about giving back, and there I was, a college graduate, helping urban Black and Latino adults read and write for the first time. According to the research of Gurin and Epps (1975), my consciousness was emulating that of Black first-generation college students in the 60s who felt a sense of responsibility for advancing the race and giving back to our communities. I definitely felt that as a young African American male in my 20s that I needed to reach back and help others. I had so many opportunities in my life because of education that I needed to "pay it forward". After a few years of volunteering I began to consider working with children and becoming an elementary school teacher. I made the decision to work with children because of the nearly insurmountable struggles faced by these adults I was tutoring and vowed that I would direct my attention to breaking the cycle of adult illiteracy by working with children.

MINING MY OWN EXPERIENCES

Existing research regarding the experiences of Black faculty, specifically males, at pre-dominantly white institutions (PWIs) have historically focused on the impact of race, gender, and class (Allen, Epps, Suh & Bonous-Hammarth, 2000; Tuitt, Hanna, Martinez, Salazar & Griffin, 2009), and not sexual orientation. As a Black gay male coming from an urban setting and now teaching at a PWI in a suburban/rural area, I teach mostly low-to-middle class, first generation white college students. They have minimal experience outside of their smaller communities and they are forced to challenge learned prejudices regarding who they think I am as a Black male from an urban background (Dance 2002; Ferguson 2001; Noguera, 2008; Toldson, 2008). This body of literature focuses on the mistreatment and mislabeling of Black males in school settings, and does not always provide a layered examination of the identities of Black males' beyond race and gender.

This auto-ethnographic paper explores the intersectionality of race, gender, class, spirituality, and sexuality, and how they inform the ways I make meaning of my experiences and journey as a Black gay male professor of education at a PWI using intersectionality as an analytical strategy (Collins, 2015). Historically, intersectionality theory has been used by feminists to research the race, gender, and class dynamics at work for women of color within society (Crenshaw, 1991; Davis, 1981; Andersen and Collins, 2012). I will be applying the theory to explore how negotiating my layered identity as a Black gay male provides a foundation for my professional and scholarly work on addressing the educational needs of diverse learners. I will examine a select number of key incidents of micro-aggression from colleagues and students that I have had to negotiate.

Incident 1

The first example of micro-aggression I will describe has happened on a regular basis since I became a teenager and is a still a part of my current experience. It is the reaction that happens whenever I walk along a pathway, corridor or hallway positioned to pass a white female. Typically, they look at me suspiciously and move past me quickly. In those moments that occur when we appear in a hallway at the same time, me leaving my office and them just walking by, it is that awful moment when their bodies tense and they move by so quickly making sure not to make eye contact. Ask any Black male of a particular age and he most certainly has experienced a moment like this. I often smile and slow down, making sure that I offer a cordial greeting their way, most are startled into a response, others move by even faster. This occurs less now after being at the same institution for six years, and according to my current and former students, “Everyone knows you, Dr. Hucks.” Still it is quite interesting how a random and seemingly benign moment of merely passing a stranger can become so racially loaded in a matter of seconds. It fits into an existing trope of the “suspect,” “threatening” or “dangerous” Black male widely held in our society. I'm sure that in my younger years, I would have thought that my neat appearance would lessen these nonverbal micro-aggressions but I have learned to accept that regardless of how long I may occupy a space or regardless of being a well-known entity, this is a part of my reality as a faculty member of color in race-based society.

There will always be students and other adults at this PWI who have attached negative traits to me solely based on my beautiful brown skin color, and it doesn't matter how I'm dressed or even how I sound. Ironically, these scared individuals in their stance of feeling threatened by me, end up actually producing in me, a momentary sense of anxiety and fear. I'm not quite sure that will ever go away completely and given the current state of affairs for Black males at any age and any walk of life, we are becoming the overwhelming victims of racist violence. All I can do, in moments like these is to remember my ancestors, who I am, and push forward.

Incident 2

The second example of a micro-aggression involves navigating my colleagues and students inappropriate interest in my personal life. The questions I field in this area put me in the awkward position of having to keep a respectful distance from most. It seems that some of my colleagues believe that they can ask questions regarding my relationship status, and if they are aware of my sexual orientation—they deem it appropriate to describe the challenges they feel I must face. I learned early on as a teacher of children that there are things regarding my personal life, that regardless of my sexual orientation, I would never offer up as fodder for casual conversation in an academic setting. The stereotypes that seem to exist regarding male teachers, especially elementary school teachers are so disturbing. Also, I know the research that exists regarding Black males (starting at a much younger age) on how our behavior is often over-sexualized.

Unfortunately, I had to deal with this as an adjunct teaching in New York City when I made compliment to a female student regarding her resemblance to a dear friend of mine, which was seemingly misinterpreted by a group of students. At the time, I assured them that I was not suggesting anything beyond a striking resemblance. Still, some students, not the recipient of compliment, chose to complain about my compliment to a colleague in a different course. After my then colleague brought their complaint to my attention, I felt compelled to go back and share more than normal about myself to prevent the misreading from escalating to drama (possible accusations of showing favoritism or inappropriate interest in a student being taken to the administration) that I believe could have potentially cost me my position, or worse, my career. I will never forget the embarrassed expressions on students faces after I revisited the incident during class, shared my own sexual orientation, and clarified it further within the context of how we learned in the course that semester how often Black males' behavior starting in elementary school is often sexualized by others in school and society.

That incident informs my current stance of not sharing every aspect of my life with students or colleagues. Some may say why not? My response is simple, if you cannot understand or appreciate me at a very basic level, I will avoid subjecting myself to your misreading, or possibly abusing, the parts of myself that I love and cherish. The barrage of prying questions always feels like people are attempting "to go on safari" in my life. Often, faculty of color are treated as an "animal in a cage" by their white colleagues, and it does not lead to true appreciation and mutual respect. The faculty of color feel judged and in some way feel like they must share these personal details in order to advance at their respective institution. Historically, racism led to the capturing of African and indigenous people displayed in what are called "human zoos" for people to observe them like animals (Crais and Skully, 2010; Popular Resistance, 2014). As a Black professor at a PWI, one is always aware of the oppressive power of the panopticon gaze by white colleagues, peers, and even students (Foucault, 1977). People need to understand that this type of overt watching and this line of questioning is intrusive and not inclusive behavior. Relationships are built over time and faculty of color at traditionally white institutions should *never* feel like they have to be an open book about all areas of their lives—the only judgments they need to be concerned about is their work. If one has minority status at different levels then the community needs to work on embracing that individual without the expectation that they will gain unreasonable access to someone else's personal life or that individual does not exist without "the white gaze" as Toni Morrison discusses regarding her writing in novels such as *The Bluest Eye* (1990). In other words, the predominant group's (white) perspective should not take precedence over the lived experiences of people of color.

Incident 3

The third significant micro-aggression example I will discuss, has to do with intentionally making someone feel like they an outsider in the community. It is in direct conflict of advocating for diversity and puts the deemed "outsider" in a potential position of resentment of the mixed message being sent to them by their colleagues at the institution. When I started working at my current institution,

I encountered many comments from some of my senior colleagues such as, "Oh, you don't understand this community." or "That's not what we do here (mentioned as a statement of permanence). My question is: how are you embracing change and diversity with statements like this? You're not. In moments like this is when the work that needs to be ongoing with preparing to engage diversity shows that the investment required may not exist. This is when faculty and even students of color make the decision to leave if the supports they need do not exist or are severely lacking. I have had to discover, in energy depleting ways that the term "community" in the wrong hands at an academic institution can lead to tremendous marginalization and isolation. I found that focusing on my work with students is a good way to not be limited by the boxes some of my colleagues construct for me.

If faculty and students of color begin to internalize this projected "outsider" status it may possibly prevent them from advancing as scholars and students. Understanding that this limiting notion of community exists, I monitor my interactions with those espousing a limiting view. But as a faculty of color, I also intentionally mentor students, especially students of color, realizing that they may not have an advocate to help them unpack their encounters with micro-aggressions. I actively work at creating spaces for meaningful interaction with students in the courses I teach and the student organizations that I serve as Faculty Advisor, such as the Kappa Delta Pi Education Honor Society.

CONCLUSION

Since childhood, depending on the context, the hyper-masculine and threatening Black male stereotype always posed a threat to my emotional, and sometimes, physical wellbeing, At times, it continues to have this similar effect on me in academia. Growing up as a Black male in an urban environment, with scripted strict parameters around my social behavior and later complicated by social class location and sexual orientation, I made deliberate and conscious choices about how I would engage with peers in school and adults in the world. This layered identity and the choices I make to share or protect my identities continue to inform my life as a professor, researcher, and faculty member.

As a member of a small group of faculty of color at a PWI, it can be a daunting task negotiating which parts of my identity could potentially be perceived by students and/or colleagues as challenging or threatening, and which parts may be perceived by them as appealing or attractive. Research that includes the intersectionality of sexual identity along with race, gender, and class will capture the nuances of experiences and actually help to intentionally empower diverse faculty members. As institutions hire diverse new faculty members they must provide ways for the existing community to learn that individuals have layered identities, and their recruitment, retention, and success will require replacing stereotypes with an understanding of intersectionality and create supportive spaces for sharing and the work to be done toward understanding diverse identities. Healthy and flexible communities are sustained because they work to embrace diverse newcomers; the community does the bulk of the work and helps co-create spaces for the newcomer to gain access and make mutually rewarding contributions.

RECOMMENDATIONS FOR PERSONAL/PROFESSIONAL TRANSFORMATIVE PRACTICE

My own journey and educational research, and the academic journeys of other African American males, have implications for the design and implementation of present and future P-16 school-reform efforts, educational policy and research, teacher education, recruitment and retention of diverse faculty and students. Where educational policy and research have primarily focused their lens solely on the achievement and outcomes of African American males at various levels of school, there seems to be a void in earlier educational reform models that have not utilized the voices or lived experiences of students as a means to engage and measure the achievement of all the stakeholders involved in student's academic success and life outcomes (Hucks, 2014). I think collective achievement theory could be applied to faculty and student recruitment and retention.

By investigating the intersectionality of race, gender, class, spirituality, and sexuality in my personal and professional narrative I have gained deeper insight and understanding to the challenges and resiliency at work in my life as a relatively successful African American male college professor at a PWI. It is always important to know history from multiple perspectives, but my life, my work, has shown me that there is power in knowing our history as only we can tell it. My personal recommendation to future generations of African American males is know your history and tell your own story.

My recommendation to educators at PWIs is to make space for dialogue in your pedagogy and curriculum for deeply understanding the lives of your colleagues, students—the hopes and dreams they share—so that you can authentically validate their experiences and invest in their current and future academic achievement and success. It will definitely require a shift in your understanding of yourselves and the privileges and access you have benefited from by being in the white majority. Diversity is about genuine engagement and it is layered and it requires continuous work, but as long as we remember that there is always more to diverse human beings than what can ever be seen on the surface,and surface level diversity (SLD) reproduces the status quo of white supremacy and dysfunctional academic communities, we will find ways to authentically and sustainably diversify higher education for the benefit of us all.

REFERENCES

Allen, W. R., Epps, E. G., Guillory, E. A., Suh, S. A., & Bonous-Hammarth, M. (2000). The Black academic: Faculty status among African Americans in U.S. Higher Education. *The Journal of Negro Education, 69,* 112–127.

Andersen, M. L. & Collins, P. H. (eds.) (2012). *Race, class, and gender: An anthology.* Belmont, CA: Wadsworth.

Collins, P. H. (2015). Intersectionality's definitional dilemmas. *The Annual Review of Sociology. 41,* 1–20. Doi: 10.1146/annurev-soc-073014-112142.

Cooper, J. E., & Stevens, D. D. (2002). *Tenure in the sacred grove: Issues and strategies for women and minority faculty.* SUNY Press.

Crais, C. & Skully, P. (2010). *Sara Baartman and the Hottentot Venus: A ghost story and a biography.* Princeton University Press.

Crenshaw, K. W., (1991). Mapping the margins: Intersectionality, identity politics, and violence against women of color. *Stanford Law Review, 43,* 1241–1299.

Dance, J. (2002). *Tough fronts: The impact of street culture on schooling.* New York: Routledge Falmer.

Davis, A. Y., (1981). *Women, race, and class.* New York: Random House.

Fasching-Varner, K, Albert, K. A., Mitchell, R. W., Allen, C. (eds.) (2014) *Racial battle fatigue in higher education: Exposing the myth of post-racial America.* New York: Rowan and Littlefield Publishers.

Ferguson, A. A. (2001). *Bad boys: Public schools in the making of Black masculinity.* Ann Arbor, MI: University of Michigan Press.

Foucault, M. (1977). *Discipline and punish: The birth of the prison.* New York: Pantheon Books.

Gurin, P., & Epps, E. (1975). *Black consciousness, identity, and achievement: A study of students in historically Black colleges.* New York: John Wiley.

Howard, T. C. (2008). Who really cares? The Disenfranchisement of African American Males in PreK-12 schools: A critical race theory perspective. *Teachers College Record, 110,* 954–985.

Hucks, D. C. (2014). *New visions of collective achievement: The cross-generational schooling experiences of African American males.* The Netherlands: Sense Publishers.

Hucks, D. C. (2011). New visions of collective achievement: The cross- generational schooling experiences of African American males. *The Journal of Negro Education, 80,* 339–357.

Hurtado, S., Alvarez, C. L., Guillermo-Wann, C., Cuellar, M., & Arellano, L. (2012). A model for diverse learning environments. In *Higher education: Handbook of theory and research* (pp. 41–122). Springer Netherlands.

Hurtado, S., Milem, J., Clayton-Pedersen, A., & Allen, W. (1999). *Enacting Diverse Learning Environments: Improving the Climate for Racial/Ethnic Diversity in Higher Education. ASHE-ERIC Higher Education Report, Vol. 26, No. 8.* ERIC Clearinghouse on Higher Education, One Dupont Circle, NW, Suite 630, Washington, DC 20036–1181.

Jackson, J. F. L., & Moore, J. L. III. (2006). Leaving Black males behind: Debunking the myths of meritocratic education. *Journal of Race and Policy, 2,* 76–87.

Ladson-Billings, G. (1995). Toward a theory of culturally relevant pedagogy. *American Educational Research Journal, 32*, 465–491.

Majors, R., & Billson, J. (1992). *Cool pose: The dilemma of Black Manhood in America*. New York: Lexington Books.

Milem, J. F., & Hakuta, K. (2000). The benefits of racial and ethnic diversity in higher education. *Minorities in higher education: Seventeenth annual status report*, 39–67.

Morrison, T. (1990). *The bluest eye*. London: Pan Books.

No Child Left Behind Act of 2001, 20 U.S.C. § 6319 (2008).

Noguera, P. A. (2008). *The trouble with Black boys … and other reflections on race, equity and the future of public education*. San Francisco: Jossey Bass.

Popular Resistance (2014). Deep Racism: The Forgotten History of Human Zoos. https://www.popularresistance.org/deep-racism-the-forgotten-history-of- human-zoos/

Rockquemore, K. A. (2016). For a diverse faculty, start with retention. *Inside Higher Education. https://www.insidehighered.com/advice/2016/01/06/how-retain- diverse*

Rowley, L. L., & Bowman, P. J. (2009). Risk, protection, and achievement disparities among African American males: Cross-generation theory, research, and comprehensive intervention. *The Journal of Negro Education*, 78, 305–320.

Steele, C. (1997). A threat in the air: How stereotypes shape intellectual identity and performance. *American Psychologist*, 52, 613–629.

Toldson, I. A. (2008). *Breaking barriers: Plotting the path to academic success for school-aged African-American males*. Washington, DC: Congressional Black Caucus Foundation, Inc.

Tuitt, F., Hanna, M., Martinez, L. M., Salazar, M., & Griffin, R. (2009). Teaching in the line of fire: Faculty of color in the academy. *Thought & Action – NEA Higher Education Journal*. (August), 65–74.

Turner, C. S., Gonzalez, J. C., & Chock, S. (2004). Faculty of color in academe. *Arizona State University*.

Turner, C. S. V., González, J. C., & Wood, J. L. (2008). Faculty of color in academe: What 20 years of literature tells us. *Journal of Diversity in Higher Education, 1*(3), 139.

CHAPTER FOURTEEN

Undone and (Mis)Recognized: Disorienting Experiences of a Queer, Trans* Educator

ERICH N. PITCHER

> Laugh and cry and tell stories. Sad stories about bodies stolen, bodies no longer here. Enraging stories about the false images, devastating lies, untold violence. Bold, brash stories about reclaiming our bodies and changing the world.
>
> —Eli Clare, 1999, p. 60

Queer and trans* histories and memories are important because of the systemic erasure of our narratives. My stories are about being undone and (mis)recognized. Contained within these stories are traces of stolen bodies, bodies no longer here. Some of us were not meant to survive (Lorde, 1995). So I tell these episodic stories with all the privileges contained within my life's history, a white, emerging middle-class, bourgeoning academic who is perceived as "male." My femininity, and my being assigned female at birth, are often negated. This negation is usually attributed to my queerness because of transmisogynistic tropes like being a "man in a dress." But my queerness is often visible, both recognized and (mis)recognized.

I am visible when walking my dogs in the early morning hours in my neighborhood, holding my partner's hand. We are two men, queering the public space. But I am undone in moments when my genderqueer trans man partner and I go out to eat and the server balks at our desire for a single check. As if our queer desire cannot enter the public sphere in this way. I am (mis)recognized when I am asked if my partner and I are brothers or twins. Our queer kinship is (mis)recognized as hetero-cisgender kinship. I am not any of the other explanations and rationalizations folks use to negate the relational trans* and queerness they observe.

FEELING THE PAST

My stories take place in the settler colonial, Midwestern United States during the early part of the 21st century. I came of age during the gay 1990s, and what will become the trans* 2000s. I was there watching Ellen come out and witnessed that first lesbian kiss on *Roseanne*. I grew up, and now live, in a world ravaged by "false images, devastating lies, and untold violence" (Clare, p. 160).

I have never known the United States to not be engaged in a sustained military conflict, nor was I a wage-earning adult during the more prosperous times in U.S. history. Events like the Gulf War, O. J. Simpson trial, the Rodney King beating, murder of Matthew Shepard, Hurricane Katrina, Patriot Act, and No Child Left Behind are all marked by lies and certain kinds of tellings. The gaps in stories told and events that occurred left spaces for queer and trans* people, like me, to resist. Before I could resist, I had to understand my own family history.

I grew up in a small town about an hour outside of postindustrial Cleveland, Ohio, at the corner of Pekin and Watt roads in Russell Township. We are country folk who lived on a dirt road. My mother dreamed up a life that was far more cosmopolitan than that little intersection that the post office calls Novelty, Ohio. This is a place that does not really exist, except in postal nomenclature. But in pursuit of more money, more things, and more fancy (don't let me down), my mother nearly worked herself to death. Despite the fact that my mother constructed our family's class status out of her imagination, our whiteness served as a critical buffer. My parents had stable employment in traditionally gendered work; my mother was a waitress, and my father, a forklift mechanic. My parents never admitted to themselves, nor to my sister and I, just how working class we really were. My parents did not go to college, but there was a clear expectation that my sister and I would.

Within this context the seeds of critical social justice activism grew. I went to Antioch College, a school built on the notion that every graduate has a moral obligation to win some victory for humanity. This led me to working professionally as a grassroots political organizer. But, the organizer life—with changing jobs every few years—was not for me. I went back to school, got a fancy degree, and went on to pursue my PhD. It was in graduate school that I learned of wisdom of queer and trans* scholar-activists.

I was just four years old when Gloria Anzaldúa (1987/2012) proclaimed the notion that changing oneself is a way to change the world. Within the context of perpetual conflict, the gay 1990s, and neoliberal times, I must take seriously the project of seeing social change as intimately connected to the way I live my daily life. Resulting from the sociocultural and historical context, it is evident that I must change myself, in order to change the world.

THINKING AUTOETHNOGRAPHICALLY WITH THEORY

First coined by Heider (1975), Patton (2004) defines autoethnography as an "autobiographical genre of writing with ethnographic research methods, integrated through both personal and cultural lenses and written creatively" (p. 47). In analyzing the autoethnographic data that details the stories presented here, I draw on what education researchers Jackson and Mazzei (2012) call "plugging in." Jackson and Mazzei propose using theory to think with data (and data to think with theory) by dissociating oneself from mechanistic coding and the desire to present coherent narratives. I think through the data I collect using a life history narrative protocol. More specifically, I plug into multiple voices, some of which are queer voices, including Ahmed (2006), Merleau-Ponty (2002), and Husserl (2001), to stitch sedimentation into the data. I draw on Ahmed to talk about the ways that the data suggested disorientation. In doing so, I constructed a nuanced assemblage of story fragments. I play in the uneasiness of telling only parts of the story, through certain kinds of impartial, impossible tellings or "typifying examples" of the queer and trans* worlds I operated within (Berlant & Warner, 1998, p. 558).

Within the data I collected for this reflexive autoethnographic essay (Ellis, 2008), I created a table of contents to think about my life history. One subtitle I selected was "Choosing another path." This was the point in my life where I chose not to follow an educational path that would have helped me to run the family business, a small-town diner. Instead, I pursued a college education in the social sciences.

Koro-Ljungberg (2015) writes about the ideas of data wants, referring to the ways that reverse knowledge flows can occur. In talking about my deviation from the expected path, these data wanted to connect with Ahmed's notions of disorientation. "In choosing another path," I chose to trod a new path, one less followed in my family, even if uncertainty emerged along that path.

The notion of the path emerged again within my life history narrative, when I described my enactment of white supremacy within a trans* collective of which I am a member. The support along the path of critiquing and living a life in accordance with my espoused values required following a different path. This "deviation [from expected reproduction of whiteness and white supremacy] leaves its own marks on the ground, which can even help generate alternative lines, which cross the ground in unexpected ways" (Ahmed, p. 20). Becoming an antiracist white person does not follow the shape of the path laid before me. My deviation is difficult and requires repetition so that the path is clearer for those who come after me.

ACT ONE: LIVING AN IMPOSSIBLE LIFE

I think of being trans* as being a kind of impossible person. Being impossible is the experience of having an identity that is unintelligible to others, or not allowable within the sociocultural constraints of a given institution, in this case, higher education (Pitcher, 2016). Spade (2011) writes, "Trans people are told by the law, state agencies, private discriminators, and our families that we are impossible people who cannot exist, cannot be seen, cannot be classified, and cannot fit anywhere" (p. 41). It is within this space of impossibility, that I, and other trans* educators exist. I wrote the following story that typifies my experience with this phenomenon:

> My admissions application to a University of Wisconsin master's degree program was delayed. After many months of waiting, and there being no action on my application, I finally emailed the department and asked about the status of my admissions. A nice Wisconsin woman wrote back, stating that my application was incomplete and would not be processed until it was complete. She writes, "We never received your undergraduate transcripts." At that moment, as I read her email I panicked, I knew that I had in fact completed my application! I scoured my inbox looking for the receipt from the transcript request and the confirmation of receipt of my application materials.
>
> After assembling my documentation, I decided I had better call the person handling admissions and make sure everything was in order. I felt even more pressure, as I soon needed to decide what I would do with respect to graduate school enrollment.
>
> So, in a shaky, frightened voice, I said to her that I hoped my application was complete and that surely there must be some kind of mistake. She said she would look again and get back in touch with me. I waited for her call. Hours, days, and finally her call.
>
> She called back to say that yes there were in fact transcripts in my admissions file but that Antioch had sent the wrong transcripts. She said, this is really odd, the institution sent the academic record of a one Erica Nell Pitcher, she laughed, are you two related? I was not laughing. She said that I would need to request the transcripts again and make sure that I got the correct records sent this time and that it was no big deal as the admissions committee had not yet made any decisions. I paused for a moment as my heart sank. I thought … "She doesn't know I exist. She doesn't even know that I CAN exist."
>
> After what felt like too long of a silence for it to not be awkward, I said firmly, "Those are my transcripts. Those are the correct transcripts. I am a trans person. I …" trailing off. The deep man voice on the phone did not match the educational record, the cognitive dissonance was palpable, even over the phone. I felt her discomfort, her shock, but I could also hear her neurons firing through the phone line, she's breathing in a labored way so as to increase the flow of oxygen to her brain, blood pumping, an effort to reduce the dissonance. She finally said, "Well that can't be. You are a man." I paused, now panicked, trying to think of how to explain the history of my body, the layers of gender, the layers of sediment. What could I say to this woman who could not imagine the possibility of my existence? My educational archive has layers of sedimentation, fine grains of sands pressing into each

other, making the layers of my gendered life, woman, butch, genderqueer, trans*, masculine, each word, each time, each self, having its own layer. Some layers blending in and becoming indistinguishable.

The admissions administrator saw just two intelligible layers of sediment. Those two layers cut across the end, like some weird demonstration object at a science museum, held up to show that, in fact, the gender binary exists, even in the soil. But from her point of view, my voice, a "male" name, could not be attached to those records, to that bachelor's degree. At this moment, I was just a fraud (Bettcher, 2007), trying to pass off some other credential as my own, suspicious.

The silence lingered on both ends of the phone.

I slowly … with the tiniest amount of available grace … said that I am transgender, "I used to be a woman. Those are my records. There's been no mistake." I cringed as I said those words, which were and are utterly untrue. It is just the layers of my life were cut open for her to see.

"So, everything with my application is complete?"

"Yes."

Click. Dial tone. As if to say, "You, sir, are out of order." As if the quarters I fed into the pay phone were insufficient currency.

THEORETICAL INTERMISSION I

Should I simply slip a few more coins in the theory phone, in an attempt to evade my own telling of a story, hiding behind theory, avoiding the personal? The shape of my body, my history, the bodily horizon is a sedimented history (Ahmed). It is not just my body with sedimentation. My mental processes, language practices leave sediments, too (Merleau-Ponty). Contained within consciousness is an "implicit or sedimentary body of knowledge" (Merleau-Ponty, p. 277). Bodies of knowledge, gender and mental short cuts are what concern me.

SEDIMENTS AND FRAGMENTS IN THE CLASSROOM

In fall 2014, I co-taught an LGBTQ Student Leadership Course. I thought that I could be as flamboyant with my gender and my gestures as I wanted. I thought this would be the classroom I yearned for, a space where my gender nonconformity could be seen. The sediments of my body revealed.

I thought I am going to feel safe. I am in power and control and my confidence is there with this topic. Safety is another one of those devastating lies.

Instead, I felt scared, in fact, terrified in that LGBTQ Student Leadership classroom. I felt dangerous, a body out of bounds. I felt that I was never saying the right things or doing the class right.

A student stood up talking about the violence directed at trans* individuals, particularly trans* women of color. While she spoke eloquently about the urgency of this issue, when she made eye contact with me, it was as if she looked through me, despite telling me a story I knew, one that I feel in my bones. I was not there.

Rather than safety, I felt disappointed. I felt invisible. Erased.

THEORETICAL INTERMISSION II

Husserl describes sedimentation in awakening and remembering as "pass[ing] over continuously or in leaps into the other layers of sedimentation" (p. 233) and "continuously integrally cohesive system of sediments" (p. 234). Applying this notion of sedimentation to gender histories, certain layers of my gender history are often "passed over," jumping instead to other "layers of sedimentation." Through these leaps, my gender becomes integrated into a "cohesive system of sediments." More specifically, in the undoing of my prior gender identities and sex assigned at birth, others fragment my history by following the continuous arc of "male" or "man." Parts of me are made invisible. Invalidated for a more linear telling of gendered histories. The fragments splinter, but only I can feel the rub of frayed bones.

SEDIMENTS AND FRAGMENTS IN THE BOARD MEETING

I am sitting at a high-top table, feet falling asleep as they dangle off the edge of the chair. Loud, terrible music is playing in the background with TVs playing seven different kinds of sports lighting up the bar. It's been a long day; I am drained, holding my head up with my hand. But it's time for another meeting of the gay and lesbian faculty and staff organization at the university. I am the graduate representative. The men at the table are all drinking beer; the women drink wine. The grads nothing, we are poor. We are talking about trans inclusivity and gender representation on the board and in our group's name. A lesbian woman says, "Of course, our name is inclusive." I say nothing. She says, "There aren't any trans people involved with our organization for us to consult on the matter." Me, still sitting silently. She continues, "If there were trans people, certainly I would know, but seeing as there aren't ANY trans people on campus, I see no problem with the name." She's looking right at me, it's a small table that we're all huddled around. I say nothing. Instead, I feel the frayed gendered history of my life scraping up against the reality of her erasure.

ACT TWO: INTERRUPTION

I am a trans* person with access to white, male privilege. People regularly read me as a cisgender male/man, despite my not identifying as such. Self-identification aside, I am bestowed with a certain authority. Disavowing my white maleness is not an option, even when I am reminded that I "do not have to *feel* powerful to experience privilege" (Sensoy & DiAngelo, 2012, p. 74, emphasis in original). While I am often (mis)recognized and undone, that does not alter the relations of power in my life. I have internalized white male dominance. Part of the internalized dominance manifests in not listening and interrupting.

> A large number of the membership of the trans* educators' collective of which I am a part was meeting at a big national conference for educators. This particular conference was fraught with many missteps regarding the handling of trans issues within the association. I felt heavy with the weight of oppressive actions made by my cisgender colleagues. My shoulders rounded forward a bit more; I was curling into myself, retreating.
>
> It is the last night of the conference and it's late. A group of us are gathered in someone's hotel room, sitting on the bed, the floor, the chairs from the patio. We are strategizing about how to handle the most recent developments. There are many long pauses and silences, sighs with the weight of the numerous disappointments. My colleague has the floor, providing some important context and background to help guide our process. Ze, a black trans person, paused just long enough that I thought they were done talking. I began to speak, talking quickly, rushed, hurried. I am tired, I want this to be over. Another colleague, a white trans person, stops me. He says, you interrupted zir. I was surprised. I felt fear deep within my bones, I fought back tears and the urge to run. I couldn't bring myself to apologize. I sat silently, unable to respond.

The racialized dynamics of my actions are important here. I interrupted, asserting white male dominance. I centered my need to be done rather than moving slowly, intentionally. My white fragility showed up (DiAngelo, 2011). I am not used to race-based stress, it is disorienting. This time, I was the one who misrecognized and undid another. I also revealed the sedimented history of white male supremacy, a history that I also take shape around.

CONCLUSION

I end at the beginning. I dare to survive and tell stories. In doing so, I must connect with a "we." Ahmed articulates the notion that solidarity does not assume the same struggle, or pain, or hope for the future. Instead, Ahmed argues solidarity about commitment and work stemming from living on common ground. We queer and trans* educators must come to understand that we do live on common ground,

ground marked by our various deviations from cisgender, heterosexual lines. We can work toward solidarity and being recognized. In becoming "we," I mean that I trod the path for you, my fellow trans* and queer kin, both known and unknown. We change ourselves so that we might change the world.

REFERENCES

Ahmed, S. (2006). *Queer phenomenology: Orientations, objects, others*. Durham, NC: Duke University Press.

Anzaldúa, G. (1987/2012). *Borderlands/la frontera: The new mestiza* (4th ed.). San Francisco: Aunt Lute.

Berlant, L., & Warner, M. (1998). Sex in public. *Critical Inquiry, 24*(2), 547–566.

Bettcher, T. M. (2007). Evil deceivers and make-believers: On transphobic violence and the politics of illusion. *Hypatia, 22*(3), 43–65.

Clare, E. (1999). *Exile and pride: Disability, queerness, and liberation*. Cambridge, MA: South End.

DiAngelo, R. (2011). White fragility. *The International Journal of Critical Pedagogy, 3*(3), 54–70.

Ellis, C. S. (2008). Autoethnography. In L. Given (Ed.), *The Sage encyclopedia of qualitative research methods*. Thousand Oaks, CA: Sage. Retrieved from http://knowledge.sagepub.com/view/research/n29.xml

Heider, K. G. (1975). What do people do? Dani auto-ethnography. *Journal of Anthropological Research, 31*(1), 3–17. Retrieved from http://www.jstor.org/stable/3629504

Husserl, E. (2001). *Analyses concerning passive and active synthesis: Lectures on transcendental logic* (Vol. 60; A. Steinbock, Trans.). Norwell, MA: Kluwer Academic.

Jackson, A. Y., & Mazzei, L. A. (2012). *Thinking with theory in qualitative research: Viewing data across multiple perspectives*. New York: Routledge.

Koro-Ljungberg, M. (2015). *Reconceptualizing qualitative research: Methodologies without methodology*. Los Angeles: Sage.

Lorde, A. (1995). *The black unicorn: Poems* (Reissue ed.). New York: W. W. Norton.

Merleau-Ponty, M. (2002). *Phenomenology of perception* (C. Smith, Trans.; 2nd ed.). London; New York: Routledge.

Patton, M. Q. (2004). Autoethnography. In M. Lewis-Beck, A. Bryman, & T. Liao (Eds.), *Encyclopedia of social science research methods*. Thousand Oaks, CA: Sage.

Pitcher, E. N. (2016). *Being and becoming professionally other: Understanding how organizations shape trans* academics' experiences* (Doctoral Dissertation). Michigan State University, East Lansing, MI.

Sensoy, Ö., & DiAngelo, R. J. (2012). *Is everyone really equal? An introduction to key concepts in social justice education*. New York: Teachers College Press.

Spade, D. (2011). *Normal life: Administrative violence, critical trans politics and the limits of law*. Brooklyn, NY: South End.

Part 5:
The Political Is Personal

CHAPTER FIFTEEN

Slam Dunk on Tenure? Not So Fast ...

CATHERINE A. LUGG

In the fall of 1996, I started my research career as an assistant professor of education at the Graduate School of Education, Rutgers University. At first, I was not an out queer professionally, though I had been out for about five years in my personal life. I was delighted to be at Rutgers since, at that time, New Jersey was one of the few states with strong civil rights protections for queer people. As a politics of education scholar and historian, I wanted part of my research agenda to track the politics of queer civil rights as they relate to public education. Once I arrived at Rutgers, I asked a supportive colleague and ally what he thought of this idea, and he was strongly enthusiastic. And so I quickly embraced an avowedly queer research agenda and got on with the business of shaping an academic career.

This reflective chapter maps out my experiences at Rutgers University as an untenured assistant professor of education working in the areas of educational administration and policy. My defining moment came when I was denied tenure in spring 2002. This denial was almost entirely based on one external letter of evaluation, which was later ruled to be strongly homophobic. In this chapter, I discuss the strategies that I and my colleagues used to overturn this decision. I close this chapter with some thoughts on the lingering effects this experience has had on me personally, as well as in my career.

IT WAS JUST A REALLY BAD YEAR

The beginning of the academic year 2001–2002 began early for me, since I needed to submit my tenure portfolio for review. After a busy—okay exhausting—summer of pulling all of the stray pieces together into what I hoped was a coherent package, I submitted it at 10 a.m. on August 7, 2001. My departmental colleagues were optimistic, telling me I would be a "slam dunk" on tenure. I was more circumspect, since at that time my school had not had great success in promoting junior colleagues, all of who conducted "nonqueer" research. That level of caution would quickly prove to be wise.

At 1 p.m. on the same day that I submitted my tenure files, I received a call at work from my youngest brother, Andy, telling me that my father had died unexpectedly that morning, a little before 10 a.m. While there was no autopsy, dad probably died of a ruptured esophagus, since he bled out, hosing the bathroom as he died. Unfortunately, our mom found him.

Besides all of the scrambling that one must do when a family member dies unexpectedly (Dad's will wasn't valid, his checkbook was a mess, etc., etc.), my wife, Mary, and I had decided to go to Vermont to secure a Civil Union. At the time, marriage wasn't an option for us—or any other queer in the United States. So, we planned to go to Vermont and be married on September 22, 2001. Dad's funeral was on September 2, which was per family tradition—funerals are to occur on major holidays.

Of course, on September 11, 2001, it appeared like the entire nation had been turned upside down. It took a few hours to locate my brother David, who worked downtown in Manhattan—it was because telephone service crashed when the Twin Towers fell. Fortunately, David never made it into work that day thanks to an unexpected car repair. While we were still deeply shocked by those events, we did make it to Vermont to be married, taking I–95 for most of the trip, which routed us around New York City, the smoke, and the horrible smell of burnt and crushed humans.

In October of that year, I managed to pick a major fight with one of my professional organizations. The University Council for Educational Administration is one of the major research organizations in which professors of educational administration are expected to participate. I had been involved since I was a doctoral student, and at that time I was serving as Rutgers' representative to a governing board. This board was going to vote on a new institutional member—Brigham Young University. As an out queer woman, I was appalled since BYU was expressly homophobic and, in the early 2000s, was still subjecting a few "out students" to electro-shock treatments in the vain hopes of making them nonqueer. So I sent an e-mail to the entire representative membership explaining exactly why I was going to vote "no." What I didn't realize is that UCEA had never turned down anyone, and a large organizational fight ensued, one that I would clearly lose in a field that has been historically homophobic (see Lugg, 2015). And so BYU, homophobic policies and all, was welcomed aboard.

In the midst of all of this professional drama, there was more personal trauma. Mary had not been feeling well all summer and now well into the fall. After a series of cervical biopsies, the doctors determined she had a hormone replacement therapy–related gynecologic cancer. The final diagnosis was made on the Monday night before Thanksgiving. Since it was a rare cancer, it was imperative that she have surgery as quickly as possible. She was operated on December 5, 2001, a radical hysterectomy, coupled with a full abdominal exploratory. It was horrendous surgery, but the gynecologic oncologist was fairly confident that it was successful. That said, given the rarity of the cancer, he wanted her to consult with a radiation oncologist to pursue further treatment. The radiation oncologist concurred and she began two forms of radiation in late January 2002.

One issue that hurt in the midst of all of this was that the state of New Jersey refused to recognize civil unions. What this meant in bureaucratic terms was that the hospital where Mary had her surgery could not recognize me as her spouse. So, when it came time to fill out the endless presurgical paperwork, Mary had to list her sister, Therese, as her closest relative—although she lived in Atlanta (!). I was but a legal stranger. That said, the hospital personnel consistently recognized us as a couple and I never had trouble seeing her when I wished.

Between December and January, while Mary was home on sick leave, I was tipped off that there might be a problem with my tenure package. Supposedly, there was a "bad letter." While I wasn't sure of the total, I probably had least 10 external letters written by top professors in my fields, each who discussed my research acumen and its influence on the scholarly fields I claimed as "homes." However, at Rutgers during that time, one bad external letter on a tenure evaluation could end a candidate's bid for promotion and tenure—no matter how glowing the other letters were—or in my case, roughly nine fabulous letters. I had easily cleared the internal levels of review, but now that my package was outside of my school, given past practices, it was likely that the upper university would act on that one bad letter and deny me tenure. I was upset with the back channel gossip, but since Mary was headed into heavy radiation therapy, it was the least of my worries. She came through the ordeal with a fair amount of fatigue, but by the end of February 2002, she had finished all cancer treatments. We just collapsed for about a week.

In April 2002, I received the official news that I had been denied tenure. And it was clear it was on the strength of a solitary letter. It didn't matter that the rest of the letters were good to excellent (per the other RU level reports), and that I had easily cleared every other level of review. While I could never actually see the letters, it was obvious, as one of the union grievance specialists put it, "You got screwed." To me, the tenure denial was a homophobic sandbagging, so I was going to grieve the decision, no matter what. Queer bashing is queer bashing, even when it occurs in supposedly rarified enclaves of academe.

The reactions of my Rutgers colleagues were priceless. They were flabbergasted, just floored, and speechless, given my research productivity. And then they quickly engaged in what I would call "the funeral." They acted like I had died, or at least my scholarly career had died, and started to talk about things in the past tense. Often, I felt like I was a spectator at my own funeral. It was really odd. I was also "busted" on rank and demoted to an "instructor." Technically, instructors aren't supposed to chair dissertations, but my dissertation load at that time was already significant. So my school engaged in a bit of "legal fiction," since it didn't have the professors with rank to assume my load. While the university listed me as an "instructor," the GSE listed me as an "assistant professor." Hence, I could continue to chair dissertations.

Perhaps the worst part of the tenure situation was the few colleagues who wouldn't speak with me—for whatever reason. It was if I had been deemed an academic heretic and hearsay is catching, so I endured a form of exile from some of my colleagues. Instead of staying in a constant state of rage—which was tempting—all I could do was to hunker down and focus on building my grievance against the upper university.

THE GRIEVANCE PROCESS: SURREALISM IN ADMINISTRATION

I had the summer of 2002 to pull together my grievance claims. I was also teaching that summer (and the following summer) because I needed to save as much money as I could if I had to leave Rutgers. While it was a stressful and aggravating process, what I quickly learned was that I had to find faults in my promotion review process that could fit into previously established criteria of "insults" to the candidate. Neither I nor my union-appointed grievance counselor (who had never lost a case) was permitted to see the external letters, which were the keys to the entire case. The situation was surreal. That the university, a public institution, was allowed to use secret evidence was a continual irritant. What I later realized is that internal faculty grievances are more like arbitration hearings than a court setting. And in arbitration, the burden is on the litigant to establish a preponderance of evidence that mistakes had been made in the review process. It's a lower evidentiary threshold than beyond reasonable doubt, but it would be hard to establish that harm had occurred without divulging the content of the external letters. So I kept sending official requests to see redacted versions of the letters (removing any identifying information), invoking my Sixth Amendment right to confront the evidence since Rutgers is a public institution. I sent these requests about every six to eight weeks. And in response, every six to eight weeks, RU officialdom kept reminding me that basic constitutional guarantees aren't that basic when it comes to an internal grievance process.

Instead, Rutgers had and still has a convoluted process of having noninvolved faculty read all of the letters and then they issue a report as to any problems contained within the letters. The reading committee did indeed find that one letter was indeed homophobic, and at that point I was fairly confident that I would eventually prevail. But the committee's report existence hinged on the good will of my colleagues, who hadn't been involved with the original process of my tenure bid, and who were willing to sacrifice a week of their time to sort through things and craft a report.

One additional irritant was the entire grievance process ground to a halt. In the midst of everything, our labor contract expired on June 30, 2002. Until a new one was ratified, all grievance actions were stopped. The good news to all of this was that the resolution of the contract was a protracted mess. So I would have at least two more years at Rutgers, until June 30, 2004. The bad news was that I would sit in labor limbo for almost two years. Also, in the midst of the contractual mess, Rutgers began to replace the upper administration. First the university president resigned. Then, bit-by-bit various upper-level administrators retired, went back to faculty, or were encouraged to move on to other universities.

By March 2003, the labor dispute was settled and grievances were finally allowed to proceed. Mine was heard over several days in May 2003. It was a fairly easy decision for the committee to make, and I won on all four charges (all relating to the homophobic letter and how it was handled by the upper level of review). But at Rutgers, winning your grievance does not mean you are awarded tenure. Instead, candidates *must reapply* for tenure and promotion, using the same package, including the same letters. In my case, this included the homophobic external letter. The grievance committee report was included in the tenure package, and the upper level reviewers were warned to ignore the bad letter. Everything went back in for review in August 2003—almost exactly two years after the initial review.

For whatever reasons, the tenure decisions came later in 2004, and it wasn't until May that I heard that I had secured promotion and tenure—though again I had been tipped off that this time the news would be good. The best news was that I would receive back pay to the year I should have been promoted or 2002—two years' back pay was coming my way. I should have been happier, I suppose. But given the craziness inflected on my life, I at least wanted interest on all of that back pay. That said, ironically, all of the upper-level officials who had denied me tenure had left their positions. After a two-year tenure fight, thanks to a confluence of disparate events, *I was the only person still in place.*

AFTERMATH

The entire promotion and tenure experience has left me highly skeptical of promotion processes, especially those deemed "merit-based," when it comes to queer and other historically marginalized academics. Clearly, if a homophobic (or racist, or sexist, or all of the above, etc.) individual wants to sabotage someone's scholarly career, there really is no better time to do so than at the tenure review. And while one can occasionally "win" after such a professional attack, it's analogous to breaking your femur. You will heal, but you will never be the same.

That said, our professional associations can play a critical role in building a network of supportive colleagues in case of "tenure hell." These individuals are critical for any scholar, but even more so for those of us who experience structural discrimination. In my own case, led by Karen Seashore at the University of Minnesota, my senior colleagues in educational administration across the country rallied and wrote the Rutgers president, decrying my tenure decision. While I had no idea this happened until 12 years after the event, and the officialdom at Rutgers would deny that my colleagues' efforts had any influence, I suspect their efforts did help.

In the midst of the grievance process, I was able to maintain my research focus and work with my doctoral students. And again, my senior colleagues ensured I was presenting my research and that I had opportunities for new research opportunities. That helped me both in the short- and long run. My career was not permanently derailed, and I was later promoted on time when I sought to be promoted to full professor. I was probably over prepared when I went up for review in late 2009. Ironically, this promotion bid was entangled in another labor dispute, and I (and all of my faculty colleagues) saw no contractually mandated raises for a few years. Yes, lightning does strike more than once.

For a few years after the tenure battle, I served as a grievance counselor for the faculty union. But I found I would become too enraged to do a good job for my unfortunate colleagues. And I was thankful my role was of co-counsel, since there were a few times I really was too angry to think clearly. So, I went where my talents are, which is to work behind the scenes when it came to actual labor strife.

One final point: Given the endless loopholes, which are arbitrary and capricious when it comes to standards for promotion and tenure, such a scenario could very easily occur today, notions of a post-*Obergefell* (2015) world aside. About half of the U.S. states have no ban on antiqueer discrimination. And even in states like New Jersey that do have such bans, the tenure and promotion process is so ambiguous and secretive that it remains fairly easy to sabotage someone's academic career. Consequently, I have no qualms challenging the homophobia of our colleagues and institutions. It really is quite simple: *Who benefits from my silence?* Clearly, not my queer sisters and brothers.

REFERENCES

Lugg, C. A. (2015). *Public schools and the politics of queer erasure.* New York: Palgrave Macmillan.
Obergefell v. Hodges. 576 U.S. ___ (2015)

CHAPTER SIXTEEN

Queering South Mississippi: Simple and Seemingly Impossible Work

KAMDEN K. STRUNK, DOUGLAS R. BRISTOL, AND WILLIAM C. TAKEWELL

INTRODUCTION

Our purpose in writing this is to recount and analyze the push for queer-positive policy at the University of Southern Mississippi (USM) over the past several years, understanding the spaces that opened for such work, and why such spaces rapidly open and close on the USM campus. We cannot begin to tell the story of our experience working for queer-positive programming and spaces, and the challenges we have encountered in that work, without first contextualizing that work within the institution of the University of Southern Mississippi, the system in which it exists, and the state of Mississippi. The University of Southern Mississippi, founded in 1910, hovers near the 15,000 mark in enrollment and has campuses in Hattiesburg and Long Beach, plus some small research sites along the Gulf Coast. It, like many institutions of higher education in Mississippi, has constant budget shortfalls, and a cycle of enrollment/financial emergencies, while struggling to find consistent quality of students and enrollment numbers. It exists in a system that places it alongside the University of Mississippi (Ole Miss) and Mississippi State University for budgeting and evaluation purposes, an unfortunate reality in many years.

Forces against change and progress can be particularly salient in the Deep South, where calls to tradition, appeals to faith, and staunch opposition to federal intervention and outside meddling in local affairs are hallmarks of how policy is made (Crespino, 2007; Shoreman & Haenn, 2009). Mississippi can, in some ways, be thought of as emblematic of the Deep South, with its strong history of suppressing civil rights (Bolton, 2005), its perennially poor outcomes in education (Education Week Research Center, 2014), healthcare (CDC, 2014), and quality of life (Bishaw, 2013), not to mention its current work to suppress the legal rights of LGBTQ citizens. Anti-LGBTQ measures have been popular with the state's voters, who approved a 2004 constitutional amendment banning same-sex marriage by a margin of more than 80%. Mississippi politicians continue to promote anti-LGBTQ measures. In February 2014, Congressman Steven Palazzo publicly criticized same-sex marriages performed on the television broadcast of the Grammy Awards (Associated Press, 2014), an action resulting in some of the first organized LGBTQ activism in the area in recent years. In November 2014, Governor Phil Bryant appealed the ruling of a federal judge that overturned the ban on same-sex marriage (WLOX, 2014), and following the U.S. Supreme Court ruling in June 2015, the same Governor Bryant attempted to resist implementing the ruling in Mississippi, despite the disagreement of the state's Attorney General (MacNeal, 2015).

At the University of Southern Mississippi, where we have worked for several years to create queer-positive policy and spaces, 9% of students identify on the LGBTQ spectrum (Strunk, Suggs, & Thompson, 2015). At USM, LGBTQ students are nearly twice as likely to experience some form of harassment or victimization on campus; are less comfortable on campus; hear disparaging comments from staff, administrators, and other students more frequently; and witness threatening behavior more commonly. In fact, more than half of LGBTQ students at USM hear disparaging comments about sexual orientation frequently on campus, and a little less than one in four has witnessed threatening behavior on the basis of sexual orientation on campus (Strunk, Suggs, & Thompson). Yet while these numbers are part of telling a story of an environment in desperate need of queer-positive policy and spaces, they also show some of the work we have done in the past few years in their mere availability.

Our experiences, as narrated in this critical memoir, with opening spaces for queer-positive work and policy at the University of Southern Mississippi begin in the fall of 2013. It is worth noting some queer-positive space existed on campus prior to that time. For example, a small gay-straight alliance had existed on the campus since the late 1980s. Also worth noting was that senior administrators attended the opening meeting of that group and considered it an adequate intervention to meet the needs of LGBTQ students up until the fall of 2013 when a number of forces converged to change that perception, including faculty pressure, changes in federal Title IX guidance, the rapid pace of change in public opinion, and the shifting legal landscape for LGBTQ rights.

THE ACCIDENTAL ACTIVIST ON THE GULF COAST CAMPUS: CATALYZING CHANGE

We begin with the story of an accidental activist in Douglas Bristol, an author of this piece and tenured associate professor of history on the USM Gulf Coast campus in Long Beach. One example of space opening for queer-positive work at USM is the Alliance for Equality, a student organization established in the fall of 2013 on the Gulf Coast campus. To provide a framework for understanding this nascent LGBTQ equality movement, the following discussion refers to the model of movement emergence that political scientist McAdam (1982) uses to examine the African American Civil Rights Movement in Mississippi during the 1960s. McAdam emphasizes three crucial factors: expanded political opportunities, the degree of organizational readiness within the minority community, and the liberation of consciousness. All three were present to some degree on the Gulf Coast campus of USM.

Having an out lesbian vice president in charge of the campus presented an opportunity that had not existed before. Progressive-minded faculty and staff members had already formed a resilient support network, which facilitated recruiting people for an LGBTQ equality movement. Although Douglas Bristol was out and had tenure, he became an activist accidentally when a younger straight colleague in his support network asked him why there were no programs or student groups for LGBTQ students. The pair met with the vice president, and plans were made to hold the LGBTQ Safe Space (known at USM as ALLIES) training program on the Gulf Coast campus in September 2013. Because this training had not been held for years on the Coast and because the vice president invited all faculty and staff to attend, the training ran out of space at seventy people. The big turnout and related publicity sparked a cognitive liberation. LGBTQ faculty, staff, and students realized they had allies on campus. The impact of the experience was particularly noticeable in students.

The training gave students a new sense of optimism about what was possible. For many students, this was the first time they had ever heard administrators, faculty, and staff talk about LGBTQ students in a Mississippi school, and the discussion focused on helping them. The ALLIES training coincided with a wave of positive news about same-sex marriage in national media. Together, this event and the news made a core group of students believe it was possible to make USM a more tolerant university. Several LGBTQ students met with Bristol and asked him to help them establish an LGBTQ student organization, which the students named the Alliance for Equality. At the student government meeting that officially recognized the organization in November, Alliance student leaders were asked to explain how the group would help students who were not gay. One of them said, "I am not gay, and I am an evangelical Christian. I am unsure about the morality of homosexuality. But I know my church teaches me it is not our place to judge others, and I know I love my gay sister. I want her to feel welcome wherever she goes. There are other allies like me on campus." The young evangelical demonstrated his belief that he would change things for the better if he spoke out on behalf of his sister.

The LGBTQ Equality movement on the Gulf Coast campus has waxed and waned since the founding of the Alliance for Equality. Once again McAdam's work points to two factors that seem to explain the outcome: the institutional response to a reform movement and the maintenance of a shared consciousness. The institutional response was largely positive. Because there were no organizations for minority students on the Gulf Coast campus, and few student organizations in general, the Alliance for Equality had little competition when it sought help and resources from the campus staff. The Division of Student Affairs organized, for the first time, a Diversity Week and a Civility Week that had programs devoted to LGBTQ students. It also awarded the Alliance for Equality the Student Organization of the Year Award for 2014–2015. Campus officials represent just one side of the coin, however. McAdam argues that the institution's response is also influenced by strength of the insurgent group wanting change, which varied on campus. The monthly Alliance events consistently drew twenty to thirty people, and the Annual Smile for Equality picnic had more than seventy-five people two years in a row. On the other hand, there was constant turnover in the student leaders of the Alliance who felt overburdened with responsibility because few students would help run the organization. McAdam contends that organizational issues pose a dilemma for social reform movements because they lose their grassroots followers. Because the university tied support to maintaining a well-run student organization, organizational issues became the priority of student leaders and the faculty advisor. Yet students had more immediate concerns than attending workshops for student leaders. They wanted LGBTQ problems addressed. Moreover, there were limits to how committed students were to seeking change. For some, just attending workshops represented too big of an outing, leading them to drop out of the Alliance. Concurrently to these developments on the smaller Gulf Coast campus were developments on the main Hattiesburg campus. Central to these openings for queer-positive work was the Vice President for Student Affairs at the time. He was first contacted in the summer of 2014 by Douglas Bristol, who was working with six faculty colleagues to get USM to join the Campus Pride Index, which rates how LGBTQ-friendly the policies and programs of more than 450 participating universities are. The vice president of the Gulf Coast had been mired in controversy, and she had been a strong advocate for LGBTQ students. After her departure, Bristol, along with colleagues on the Hattiesburg campus turned to the Vice President for Student Affairs to work for change at USM. Bristol and a lesbian faculty colleague met with the vice president in the summer of 2014. Although the vice president said he was open to a process of incremental change based on meeting a national standard, he would not commit to working to get USM to participate in the Campus Pride Index. By way of explanation, he pointed out that USM had had a Gay-Straight Alliance on the Hattiesburg campus since 1986. He had attended the first meeting of that group and made positive comments, which found their way into the student newspaper. Then a state legislator had copies of the article distributed to every member of the Mississippi legislature. The vice president was vague about the repercussions of these developments, but he told the story as if it were a cautionary tale. This senior administrator made it clear that he feared a political backlash over the controversial subject of LGBTQ students.

THE QUEER QUANTITATIVE METHODOLOGIST: BRINGING DATA AND FRUSTRATION

Our story of queer-positive work continues through the perspective of Kamden Strunk, another author of this work who was, from May 2013 through May 2015, an assistant professor of educational studies and research on the main Hattiesburg campus of USM, and is a director of the Research Initiative on Social Justice and Equity (RISE). This pairing placed Kamden in the position of regularly engaging in queer research and advocacy, especially in Mississippi and regionally. Following developments with Douglas Bristol and his interactions with the Vice President for Student Affairs, the vice president subsequently met with the LGBTQ student organizations on both campuses of the university, with interested faculty, funded an LGBTQ scholarship, agreed to provide additional training for campus police, and to appoint a commission to redesign the campus ALLIES program and make policy recommendations. One pivotal moment, in our estimation, in opening some space for these conversations was a meeting early in the fall of 2014. During this meeting, the vice president asked Kamden Strunk to attend and to have the perspective of a researcher. Through the course of this conversation, the idea of a campus climate survey was hatched among the group. The same administrator would later tell other faculty (whom he was apparently unaware were acquainted with us) that he felt confident the survey would show the climate was essentially positive and affirming for LGBTQ students—that there was no problem. In our report of those survey results, from which we selected the above-reported findings, we found deep problems (Strunk & Suggs, 2014). Nevertheless, it was at that meeting that the administrator asked us to complete a campus climate survey to evaluate whether intervention was necessary and to what extent change was needed in policy and practice. That campus climate survey became a necessary leverage point for further conversations—what the administrator apparently believed would be a way to dissuade our attempts to work for queer-positive policy became a way to persuade him and others of the need. This led to faculty senate resolutions calling for action to improve the climate for LGBTQ students (Gulf Coast Faculty Council, 2015; Faculty Senate, 2015).

This work was not without frustration. In fact, after the publication of the final study report in 2015, one particular USM administrator made attempts to discredit the results of the survey. This was initially through contacting the Institutional Review Board to ask them to investigate the ethics of the climate study. When this failed, the administrator moved to directly contacting coauthors of the report, who had provided expertise in introductory sections of it. The administrator further contacted Kamden Strunk on multiple occasions in apparent attempts to gain inappropriate access to identified data, contact information for participants, and to request contact information for people who had received the report (which was impossible as it had been distributed by the Faculty Senate to all faculty). Nevertheless, the report was public, accessible to all, and on the USM website. Some action was necessary—the Vice President for Student Affairs, who was at least superficially supportive throughout, appointed a commission to examine training programs such as ALLIES as his solution.

THE STUDENT AFFAIRS STAFFER: WORKING WITHIN THE SYSTEM

We tell the next portion of this story through the perspective of William Takewell, who for several years worked in the Division of Student Affairs at USM, and was employed there throughout this period. William was a member of the vice president's commission on LGBTQ initiatives, which had specific responsibility for analyzing and improving the university's ALLIES training and included faculty and staff from across the institution representing a variety of academic departments and functional areas of student affairs. The taskforce also included two authors of this chapter. Most of the members of the taskforce felt comfortable identifying openly as either a member of the LGBTQ community or as an ally to the community. The taskforce worked to establish what the needs were on campus for the ALLIES training program by including students from the campus's Gay Straight Alliance on the taskforce, and discussing openly with them what they felt the campus was lacking in regards to LGBTQ+ inclusivity. The meetings of the taskforce occurred in tandem with the faculty-led campus climate survey to assess the experiences of LGBTQ individuals. Of important note is that at the time the climate survey was issued and the taskforce assembled, there was no administrative office, support person, or official LGBTQ+ initiatives available on the USM campus for students, staff, or faculty. While an ALLIES training program was available, the program began a review process in November 2014 to assess the effectiveness and accuracy of the program. These recommendations were informed by the campus climate survey (Strunk & Suggs; Strunk, Suggs, & Thompson), and also from the taskforce's interactions with LGBTQ+ students who were able to attend its gatherings. Recommendations included revising the mission statement of the ALLIES program, creating two levels of the training—one for incoming students and employees, and one for those wishing to become allies-advocates—finding a permanent home for the training within Student Affairs, and creating a plan for ongoing success of the program, among other suggestions.

The taskforce offered up its recommendations in late April 2015. However, the 2014–2015 school year included multiple changes to the landscape at USM: A financial crisis calling for large across-the-board budget cuts emerged due to declining enrollments, the Vice President for Student Affairs announced his retirement, and for a number of reasons, several faculty working on queer-positive policy proposals left the university. Since the taskforce offered these recommendations, there has been a lack of communication as to what will happen next for the ALLIES Program and for LGBTQ+ issues on campus. Transitions in key faculty, staff, and administrators likely explain some of this lack of movement. It parallels a lack of movement on other initiatives which, at one point, seemed inevitable. One example is conversations that began about trans-inclusive housing policies. These seemed inevitable and simple in the spring of 2014, but going into the summer of 2015, they seemed a distant hope unlikely to materialize. However, there are some positive changes as a direct result of the taskforce's work and the publicity of the campus climate survey. Students seem to be more aware of what is going on with campus in regard to the issues of diversity and multiculturalism, and there has been interest shown by a variety of students to establish programming and initiatives that are inclusive and protective of all students.

WHAT HAPPENED? AN ANALYSIS OF INSTITUTIONAL RESPONSES TO QUEER-POSITIVE POLICY WORK

Our analysis, in looking back at the past years of working for queer-positive policy at USM, is that many of the challenges that are supposed to explain why reforms were not enacted seem to be illusory. While budget shortfalls at the institution were all too real (and remain a threat to the institution on an ongoing basis), the reality is that the majority of the reforms called for would not have cost money at all. One example is our strong and insistent suggestion that housing policies for trans* students be written down and made accessible to prospective and current students online. Student Affairs has a standard way of working with such students, so no new policy would be made, but merely working policy would be written down. And the cost of the paper to write it on or the server space to put it online is surely not the objection. Others that we asked for would cost extremely small amounts of money—a notion often met with questions about which student groups such funds might be "taken from." We tend to reject the idea that a $500 program across an institution with an annual budget of $278.7 million for 2015 (USM, 2015) would be unsustainable or would require cuts to programs for students of color, as seems to be the implication. Instead, we suggest that two forces are at work in these institutional tactics to avoid queer-positive policy work: (1) Institutions can, by putting the interests of marginalized groups against each other, diffuse the energy and activism that would otherwise be behind a single policy push. In other words, when faculty who might be for queer-positive policy learn that its enactment would (somehow) lead to fewer resources for women or students of color, some are likely to lose interest in that policy fight. Even though such dichotomies are likely false, they are powerful in diffusing the interests of people who are otherwise interested in such changes. (2) As the Vice President for Student Affairs suggested in his meetings with us, institutions subject to extremely conservative legislatures may look for ways out of doing queer-positive work. The vice president at USM referred to a fear of "going too far" and "catching attention" of legislators. In other states, such attention has not been good for colleges. In one example, South Carolina legislators cut funding to two institutions because they assigned readings viewed as queer-positive (Wilson, 2014). In an environment where funding is scarce and cuts constant, such attention can truly be devastating to the institution.

We write this today from an interesting position. While all authors of this piece were at USM working for queer-positive policy over a period of years, today only one of us remains at the institution. Looking back, we are left to wonder how what seemed so simple at our initial meetings with administrators became so complex and seemingly impossible: creating some meaningful queer-positive student policies. The institutional response was in some ways typical: We need more time. We need more data. We don't have the money. We don't have the legislative support. Yet, in other ways, the institution seems to have inadvertently set a path for itself that will be difficult to undo. The data, now public, available online, on the institution's own website, led to faculty senate resolutions calling on the president to act. Next year, they plan more research (by an outside firm instead of by faculty researchers), perhaps to buy more time before any real action, perhaps hoping for better outcomes from different data.

In general, we view three cooperative forces as being at work in institutional responses to our work for queer-positive policy at USM: (1) There is a general institutional resistance to change, particularly in the South, and even more so in Mississippi. (2) As evidenced in statements by the Vice President for Student Affairs and other administrators, there is a real and valid fear of going too far with queer-positive policy work. This fear is rooted in legislative reprisal for being too easy on gays and the gay agenda. This is evident in the vice president's anecdote about the newspaper with quotes from him about the Gay Straight Alliance being on the desk of every state legislator, and recent efforts in South Carolina to cut funding to colleges perceived as too gay-friendly. (3) These two instincts lead colleges to play a zero-sum game in which they pit marginalized groups against each other to fight for small amounts of funding. This, quite naturally, diffuses the energy to work for policy that benefits diversity and campuses that embrace and welcome all, as students and faculty are forced to choose who to support.

While recognizing these factors as the reality in which we work and exist and that administrators and policymakers are embodied beings who take on the expectations that saturate the culture around them, we reject these dialogues. We know that colleges can fund initiatives that benefit women, students of color, students with disabilities, and LGBTQ students, particularly when such initiatives are so inexpensive, and often free. We know that there are ways to work *with* legislators, even in religiously and politically conservative environments, instead of *around* them to work for student recruitment, persistence, and success, instead of denigrating, ignoring, and marginalizing some students. We call on administrators, faculty, staff, and students to be bold in working for queer-positive policy while being attentive to ensuring all students are welcome, safe, and successful, and to be brave in explaining and advocating for that work with their boards and legislators.

REFERENCES

Associated Press. (2014, November 28). Mississippi appeals ruling in same-sex marriage case. *Jackson Clarion-Ledger.* Retrieved from http://www.clarionledger.com/story/news/2014/11/28/mississippi-appeals-ruling-in-gay-marriage-case/19627297/

Bishaw, A. (2013). *Poverty: 2000 to 2012. American community survey briefs.* U.S. Census Bureau. Retrieved from http://www.census.gov/prod/2013pubs/acsbr12-01.pdf

Bolton, C. C. (2005). *The hardest deal of all: The battle of school integration in Mississippi, 1870–1980.* Jackson, MS: University Press of Mississippi.

Centers for Disease Control and Prevention. (2014). *Statistics of the state of Mississippi.* Retrieved from http://www.cdc.gov/nchs/pressroom/states/MS_2014.pdf

Crespino, J. (2007). *In search of another country: Mississippi and the conservative counterrevolution.* Princeton, NJ: Princeton University Press.

Education Week Research Center. (2014). *Mississippi state highlights 2014: District disruption and revival: School systems reshape to compete and improve* [Special supplement]. *Education Week's quality counts 2014.* Retrieved from http://www.edweek.org/media/ew/qc/2014/shr/16shr.ms.h33.pdf

Faculty Senate (2015). *Faculty senate resolution #6, 2014–2015.* Retrieved from https://www.usm.edu/sites/default/files/groups/faculty-senate/pdf/resolution_06_2014-15.pdf

Gulf Coast Faculty Council (2015, February 2). *Letter of support.* Internal campus document.

MacNeal, C. (2015, July 1). Mississippi AG asks to stop defending guv in gay marriage case. *Talking Points Memo.* Retrieved from http://talkingpointsmemo.com/livewire/jim-hood-phil-bryant-mississippi-gay-marriage

McAdam, D. (1982). *Political process and the development of black insurgency, 1930–1970.* Chicago: University of Chicago Press.

Shoreman, E. E., & Haenn, N. (2009). Regulation, conservation, and collaboration: Ecological anthropology in the Mississippi delta. *Human Ecology, 37*(1), 95–107.

Strunk, K. K., & Suggs, J. R. (2014). *Research update on findings from the USM campus climate survey: Results related to LGBTQ students.* The University of Southern Mississippi & Research Initiative on Social Justice and Equity.

Strunk, K. K., Suggs, J. R., & Thompson, K. (2015). *The USM campus climate survey: Findings and recommendations.* The University of Southern Mississippi & Research Initiative on Social Justice and Equity.

University of Southern Mississippi. (2015). *Summary of revenues and expenditures.* Retrieved from http://www.usm.edu/sites/default/files/groups/office-fiscal-planning-and-analysis/pdf/summary_of_general_and_auxiliary_fund_revenues_and_expenditures_2015.pdf

Wilson, R. (2014, February 21). South Carolina legislators cut university funding over gay-themed books. *Washington Post.* Retrieved from https://www.washingtonpost.com/blogs/govbeat/wp/2014/02/21/south-carolina-legislators-cut-university-funding-over-gay-themed-books/

WLOX. (2014, February 5). Protestors want apology for Rep. Palazzo's gay marriage remarks. *WLOX.* Retrieved from http://www.wlox.com/story/24647058/protestors-want-apology-for-rep-palazzos-gay-marriage-remarks

CHAPTER SEVENTEEN

Smear the Queer: A Critical Memoir

SCOTTY M. SECRIST

INTRODUCTION

This is a piece of art, because I am an artist. I am an artist of many media. I draw. I paint. I play piano. I am also a scholar. My professional training in higher educational research has conditioned me to express my thoughts in very particular ways. However, you will not find a nice, tight argument, wrapped with a bow, in this piece. Actually, this piece is an artistic experiment, one in which I infuse my body and my voice into an artifact for others to view and ponder.

I have been greatly inspired by Gloria Anzaldúa's *Borderlands/La Frontera: The New Mestiza* (2012). While the concept of borderlands is quite powerful and can probably be applied to many of the stories that I share in this piece, I hesitate to make such comparisons. Rather, I draw inspiration from Anzaldúa's way of working and thinking, her methods and methodology. For this piece, I dig deep, drawing upon both my past experiences and my interpretations of those experiences. Throughout this essay, I try to honor my spiritual experiences. In short, Anzaldúa has challenged me to be open and vulnerable, and to find my voice in doing so.

Vulnerability is a form of violence. When we think about vulnerability in education, we usually think about a person choosing to reveal something very personal about themselves, to share it with others for the sake of learning. Obviously, when people share these kinds of personal narratives, they are choosing to pick a scab off of a wound. What people don't usually think about is all of the violence the person experiences in making the decision to be vulnerable. Often, they will play out every imaginable scenario in their head to prepare themselves for any potential backlash. They live all of those scenarios, and they feel the pain, heartache, and misery associated with the worst possible outcome. But somehow, they come to the decision that airing their wounds will be more beneficial for them and for others than not doing so.

I suppose that is what I am trying to do here. I provide some stories from my own experiences. Some of them are hard to tell. All of them inform my thinking and my orientation toward my work as an administrator, as a scholar, and as an educator. Harjo (2012) writes, "For me drawing was dreaming on paper," (p. 48), and "I loved poetry. It was singing on paper" (p. 50). As an artist *and* a scholar, I give this to you as my dream and my song.

INTRODUCTIONS: HELLO, MY NAME IS ...

This might be another cliché name story, but I've been thinking about names differently because my own has become a site of contestation. And let me be clear, my name has not changed. Other things have, like my research agenda, my professional capacities, the degrees I hold, my geographic location, my income, my professional aspirations, my body, but my name hasn't. I've always gone by Scotty. For purposes of full disclosure, my legal name is Scott. But everyone has always called me Scotty, ever since I can remember. I was my grandmother's favorite grandchild (at least that's how I remember it), and through her final days, she called me "my Scotty." She passed away the summer before I started my doctoral program after a long battle with osteoporosis-related complications. In fact, I was with her most of that summer, and in many ways I was her caretaker.

That August, I moved to a shitty apartment in downtown Lansing, Michigan. While I was preparing to move, my mom and my aunts hired an in-home medical service for my grandma. After a week in Lansing, I got a phone call from dad letting me know that she had passed. I loved her. I was heartbroken, and I felt a huge amount of guilt about leaving. I was her Scotty, and I left.

Maybe that is why I almost had the meltdown after being told that I should start going exclusively by Scott. Before coming to Lansing, people asked me if I preferred Scotty or Scott. I usually said something like, "Everybody calls me Scotty, but I suppose I'll answer to either." Looking back, I suppose these were subtle ways of people telling me I should go by Scott, but those hints didn't really sink in. During my first year in my doctoral program, people holding a rather large amount of institutional power and influence felt the need to have a very serious conversation with me about my name.

A few months into my program, I was just getting my footing in my administrative, on-campus job. My supervisor retired midway through the year, so my direct report line shifted to an individual who had just started in an executive-level position. We had been building a rapport for many months before he officially began in his new position. I confided in him my professional aspirations and my need for mentors on the campus. I told him I wanted to do queer work. I recounted the story of how I came to the higher education and the student affairs profession. I completed a bachelor's degree in biochemistry, thinking I wanted to go into the medical field. However, during my time as an undergraduate, I was extremely involved in new-student orientation programs. I discovered that there were people who devoted their lives to college students' success. Upon graduation, I was hired on in the orientation and first-year student services office at my undergraduate institution, but I made a decision that at some point I would focus my work on LGBTQ students and/or queer scholarship.

After telling him this and giving him my history, my new supervisor had a troubled look on his face. My heartbeat accelerated and my stomach twisted in knots. In that moment, I imagined him telling me not to tell anyone else about that desire and to not bring it up to him again. But the conversation didn't go in that direction … entirely. Rather, he started with flattery. He told me that he had seen my resume and that I had some great professional experiences working in broader areas of college student success initiatives and student leadership development. I agreed. He went on to say that if I had aspirations of someday rising to an executive-level position, that I should be sure to make strategic career decisions and not fall into the trap of being pigeonholed into a single type of student affairs professional. Rather, I should consider trying to enhance my experiences working with student success and leadership development broadly, because it shows versatility. I will comment on versatility later.

I can't recall if it was during the same meeting, or if it was during a meeting a week or two after, but he asked if my legal name was Scotty or Scott. I told him that it was Scott but that I had always gone by Scotty. For some reason, though, I refrained from telling him that I was fine being addressed as either. In this moment, I realized that I was not fine being addressed by either Scott or Scotty. He went on to tell me that I should probably consider signing my emails and introducing myself as Scott. His rationale was that because I had certain professional aspirations, I would probably be taken more seriously on this campus, and more widely, if I went by Scott. He said that "Scotty" might seem less professional to some, and folks in upper-level administrative positions might not take me as seriously. He went on to say that "Scott" connotes a more mature and seasoned professional persona. However, he ended the conversation saying that it was completely my choice and that he would support me no matter what I decided. I should just let him know if he needed to include the "y" or not.

Needless to say, this experience triggered a good deal of cognitive dissonance. But I coped, as I had for many years before, by pushing it aside and assuring myself that others are inherently filled with good intentions, regardless of the impact they have on the world. These conversations sat with me for a long time. They played over and over in my head. I did not know how to make meaning of them, but I knew they meant something. After all, this person is someone I asked to mentor me. I truly believe, to this day, that this person was acting in what he thought was my best interest. But, they were conversations that had never stuck with me like this, in this most uncomfortable way. The fucking "y."

NIP/TUCK

A scalpel cuts into my skin. It burns, ironically. The scalpel is a cold, clinical hunk of metal. But that's not what I feel. I feel the burn slicing into my skin. It cuts precisely around the problem spot. It hurts. The pain is sharp, but I know it will get worse before it gets better. Then I hear the powering on of the bone cutter. The saw traces the scalpel cut, but this time I feel the pressure of the surgeon pushing it hard into the bone. I can feel it because there aren't any anesthetics. There aren't any anesthetics because I chose this. This is an elective surgery. I chose this. This is my decision. I am choosing to have this cut off from me, cut out from me, from my body.

Through my screams, the loudest I've ever screamed, the sound of the saw buzzes without fail. I can hear my blood splattering on the walls, on the surgeon's goggles and face mask. And then, a crack. It's done. I can feel a rush of cold air sweep over the open wound. It's done. The procedure is complete. It is forever cut from my body. All that I was, will never be again. I am forever different. But I am different, changed forever, and now I can be what I think I want—what they wanted.

WHO AM I KIDDING ...

I probably keep the "y" for nostalgic reasons. It does represent my youth; every time my grandmother called me "her Scotty," I was reminded of my generational place in my family. I've never been a morning person, so every day before school, my mom would walk into my room and softly say, "Scotty, it's time to get up." My brothers, in their typical straight-jock style, were always introducing new nicknames. They called me "Scotty-dawg," "Scotty-the-body," and many others. I remember getting scolded in fifth grade because I was running in the student council elections, and I hung on every bathroom door posters that read "Before you go potty, vote for Scotty!" I remember some of my classmates called me "Scotty-too-hotty," which subsequently became my first ICQ screen name. The "y" was part of my youth. It was with me, following me around through the good and bad.

I also think that my "y" is related to my queer. When I think about the first time I woke up with another man, I remember him saying, "Morning, Scotty." I remember being 19, walking into my first gay club in Ann Arbor, Michigan, with my best friend, where she introduced me as "Scotty" to all her gay friends. I remember the first time a man said he loved me, "Scotty, I love you." I remember my first gut-wrenching, heart-shattering breakup; "I'm so sorry, Scotty, but this just isn't working for me right now." I remember my youth and my queerness as Scotty.

Maybe, though, I am just reading too much into all of this. After all, I did sign up for this career path. Higher education is my passion. I want to be taken seriously. I want my work to be acknowledged. I want my thoughts to be heard. Sara Ahmed (2013) describes institutionalization as fading into the background, becoming part of the environment that nobody notices. However, dropping the "y" seems like a whole lot more than deleting a letter from my email signature. It seems like trying to become part of the institution and leaving whole parts of my life behind.

FAGGOTRY FOR SOMETHING

a poem

"Hi, I'm Scotty."
And that's all it takes …
From that simple utterance,
You know
I'm Gay,
a Homo,
a Queer,
a Faggot.
My faggot voice
Tints every word I say.
It warps your view of me
So that everything I do is faggotry,
And because I do faggotry,
I am faggotry.
And before you know it,
all I can ever do is faggotry,

because I am faggotry.
For a long time,
I ran from faggotry.
It was something I didn't want to be,
So it was something I tried not to do.
And if it was something I didn't have to do,
then it was something I could choose.
So, I chose to run.
I hid.
But from what?
Why was my faggotry so hard to escape?
"Hi, I'm Scotty."
Oh yeah …
There it is.
The Gay lisp.
The Homo Intonation
The Queer sound.
My faggot voice.
Try as I might, I wasn't going to be able to change that.
So, I took up that old adage,
"If you can't beat 'em,
beat off with 'em!"
And beat off I did!
Along with lots of other fun things.
With guys,
boys,
bears,
Sirs,
cubs,
otters,
tops,
bottoms.
In the backseats of cars,
hotel rooms,
hotel pools,
hotel elevators,
In random apartment complexes,
at movie theaters
In bathhouses and frat houses.
You name it, I probably fucked it, on it, around it, or near it.
After a while though

the gratification from my almost-nymphomaniac tendencies
and certainly risky decision making
wasn't sustaining enough.
Sure, fucking in a classroom after hours
or at work in a much older faculty person's office constituted some kind of resistance.
It felt like I was making some kind of statement. But for what?
"Hi, I'm Scotty."
Hear it?
It's there.
The faggotry.
It's in my voice.
What I didn't realize,
While I was out fucking for the cause,
Is that I wasn't just doing faggotry while I fornicated.
Somehow I created,
As false and imaginary
Two worlds.
One where my dick and tongue did faggotry,
And another in which I, Scotty, didn't.
Then, one random day,
In an agonizing moment of having to introduce myself
Knowing that my secret's out of the bag every time I speak,
The space that I tried to keep between those two imaginary worlds evaporated.
Planets collided.
That way of being, those two worlds, those two ways of being
were suddenly ripped from me.
And that's all it takes.
From that simple utterance,
You know
I know
I'm Gay,
a Homo
a Queer
a Faggot.
My faggot voice tints every word I say.
It warps your view of me
so that everything I do is faggotry.
And because I do faggotry,
I am faggotry.
And before you know it,

all I can do is faggotry.
But now, I don't resist my faggotry.
I don't run from it.
I don't choose to hide.
Instead of resisting faggotry,
I take it up as a form of resistance.
I resist a world that assumes I'm straight until I introduce myself.
I resist a world that
Shames
Punishes
Murders
Those who do faggotry
because they are faggotry.
I resist that world with every fiber of my being,
Not just with my cock, cum, and mouth.
I use my mouth,
my tongue,
my voice,
I use my entire being, my whole body to do faggotry
to resist.
I do faggotry for something more than personal gratification.
I do faggotry for something else.
I do it so that when I enter a room,
I am both welcomed AND expected to be there.
I do it in remembrance of my forefaggots,
And I do it to broaden the horizons of possibilities for all the little faggots to come.
When I speak,
I speak faggotry.
When I introduce myself with,
"Hi, I'm Scotty,"
I do so mocking conventional norms,
Infusing my faggotry into the seams of everyday life.
My cordial introduction isn't cordial at all.
"Hi, I'm Scotty."

MY BOD(Y)

See, the "y" actually fits my voice. When I speak, the tone of my voice is a clear tell. Everybody knows I'm queer when they hear my voice. What I have noticed, though, is that while the "y" has fit my voice since primary school, the "y" does not actually fit my body anymore. Or maybe my body does not fit the "y." What I mean by this is that part of the reason people question the "y" was that my physical body did not align with what they thought a "Scotty" should look like.

In high school, I was a diver. I was actually quite good. I was the only male athlete in my grade to make it to the state finals in any event. I still hold the record. Pretty macho, right? My success as a diver-athlete did not assuage the constant, daily microaggressions. Apparently, jumping off of a board and flipping around in the air in nothing but the tiniest of speedos only assured my peers of my queerness. But I did it anyway because I was good at it, and I loved it. I loved when the entire natatorium would quiet when I stepped on the board. I loved standing there, my body fit, tight, and smooth. My body was a spectacle. I put myself out there to be judged.

My physique changed a bit in college, but my fitness held throughout most of it. I started growing more body hair, but my time of coming out coincided with the era of manscaping. Thus, I usually kept a pretty smooth appearance. Overall, I stayed in pretty good shape, maintaining a 32-inch waist. It was not until my first year of work after graduation that I woke up one morning and noticed that my shape had changed significantly. My 32-inch waist grew by 8 inches. My hipster skinny pants became a thing of the past. My body started sprouting hair in all kinds of places. Perhaps not so ironically, my hairline had started to recede significantly. I know that I am making myself sound like some kind of ogre, but honestly, I felt like one day I just woke up in somebody else's body. This body was one that would not fit in at my favorite gay/twink clubs. I was no longer the hot new twink on the gay hookup sites. I was what they meant when they said, "No fats." But I looked pretty masculine. I remember one guy I dated told me that he liked "bigger bear guys." He meant it as a compliment. I didn't take it as one.

That's what I mean when I say that maybe my body doesn't fit the "y" anymore. I had known my gayness in a very particular way. The way I knew to be gay at that point in my life was white, twinky, promiscuous, sexist, classist, and transphobic. When I perceived that my body had changed in a way that left me no longer an object of many people's desire, I began to see that my body did not fit in that definition of gay. My changing body has altered others' perceptions of me, which in turn have altered my perceptions of my own queerness.

So I considered dropping the "y," like I dropped those skinny hipster jeans and the pretentious hairstyles. I was beginning to see that my body was becoming more like those of my middle-aged, middle- to upper-class, white, straight, male colleagues. Maybe that's what I could become. Maybe someday, this body would take me to the head of a classroom as a beloved professor, or to the administration building as the provost or president of a university. This body, the not-gay-enough, average-white-dude body, might open some doors for me, much like when Sara Ahmed describes in *Queer Phenomenology* as an "approach to how bodies take shape through tending toward objects that are reachable, that are available within the bodily horizon" (2006, p. 2). Maybe a year working as a higher education administrator served as a reorientation that ultimately reshaped my body and my bodily horizon.

It's possible, but my voice stayed very much the same. A dear friend of mine once told me, in a joking manner, that when I speak, my purple chiffon purse spills out and the world is suddenly all glitter and rainbows. In other words, my voice is still queer. You can hear my queer when I speak. My voice holds on to that youthful, gay "y." Even if my body takes on the shape of an upper-level higher education administrator or researcher, my voice gives me away. The only way to hide my queer is to be silent, to remove the "y" from my email signature and to silence my voice from the places my body finds itself.

The interesting thing about voice, though, is that it is of the body. Our diaphragms push air from our lungs over our vocal cords, causing them to vibrate. These vibrations produce sound. Vocalizations reverberate through the atmosphere and into other's ears. Voice, then, is literally our bodies vibrating in ways that others can perceive. And once voice is released into the world, the space is forever imprinted with those vibrations. In relation to the more metaphoric voice, voice can be understood as the individualized interpretations of culture manifested through the body moving and responding to either reify that culture or to resist it. In that way, my body is moving as I write this paper. My fingers tap across a keyboard. These words are my vocalization both in resistance and in compliance, set free into this world, carrying with them my voice, my body, and my "y."

SMEAR THE QUEER

To remove my voice is to remove the paths that my body has traveled to get to this point, and without embodying that history I can't really make a contribution to any body of literature. Which brings me to the conclusion of this queer tale. In case you are fortunate enough to not have encountered the childhood game called Smear the Queer, it goes something like this: In middle and high school, the pretty jock-boys, the ones you secretly lusted after, would form a circle around the weak, outcast queer. Then the boys start chanting, "Smear the queer! Smear the queer!" as they violently push the queer bouncing from one bully to the other, leaving the poor queer smeared on the ground for the rest of the straight world to walk over as they pass by. For me, smear the queer was actually a part of the institution. I played football in seventh and eighth grade. Don't ask me why. I still don't actually know how that happened or how I survived it. One of the early activities that our coaches had us do was a drill called "Smear the Queer." The drill was identical to the bullying tactic, but it was meant to get the players used to being pushed around and disoriented in full gear. Everyone had to be the queer. The only difference was, when the drill was over, I was the only one who was still the queer.

As traumatizing as that experience was, it has stuck with me, much like my faggoty voice and my queer "y." Like I said in the introduction, this piece is meant to be an artistic experiment. So, I'm taking Smear the Queer back. I am using it as a form of resistance. I have made a decision about my "y." I am keeping it. I have made a decision about my voice. I am going to speak. By speaking and being heard, I smear *my* queer. By going by Scotty, I smear queerness in every interaction. And I do this while insisting on being taken seriously. I do this while insisting that my work in education is valuable. In naming my own body, I insert my voice into a queer conversation about education. I will not silence my voice or alter my queer body so that my work aligns with certain methodologies and theoretical perspectives like someone tells me it should. Where I go, my voice, my "y," and my queer go. And I will not smear that queer on the ground for others to step over and not notice. No. I will smear that queer in my writing, my research, my presentations, my classrooms, at professional conferences I attend, and in meetings with executive administrators. I will smear it like I smear paint on a canvas or words in a poem. And I will allow that queerness to be a spectacle for others to view and to ponder.

REFERENCES

Ahmed, S. (2006). *Queer phenomenology: Objects, orientations, others.* Durham, NC: Duke University Press.

Ahmed, S. (2013). *On being included: Racism and diversity in institutional life.* Durham, NC: Duke University Press.

Anzaldúa, G. (2012). *Borderlands/La Frontera: The new Mestiza.* San Francisco: Aunt Lute.

Harjo, J. (2012). *Crazy brave: A memoir.* New York: W.W. Norton.

CHAPTER EIGHTEEN

"I heard it from a good source": Queer Desire and Homophobia in a South African Higher Education Institution

THABO MSIBI

INTRODUCTION

Universities, like schools, are heteronormative sites (Renn, 2010). From the way in which knowledge is structured to the way in which social relations are organised, including the type of relationships that is legitimised, universities are heavily imbued in processes that legitimise and exclusively recognise the normalisation of heterosexuality, often leading to a systematic erasure of other identifications. So pervasive is heteronormativity that faculty and students claiming identifications outside heterosexuality often find themselves excluded, constrained, and policed. While there have been significant gains in terms of queer rights and visibility in higher education spaces in some Western contexts, it cannot be denied that the situation of queer[1] subjects still remains precarious in most institutional spaces across the globe. While several studies have highlighted the challenges encountered by students in higher education institutions and residential halls, little work has been undertaken with a particular focus on the experiences of queer academics in higher education institutions. Yet, as Bennett, Hill, and Jones (2015), in the context of Australia; Ozturk and Rumens (2014), in the context of the United Kingdom; and Maritz and Prinsloo (2015), in the context of South Africa show, the heteronormative condition persistent in many university spaces remains a challenge for queer academics who often have to adopt various identity management and negotiation strategies in order to be respected by students and their peers (see DeJean, 2010).

The challenges highlighted above get even more complex when the issue of romantic liaisons between academics and students is considered. Sikes (2006) has argued in the context of heterosexual high school relationships between teachers and students that teacher-student sexual relationships are often accompanied by a "moral panic" that is triggered by a fear of paedophilia and abuse from the parents, media, and government. In the United Kingdom, where sexual engagements between a teacher and a student below the age of 18 are criminalised under the Sexual Offenses Act of 2003 (see Sikes, 2006), despite the legal age of consent being 16, such triggers produce a salacious and titillating interest, with any such relations surrounded by notions of abuse and scandal (Sikes & Piper, 2010), regardless of the context. While South Africa does not necessarily respond in the same way as the United Kingdom to such relations, largely due to normalcy of such heterosexual relations, despite their prohibition by the South African Schools Act of 1996, it is more relations between same-sex individuals that yield such public repudiation. In the context of same-sex relationships in higher education, this scandalous positioning is sustained, with many South African academics remaining private about their same-sex identities and their relations with students, if they exist.

While erotic desire between teachers, those in a position of authority and therefore perceived as powerful, and students, often falsely positioned as powerless, is constantly present in university spaces (see hooks, 1994), university space is often constructed as a cold, loveless space—a space where students often innocently sit eagerly awaiting the "wisdom" and knowledge of their professors whose interest is only on the subject matter and not the attractive bodies that sit in front of him or her. In instances where transgressions (hooks) occur: where pleasure, love, intimacy, and desire are explored, such explorations are often hidden, or, if public, positioned as abusive, inappropriate, and scandalous, especially when they occur between faculty and student of the same sex. While this is not to suggest that heterosexual relations are not excluded from this moral gaze (clearly this is not the case given the panic around sexual harassment in U.S. universities in 2014 and 2015, leading to numerous universities, including Harvard, Yale, and Connecticut, strengthening their sexual harassment policies by banning consensual sexual relationships between faculty and undergraduate students; see Rhodan, 2015), same-sex relationships are often are doubly scrutinised; the idea of a relationship between an academic and student is viewed scandalously, while the same-sex nature of a relationship is sensationalised and judged as morally bankrupt. It is this double scrutiny that this chapter seeks to explore.

Drawing on a personal narrative of a horrendous, painful, and professionally and physically compromising experience of being falsely accused of abusing my partner who happened to be a student at the university in which I work, I highlight the systemic ways in which university spaces are heterosexualised (Taulke-Johnson, 2010) as well as the damaging ways in which the double gaze highlighted above works to victimise queer academics who engage in sexual relationships with students. I also showcase the double standards that are applied to "other" same-sex love, often in direct violation of established university policies and processes. I also explore the covert and overt ways in which same-sex love is erased and rendered "dirty" in higher education spaces. In doing this I position the heterosexualised university space as a risky space for queer expression and consensual, policy-affirmed love between faculty and students who are queer.

METHODOLOGY

Working with sex is and continues to be an ethical nightmare for many researchers (Sikes, 2010; Irvine, 2014). This is because sex continues to be constructed as "dirty" in public discourses and spaces, yet passionately enjoyed in private spaces. It often is socially accepted to do sex—in private—while talking about sex is often not encouraged. This is more so the case when sex involves individuals in formal institutions such as schools, universities, and other areas of formal employment. Writing about the ethics of doing sex work in schools, Sikes (2010) notes:

> Researching, and even proposing to research, anything to do with sex in schools does, however, raise a myriad of difficult questions whilst also attracting unpleasant attention to the supposed motives and preoccupations of the researchers. When the issue under consideration involves actual or purported sexual contact between teachers and students, the challenging questions and the attention both seem to increase exponentially and in degree. (p. 143)

Conducting research on romantic liaisons between students and teachers can easily be construed as "sick" and depraved. This sense of "sickness" is additionally emphasised when one is the subject of inquiry as questions around intent often abound. Such work can easily be construed as seeking to advance some immoral and questionable conduct or, in the case of this chapter, an attempt to seek a form of redemption. I am cognisant of these troubling ethical concerns and have therefore adopted a methodological approach that is not shy from claiming and affirming subjectivity, and that centres on the individual experiences from the gaze of the person telling the story. Autoethnographic work is primarily concerned with the researcher's subjective, often personal, experiences. As Ellis (1997) shows, it enables for reflexivity, providing an opportunity for the researcher to engage with the state of his or her emotional self. Autoethnography does not seek to present objective truths but rather seeks to foreground the memory, story, or experience of the researcher. Like narrative work, autoethnographic research can be deeply therapeutic, allowing the storyteller to engage with painful, often untold, difficult stories.

I rely on my own memory and knowing very well that what is presented in this discussion is not necessarily an objective truth. Rather, I present an account about myself, recognising the biases that come with this positioning. That narratives are subjective and therefore cannot be generalised forms the premise of autoethnographic work (Goodson & Sikes, 2001) and, therefore, this chapter.

Given my relative closeness to this issue, as well as the sensitivity of the issues highlighted, including the fact that the matter is still ongoing, I borrow from Sikes and Piper's approach of allowing the narrative to "speak for itself." While I use a theoretical framework to foreground the argument of the paper, I deliberately avoid presenting a critical analysis of the narrative presented. Instead, I invite the readers to engage with, interrogate, and analyse the information themselves. I wish for the data, in this case, narrative, to speak for itself, understanding very well the limitations of this approach (see Anderson, 2006, for a critique of autoethnographic work that does not provide deep analysis). By virtue of presenting my story, I already select the memories I wish to prioritise, the details I wish to emphasise, and the words I wish to use, thereby leading the reader to a particular understanding that I desire. This is acknowledged as a shortcoming of the chapter. However, I am cognisant that human agency and diversity of thought allow for multiple understandings and interpretation of stories. It is this potential that I appeal to. While my approach may appear to be lazy, I argue that being sensitive to one's biases when telling personal stories is critical for an autoethnographic piece that is cognisant of its location and the politics of such a location. I deliberately choose therefore not to explain myself and my actions through my own reading or analysis of the story presented. Instead, I allow you, the reader, to make your own judgements, interpretations, and analyses.

THEORETICAL FRAMING

This chapter draws on Foucault's (1975) notion of the panopticon and seeks to showcase the various ways in which heterosexual power polices, regulates, and governs queer bodies in higher education institutions. In his book *Discipline and Punish*, Foucault uses the panopticon, a tall tower in the middle of a courtyard that surveils prisoners in prison, to showcase how power functions to regulate bodies. In the tower, the guards have the regulating power to see the presence and actions of prisoners, while the prisoners remain oblivious to the presence or absence of the guards in the tower. In this way the tower functions as a policing mechanism through both the presence of the guards and also through its own presence as the prisoners begin regulating and policing their own actions, believing that the regulating eye of the guards is present in the tower.

Like the panopticon, it is argued in this paper that heteronormativity and its taken-for-granted natural status offer a powerful technique to police and regulate queer bodies in institutional settings. Heteronormativity becomes the mirror through which human actions are judged and regulated. Any behaviour deemed incongruent with heterosexual norms is policed and heavily penalised. The power of heteronormativity lies in its reliance on a patriarchal condition, a condition that is heavily connected to the power of the state in regulating people's bodies and sexualities. This power is manifest in the proliferation of laws and policies across the globe that seek to regulate human sexuality. Human sexuality, passion, pleasure, exploration, and desire become positioned as improper, unacceptable, and in need of regulation, especially for bodies that do not fit the norm. As Foucault writes:

> The domain of panopticism is, on the contrary, that whole lower region, that region of irregular bodies, with their details, their multiple movements, their heterogeneous forces, their spatial relations; what are required are mechanisms that analyse distributions, gaps, series, combinations, and which use instruments that render visible, record, differentiate and compare: a physics of a relational and multiple power, which has its maximum intensity not in the person of the king, but in the bodies that can be individualized by these relations. (p. 208)

Understood in Foucault's terms, heteronormative power is therefore discursive and ever present. It regulates behaviour, sets the rules of engagement for sexualities and allows for the policing of individual bodies by others and also by the individuals themselves.

The narrative that follows highlights the various ways in which heteronormativity is supported through actions, inactions, and rules of engagement in higher education spaces. It shows how institutional policies and processes that attempt to undermine the technical and ubiquitous power of heterosexuality in turn become undermined and negated, just for the judging gaze of heteronormative power to have the last say.

SHE HEARD IT FROM A GOOD SOURCE

It was a Tuesday afternoon when a knock came through the door as I sat with my masters students for supervision. The face that came through the door was familiar, accompanied by a familiar smile. The knocker greeted and apologised for interrupting me. Buhle then requested me to call later on as there was something important that needed discussing. I agreed. With little worry, I continued the supervision session and forgot about my visitor.

I arrived home around 8 p.m. that evening. I had dinner and treated myself to an hour of television as usual. I then headed to the bedroom to initiate my evening writing. Around 9:30 my phone rang. It was Buhle, irritated that I had not returned the call like I promised I would. I apologised; I had simply forgotten due to my failing memory. Buhle sounded very concerned as he said: "You must promise me that you won't overreact if I tell you this and that you will act professionally." I was cautioned. I gave my assurance and was then informed of what would be life-changing information.

Buhle had attended a postgraduate honours[2] class, Educational Psychology. The subject of the discussion was abuse. Students were presenting on the abuse of children in school by their teachers. The class was discussing about how to deal with child abuse in schools when the academic leading the discussion informed the students that the abuse they were talking about was not only isolated to schools but was in fact also happening at this university. The students were then told that there was a gay academic senior member of staff, who was involved with a male undergraduate first-year student in a sexual relationship. The students were further told that the staff member concerned had a history of being involved with students as he had had a relationship with another student from another university. When this initial relationship soured, the academic turned to a student on campus. Buhle recalled how the students began questioning the academic concerned on her claims of abuse in the relationship. She informed them that the relationship was abusive because the academic staff member was using his power by taking the student on holidays and paying for his university fees. The students enquired whether the staff member was teaching the student, and they were told that this was not the case. Students further asked on the accuracy of the information presented and were told by the gossiping staff member that she heard this information from a very good source. When the students started seriously disagreeing on the claims of abuse, Buhle told me that the staff member then changed the subject. Given the fact that there was no other known academic staff member on campus who is open about his same-sex relationships other than myself, Buhle was very concerned that his peers would be able to link the story to me and that this had potential to damage my reputation. It was clear to Buhle that the information given was adequate for any student with the knowledge of campus staff to reasonably conclude that it was me being spoken about.

I sat on the other side of the line trying to compose myself, given the horror of what I was hearing. There was no doubt that it was I who was being referred to. Indeed, I was romantically interested in an undergraduate student. I had shared this information with two close colleagues at work and a few students who were close to me, as I was worried about the ethics of being involved with an undergraduate student in the same institution and had never been in a relationship with a student before. I had met Mondli, my partner, on Facebook by chance. A friend of mine had tagged herself on his photo, leading to his photo appearing on my newsfeed. I was immediately drawn to his handsome yet unassuming look. I had checked his details on Facebook and had noticed that he was a student with us. I had not invited him to be a friend, precisely because I did not want to be in a relationship with a student on campus. Little did I know that I would meet him physically by chance a week later when a colleague's car battery went flat after a weekend meeting, and we were forced to proceed to a nearby fuel station to buy jumper cables. As we drove into the fuel station Mondli was standing outside all by himself. I was naturally and immediately attracted to him. I asked him to invite me on Facebook, which he did, and we began communicating. Unfortunately, however, he was going home the following day as the semester had ended. He would only return to campus a month later. I used this time to consult with close friends and my most trusted students. Buhle was among the students I had consulted. This is why he had been so offended when the academic staff member presented falsified information about me in class. While Mondli and I were at an initial stage of relationship building, I have never paid a single cent towards his fees and had never taken him on holiday. I wish I had taken him on holiday, but there simply was no time.

When Buhle told me this story I immediately knew who the good source was. There were two close colleagues that I had personally introduced Mondli to. The one colleague I trusted completely as we had been friends for some time. I had shared much more personal information with her before and she had never seen the need to disclose any of that personal information to anyone. The other colleague was queer and often shared her own experiences with me, but, while I considered her to be my friend, we were not too close as our friendship had only started a few years back. She also was in the same department as the colleague who had just presented falsified information about myself to a class full of students. I was understandably very disturbed: how could trust be violated this way? I thanked Buhle for the call, giving assurance that I would not disclose my source to anyone. That night I sat up in the bed frustrated, angry, and disillusioned. I was angry that someone had the audacity to present me as an abuser to a class full of students. I was angry that I was being constructed as an abuser, yet I had not violated any law or policy of the university. In my consultations, I had studied the university's policy very carefully. It allowed for relationships, as long as one declares. It even explicitly noted that nondisclosure was not necessarily an offense; it was conflict of interest that was an offense. I was sure that there was nothing to declare, and even if there had been something to declare there was no conflict of interest as I did not teach Mondli. In fact, prior to my Facebook sighting, I did not even know that an individual like him existed on campus and he did not know anything about me. I was fuming that relationship with Innocent, my former partner of five years, had also been presented as abusive, despite the fact that we were only a few years apart.

His only crime was being a student. We lived together and loved each other; our relationship was public knowledge. So loving was our relationship that when we broke up, he continued to live with me whilst he completed his studies. How then could someone with no knowledge whatsoever of my relationships judge them as abusive? I was confused and unsure how to react.

After contacting a few close friends about the matter, it was clear that I needed to confront the colleague about the issue. I wrote an email and we scheduled a meeting for Thursday that week to discuss "teaching" issues. My very close friend advised that I record the conversation because I was her line manager and did not want to be misinterpreted and misquoted after the meeting. This proved to be lifesaving.

THE MEETING

Before I initiated the meeting, I explained to the colleague that the matter was serious and requested for the conversation to be recorded. She agreed to this. In order to protect Buhle, I presented the matter as if a number of students had been to see me on the issue. I highlighted what had been presented to me and my concern as division head that a serious matter such as this had not been reported to the relevant university authorities in spite of the existence of sophisticated and effective tip-off mechanisms in the university. I noted the importance of her naming the colleague concerned in order for the matter to be reported to university authorities. She initially acted surprised and attempted to deny that she had positioned the relationship as abusive. She said a number of disjointed sentences and couldn't present a coherent defence for her actions. She claimed she had presented the matter as a case study and had no knowledge that the students could make out who it was that was being referenced. I was calm in all of this but was internally fuming with disbelief. She continued to go around in circles seeking to deny what had happened until I asked her decisively whether she had shared the information with students that Buhle had claimed was shared. She indicated that indeed she did share the information, but it was not maliciously intended. I asked her for the name of the colleague that she was referring to, at which point she stood up and told me that the next time she'd see me would be with her attorneys. I thanked her and reminded her that the meeting was not meant to be antagonistic and that it was a fact-finding meeting. I reminded her that the meeting was recorded. She asked the point at which the meeting was recorded; I reminded her that it was from the beginning. At this point it seemed as if she finally noticed that she had no escape. She told me that she meant no offense and eventually got to the point of apologising. As I had no interest in taking this matter forward, primarily because I believed at that stage that she had made an honest mistake, I asked her to simply correct the information the following week. She made clear inferences that it was me she was talking about, and I reminded her of the university's policies and the lies in her gossip. Indeed, it was my friend who had shared my personal information with her and she decided to add further lies. I did not care that she had outed my relationship with Mondli. It really didn't matter to me. I was concerned that she had presented false information, which needed correcting. She agreed to correct the information in the next session. She left the office ever so apologetic.

PLAYING THE VICTIM

After this meeting, things fell apart. She ran in tears to my "friend" who had disclosed the relationship to her. She resigned as the discipline head and initiated a frenzy of gossip by colleagues against me. Things went from worse to worst. There were corridor talks amongst colleagues. I heard of colleagues in other divisions being called to be informed about me. Some close friends came to enquire. She positioned herself as a victim and many colleagues bought into this. The narrative I was later to hear was that I had victimised her and had ambushed her during the meeting. There were a number of sympathetic ears she could count on as a heterosexual woman being victimised by this queer "dirty" line manager. That I didn't discuss this matter with any person in the entire school other than my very close allies meant that there were no counternarratives to her victim positioning. Seeing that the matter was going out of hand, I reported the issue to the dean, who promised to call the meeting between the colleague and myself in order for the continuation of working relations. Again, at this stage, I did not see the need to formally act as I just wanted this entire matter to go away. I did not want Mondli to be known and victimised. I wanted to protect him. I therefore agreed.

A meeting was scheduled for Tuesday the following week. I arrived at the meeting and found the dean and the human resources manager present. The colleague concerned was not there. I was told that she had indicated that she couldn't attend the meeting as she was traumatised. I was shocked that she had been allowed to give this excuse as the person who really was traumatised was me after all her actions. Still, I sat and listened. The HR manager at this stage was very clear: there had been no violations on my part and the colleague needed to be present in the future meeting. Little did I know that this would change when the colleague's union got involved, a union that has queer individuals in its executive committee.

After the meeting on Tuesday, I received a frantic call from Buhle. The colleague concerned had been to class with the academic leader for teaching and learning, who happens to be in the same department as her. They had asked the students to complete a questionnaire, where students had to write their names and sign, responding to whether they made any connections to the "case studies" previously presented to specific individuals. Buhle, like all students in the class, had signed that there were no connections made, in fear of being discovered. I was livid at this recent unethical action, which was given institutional approval via the presence of the academic leader for teaching and learning. I wrote to the dean to raise my concerns about this, noting that while I was open to reconciliation, this move was prompting me to take formal action.

The weeks that followed were so troubling that I decided to formally pursue a grievance process. The colleague concerned had re-created herself as a victim and her union was writing as if she had launched some formal process against me, which was bizarre and highly stressful. She then began a process of attacking me and undermining me by copying members of her department in the communications with her union, unfairly attacking me. The university was notified about this and there was no action. In one of the emails, I was accused of abusing my authority and attacking her department because in my division report, I requested colleagues to familiarise themselves with university policy and to avoid thinking of our students as children. This was a general point I made about staff conduct. A denigrating email was sent to her union and then forwarded to the entire discipline.

Through all this there had been no meeting as I had to go to Mauritius for doctoral teaching, and she did not want to attend any meeting without her union. When the date for the meeting was eventually scheduled, I received a barrage of emails attempting to deny me representation from her union. As my representative was an honorary staff member instead of being a full-time staff member or a union member, her union argued falsely that the university policies and labour laws prohibited such representation. Insinuations to the effect that I had a charge to answer to were also made by her union. I received no protection from the university. I asked for clarity from our HR manager and dean concerning policy requirements in terms of representation and the claim that I had a case to answer and received no response. I felt alone through this entire struggle, apart from the support I was receiving from close friends. I was even starting to doubt myself. I thought maybe I was guilty of something, but I honestly did not know what it was that I was guilty of. I thought of resigning but then thought that this would appear as an admission of guilt. If I did not have incredible support from friends, I would have been hospitalised. Through this entire process my health was in a bad state. I could not sleep at night and was on sleep medication. I had developed lumps on my tongue due to stress and had to have surgery as we feared cancer. I was depressed. I lost passion for work and for relationships. I felt empty, unappreciated, and unsure of my existence.

On Monday, the day of the meeting, I had not received input on representation. I had also not received input on the supposed charges against me. I was angry and troubled. I tried without success to call the HR manager prior to the meeting.

I eventually was able to speak to the acting executive director for HR to ask about representation requirements 15 minutes before the meeting. The acting executive director confirmed that I was correct in my interpretation of policy and that the unions were wrong. At this stage it was too late to have my representative present. I attended the meeting alone, without representation, and informed the dean who was chairing the meeting of the ruling from the executive director. I was told that the executive director needed to write something formal around this, and I was surprised as to why this clarity had not been sought by the chair before the meeting as I had enquired about this. Nevertheless the meeting proceeded. The dean asked the two of us what we wanted at the end of the process. I wanted this entire thing to be over. I indicated that I would only withdraw the grievance if three conditions were met: if she corrected the information as per original agreement, if she sent a written apology, and if she circulated the apology to her colleagues in the department whom she had involved in the matter via her email communication. Her demand was to be moved to another manager or school. I was not going to allow this as she had told colleagues that she would be moved. This would have created the impression that she was moved because I had done something wrong.

December 2014 ended with me depressed and feeling unsupported by the institution. My health was fragile. In January of the following year, I decided to pursue the matter more vigorously in order to bring about a conclusion. I requested for the matter to be escalated as it had not been resolved at the school level, in line with the policy. Her union objected to this as they now wanted an alternative dispute resolution (conciliatory) process instead of the more serious process I was now pursuing. They started attacking the dean, who chaired the matter at school level, claiming that he was biased against them. Instead of having a grievance hearing as mandated by policy, and I believe in fear of the union, the university appointed the dean of law to be a neutral dean to hear the matter again. Before the meeting, my accuser had sent yet another email to her discipline, this time against the acting discipline coordinator and myself, telling us to "go to hell" because I had asked for a meeting with the discipline head to discuss the importance of staff to keep to the university's leave policy. The email was a serious case of insubordination, containing slanderous statements. I brought this email to the attention of the dean, who forwarded it to the human resources manager, and again nothing was done.

THE INFORMAL HEARING

The dean of law was mandated to chair the informal fact-finding meeting. She held the first meeting with my accuser and me the following week. I was told that my accuser was happy to work with me and that she respects me. I was also told that she had told the chair that she understands how I could have been upset.

She wanted us to work together again and would be happy for an alternative dispute resolution process. I burst out with laughter at hearing all this information and was so upset that I began crying at the level of abuse this colleague was directing at me. I presented the dean of law with facts and all the evidence pertaining to the issues. To say that she was shocked by the contents of the emails would be an understatement. She advised that I withdraw the grievance process and launch a formal disciplinary process as the behaviour exhibited was completely unacceptable. I left the meeting feeling affirmed for the first time.

AND NOTHING HAPPENS

In May I launched the disciplinary process as my accuser had unfortunately lost her brother and I wanted to give her space to heal. This was followed by emails from both myself and my dean to human resources asking for an update on the process. I kept on being told that the process was moving forward, until a point that human resources stopped responding. A year and four months later, the matter remains unresolved. This is despite an independent chair clearly instructing human resources to act and the continued violation of university processes by the individual concerned. I hear informally that the matter has lapsed, but no one in the institution has had the courage to formally notify me of this. This is despite writing to all human resource and college management layers for an update on progress. I wonder whether it is my age (I'm only 32), my race (Black), or my queer sexuality that have allowed the university to violate my dignity in this way. I wonder how it is that this matter has been allowed to drag on in the manner that it has when the facts are so clear. My view is that the matter was deliberately made to lapse. I have now escalated the matter further and intend on pursuing the matter to the constitutional court, if need be. I will not rest until justice is served.

CONCLUSION

As I bring this chapter to a close, I invite you, the reader, to provide your own analysis of the situation. In guiding your thinking in this regard, I wish to pose the following questions: why is it that an academic staff member can find it perfectly and ethically acceptable to present false gossip about another academic staff member in the same institution and division to a class full of students? How is it that an individual who has deliberately violated another can successfully play victim and receive the support of colleagues in the university? How is it that the same individual can flout university policies and be left unpunished? How is it that an independent, qualified dean can recommend serious action against an individual and have such recommendation ignored by the university's human resource division? Would the experience have been the same had the case involved two consenting heterosexual individuals? I invite you dear reader to attempt to answer these questions. For me, what the above highlights is the pervasive and systemic manner in which heteronormativity finds legitimacy. My claim remains simple in this chapter. University spaces are deeply heterosexual spaces, spaces where heteronormative power regulates behaviour. Consensual same-sex relations involving academic staff and students become one of the vehicles to demonstrate the regulating power of heterosexuality. While it cannot be denied that power imbalances exist in student-teacher relationships, it is my view that in the case highlighted, abuse was never a feature. Instead the heteronormative power of imagination took control, enabling a stereotypical construction of my relationship, which clearly was unwarranted. It is clear that lies, dirt, and scandal surround same-sex love. This is in part because of the disruption of the discursive power heteronormativity that same-sex love presents. If heteronormative power, an ever-present power that informs the nature of engagements in higher education institutions, is not troubled, bodies outside the hetero norm will continue to be excluded, surveiled, and marginalised.

NOTES

1. While I use "queer" to refer to identifications outside the hetero norm, I am cognisant of the limited use of this identification, especially in contexts such as South Africa.
2. An honours is an independent degree South African students are required to complete after finishing their bachelor's but prior to commencing with their master's degrees. An honours qualification is usually one year and introduces students to research in their respective fields of study.

REFERENCES

Anderson, L. (2006). Analytic autoethnography. *Journal of Contemporary Ethnography, 35*(4), 373–395. doi: 10.1177/0891241605280449

Bennett, R., Hill, B., & Jones, A. (2015). In and out of the cross-cultural classroom closet: Negotiating queer teacher identity and culturally diverse cohorts in an Australian university. *Higher Education Research & Development, 34*(4), 709–721. doi: 10.1080/07294360.2015.1051008

DeJean, W. (2010). Courageous conversations: Reflections on a queer life narrative model. *The Teacher Educator, 45*(4), 233–243. doi: 10.1080/08878730.2010.508262

Department of Education. (1996). South African Schools Act, 1996. Retrieved from http://www.education.gov.za/LinkClick.aspx?fileticket=aIolZ6UsZ5U%3D&tabid=185&mid=1828

Ellis, C. (1997). Evocative autoethnography: Writing emotionally about our lives. In W. G. Tierney & Y. S. Lincoln (Eds.), *Representation and the text: Re-framing the narrative voice* (pp. 115–139). Albany: State University of New York Press.

Foucault, M. (1975). *Discipline and punish: The birth of the prison*. New York: Vintage.

Goodson, I., & Sikes, P. J. (2001). *Life history research in educational settings: Learning from lives.* Berkshire: Open University Press.

hooks, b. (1994). *Teaching to transgress: Education as the practice of freedom.* New York: Routledge.

Irvine, J. (2014). Is sexuality research "dirty work"? Institutionalized stigma in the production of sexual knowledge. *Sexualities 17*(5–6), 632–656.

Maritz, J., & Prinsloo, P. (2015). "Queering" and querying academic identities in postgraduate education. *Higher Education Research & Development, 34*(4), 695–708. doi: 10.1080/07294360.2015.1051007

Ozturk, M. B., & Rumens, N. (2014). Gay male academics in UK business and management schools: Negotiating heteronormativities in everyday work life. *British Journal of Management, 25*(3), 503–517.

Renn, K. A. (2010). LGBT and queer research in higher education The state and status of the field. *Educational Researcher, 39*(2), 132–141. doi: 10.3102/0013189X10362579

Rhodan, M. (2015, February 5). Harvard bans sexual relationships between students and professors. *Time.* Retrieved from http://time.com/3697799/harvard-sexual-relationships-students-professors/

Sikes, P. (2006). Scandalous stories and dangerous liaisons: When female pupils and male teachers fall in love. *Sex Education, 6*(3), 265–280. doi: 10.1080/14681810600836471

Sikes, P. (2010). Teacher-student sexual relations: Key risks and ethical issues. *Ethnography and Education, 5*(2), 143–157. doi: 10.1080/17457823.2010.493398

Sikes, P., & Piper, H. (2010). *Researching sex and lies in the classroom: Allegations of sexual misconduct in schools.* London: Routledge.

Taulke-Johnson, R. (2010). Assertion, regulation and consent: Gay students, straight flatmates, and the (hetero)sexualisation of university accommodation space. *Gender and Education, 22*(4), 401–417. doi: 10.1080/09540250903341104

Part 6:
Queered All the Way Through

CHAPTER NINETEEN

A Profound Moment of Passing

DAVID LEE CARLSON

Gliding into Rapid City regional airport, snow drapes the surrounding hills and cloaks the prairie. A drab, dingy frozen steam hovers and lingers in the crisp, frigid air. Horses and cows stand unbothered and unconcerned as a slight, brisk wind puffs around them. Cars traverse the gravel country roads and newly paved city streets. People seem to be nowhere and everywhere as they journey through life withstanding and, in some cases, relishing the raw and frosty locale. It was early July, and my mother's twenty-year battle with Parkinson's disease was beginning its final scene. My heart ached at my mother's condition, fumed over the injustice of her plight, and my joints trembled in anticipation of what likely awaited me when I arrived at her bedside. The judicious, yet unmet demands and requests that render this able-bodied man paralyzed and helpless became too staggering to perpend. I recall the time my mother handing me a copy of Leo Buscaglia's book *Loving Each Other* (1986) one morning in response to a conversation we had. I could not understand why I didn't want to date girls. The unsettling, confusing, and terrifying absent feelings and attraction for them mortified me; but she understood more than I did what I was going through. Here, at this moment, during this time, I became acutely aware of the importance and relevance of memory and place. Specifically, the province my fragmented and distilled memory and my place of belonging in the world as imposture, as settled ground, and as a modest vista assumed in my life. It was actually early July and the sun poured its warmth across the plains and the streets beamed with vitality and the people meandered. Yet, my memory of my hometown will always be a very cold place.

Jogging along a gravel dirt road about two miles from my father's horse ranch, the cold gray sky offered relief from the oppressive heat that usually awaits those of us who sojourn to the sacred plains of South Dakota. A cool breeze relieves me of the scorching and arid heat of the desert valley of Tempe, Arizona. A four-mile run seemed rather easy after twelve weeks of already intensive diet and running regimes in pursuit of a finish in my third marathon. Forty minutes, there and back, was all it required. The act of running outdoors is a spiritual experience. My body and nature coagulate into a sweet honey, mango, and earthy floral mixture. My body challenges my mind and pushes me to confront and endure the elements. Sometimes when I become dubious about my fortitude to complete a course, confidence gains momentum over doubt and anxiety, and the more I devote myself to this holy event. Running reminds me that I can travel; it represents self-independence, self-competition, and self-flight. The sunflowers and lilacs that parade along the roadside ignite my senses, put me in place, and awaken my memories.

The sweet and rustic scent of the weeds, hay, and wheat recall my early same-sex desires. They remind me of crushes, fantasies, and heartbreak. They reflect the evanescence of desire and the elusiveness of satisfaction. Scent entices me, excites me, arouses me, and simultaneously evades me, leaves me in a flash, in a whisper, in a fleeting moment. The pure sensual elixir of the South Dakota prairie mocks my desires, troubles them, and confuses them. Further along the way, the rocks crush about my feet as I traverse and maneuver through the hilly road. I notice the medley of marble that both comforts and strengthens my legs as I jog along the rugged trail. It is here at this moment that I think about the importance and relevance of diversity in my life. I am an assortment of selves and the world around me presents itself to me similarly. Multiformity grounds me, drives me, and guides me. It is also what sustains and enhances my world. It structures and necessitates social justice.

The solid and durable rocks remind me of the time I sat in a graduate seminar on multicultural education with a group of preservice and in-service teachers at a rather prestigious teachers college in New York City and, during a one-week section on LGBTQ Issues not one student (besides myself) used the word "gay" in the class discussion. Instead they employed the phrase, "If one of my students were it, then… ." I learned about being an "it" and how a group of individuals can treat your desires, the way in which you express the most intimate parts of yourself, as an object, as a dodge ball. It was not a good feeling. Although I knew what it meant to be gay by that point, the experience with those students on that night in that hot classroom in Horace Mann Hall taught me what it meant to be straight. And I feared for the many gay students these teachers were about to teach. It also ignited in me an impatient punch to contest and clamor against the subtle yet overt biases many within education assume about queer individuals. When I approached the professor after class about why she never corrected her students, she replied, "Why didn't you?" This was a really severe way to learn a rather tough lesson about the taboo that is sex and sexuality in secondary schools and about the "tools of the master."

Along similar lines, the callous pebbles beneath my feet recalled the time when I wanted to "come out" to my ninth graders during my first year of teaching in Brooklyn, New York, in 1997. Hearing students launch homophobic pokes at each other all day became tiresome for me during my first semester of teaching. When the principal learned of my decision to come out, he called me at home the night before and warned me against it. He argued that the students would never respect me and that I would be unable to get much teaching done this year. Out of deference and naiveté, reluctantly, I conceded. I hid behind the proverbial rationality of "My sexuality has nothing to do with my abilities to teach, and if my sexuality gets in the way of any of my students' learning, then it is unethical of me to reveal it." What I failed to realize was that telling them could have taught them many lessons, and that being perceived as "straight" does not protect one from the blatant and horrific affects of bigotry, even those who appear to be quite innocent or naive. I learned to categorize and demarcate sections of my life into sandboxes, and I knew who I was in each one in order to be successful. Passing and scoring well on tests remained the subtext of the dramatic gestures of the day.

As I turned the corner to head back home to my dad's house, I stared at the horizon out yonder. It is here that I think about how light and matter dictate and demarcate the geometry of spaces. And off to the left I see a rather large barn; it interrupts what seems to be a seemingly seamless plain. I wonder if I were the only one of my childhood friends to see the barn. So much exertion transpires to ignite a disturbance, and yet it can materialize in an instant, and if done well, it sticks, stabilizes, and proceeds to form. It is probably rather trying to be the pariah on a plain, but this waif anchors the plain, and it is the place of return in search for wisdom, for sanity, worth, and hopes. It is here that I think about how vital it has been for me to be out, to be with others, to contest and challenge homophobia, and to rally with and advocate for other marginalized groups. I remember my students in Brooklyn who made fun of gay people in my classroom, who later learned about my sexuality, are now friends with me on social media, like many of my posts, and still consider me an influential teacher. They learned their lesson and so did I.

They travel with me as I turn the corner to head into my father's driveway at the end of my run, and I think about this year: I turned the tender age of 45. This year experienced many firsts: I sold my first house, I finished my first book, and

I witnessed firsthand a member of my immediate family sunsetting in dramatic fashion. I did something else for the first time, too.

You see, every time I teach a methodology course, I begin the first session by asking students to take out a sheet of paper and to take notes, any notes on my presentation. I tell them the story of a young boy who lived until the age of nine in a small farming community of 400 people in South Dakota where he nurtured his innate love for art, music, and sports. His father was a chef in the U.S. Navy for 21 years; his birth-mother matured in Washington, D.C., and they owned a restaurant and a ceramic shop in this quiet prairie town. This young boy won local and state awards for his art projects and took a piece of clay that none of his siblings wanted and fashioned it into a blue ribbon at the central state fair; and how he won a first in a music competition for the French horn; and impressed my manly father of his athleticism at catching and hitting a baseball. I tell them about how my parents divorced and we moved to Rapid City, a much larger city with my new mom. Here is where I grew up to play football, basketball, track, and of course baseball. I played on several all-star teams and struggled in school. I tell them about working at Wendy's throughout high school to pay for clothes and gas, the joys of sophomore English, and the discipline it took to excel in advance composition class my senior year when I composed my final research paper on sex education in high schools. I tell them about going to college and how I majored in English because I could not imagine a semester without reading literature and how it was a study-abroad opportunity where my brilliant professors taught me how to teach myself and that learning entailed confusion, consistency, and, most important, camaraderie. I tell them about how my grandfather's rotary phone and bulky yellow pages helped me to land my first position as an English teacher and how it was in graduate school at American University studying literature that, in Betty Bennett's seminar on the Shelley Circle, sparked my desire to be a professor. So knowledgeable, wicked smart, unbelievably generous, and she championed her students like a tough coach, Dr. Bennett had what I wanted. I tell them the story of how teaching high school in New York City changed my life, where poverty and inequities soaked every fiber, drenched every aspect of schooling; and how children in Brooklyn and the South Bronx infused me with an ecstatic life force that departed the day I exited the high school classroom. And how graduate school pushed me in unimaginable ways but forced me to mature emotionally and intellectually, where reading the work of Michel Foucault help me to untether chains between sexual practices and truth to show me that I am freer than I perceive to be. And how being a professor is the most magical and yet difficult job I have ever had. All of this and much, much more.

But for the first time in my life I spoke openly and with conviction in my college classroom about my personal and scholarly passion for queer theory and the plight of the LGBTQ community. And I told my students that I am gay and how I weep every time I read about queer youth committing suicide because the gay rights movement fought to prevent queer youth from feeling like I did when I was an adolescent: alone, dismissed, frightened, and humiliated. And I tell them about how sex education, as well as the curriculum, needs to be inclusive of queer voices; and I tell them that one of my biggest concerns is ensuring that queer youth learn the history of LGBTQ people; and how as a queer academic it is my responsibility to try to address these issues. Some experiences deliberately get deleted from the story, such as how feelings of impotence and embarrassment surfaced when as an assistant professor, homophobia and bigotry rang through the hallways and faculty meetings, and about how a senior administrator strongly suggested to the grant administrator to slash my line from the grant due to concerns about how the funder may react to my primary research focus on queer studies. I tell them that tenure afforded me the privilege to redirect my scholarship from methods of teaching English to queer theory and LGBTQ studies. And, finally, I share with them about my current research and about my partner, our four dogs, marathon training, and devotion to baseball, music, and the arts.

My story as a gay man, as an academic, as a teacher-learner revolves around my innate capacity to make sense of my place in the world, my queer (s)place in the world. Who I am in specific and peculiar (s)places, and how gathering and collecting materials around me sustain a wonder about (s)place, apprise and instruct the manner with which I fashion myself now. So much of what I have learned about the world and who I have become germinated from the farmland of South Dakota. Queerness originates from the sensuality of the prairie, from the grittiness of the farm, and the amalgamated colors of sunsets, Mother Nature's exquisite and asymmetrical floral designs, the complex rhythms of history, and the intricate intermixing between plant and animal life. Queerness is homegrown food, well water, and the sights and sounds of the unpredictable plains. It is acknowledging one's part in the dramatic embodiment of the liminal generation of gay men, between the AIDS/ACT UP era and the marriage equality movement. And it is staring at the gracious and magnanimous vast land and answering my mother's first question out of her mouth with poise and heart the day I arrived when she asked, "Do you have someone special, yet?" and I responded, "Yes, mother I do. He's really sweet and we are very happy. Please don't worry, I won't be alone." To which she replied, "Oh, I wasn't worried, just making sure." And as I think about my run a tear streams down my face and I pause to look around and notice my father's red barn in front of his house. As my run concludes, the sun begins to burn the somber clouds and I ponder the day ahead with my mother and the aid and comfort she needs to present her last remaining gifts to us. The mnemonic chill begins to subside in this moment of profound passing.

REFERENCE

Buscaglia, L. (1986). *Loving each other.* New York: Ballantine.

CHAPTER TWENTY

Being Queer in Academia ←→ Queer*ing* Academia

DANA M. STACHOWIAK

Queer is who I am. It is how I behave. And how I *mis*behave. Queer is what I embody. Queer*ing* is my way of mind, of body, and of soul. Queer*ing* is how I work. It is how I disrupt. And it is how I stay sane. This chapter is intended to be queer and to queer. What follows are queer stories of my life and work, experiences of queering and being queer, from my pre-academia life to my current life in academia as an assistant professor of diversity/multicultural education.

BEFORE I WAS AN ACADEMIC, OR, WHEN I WAS A QUEER TERRORIST

"Now, we know you aren't going to call any media outlets and make a big deal out of this," he said, hands folded, prayerlike, on top of his oversized cherry desk. His voice was smooth, with every word he said edging slowly over the coil of his southern drawl. He had a serpentine smirk, and he squinted his eyes like he was trying to put me in a trance.

I stared, wide-eyed. Nodded in agreement. I looked at the Bible on the corner of his desk, darted my eyes between his squinted eyes and praying hands. I just kept nodding.

Just like that, the public school district took the conference funding they previously awarded me and pulled it away. I could still go and present my work, but now

I had to pay for it on my own and had to dock a personal day. I knew it was wrong, to pull the funding, but I didn't quite grasp what he meant about not making it a big deal—such a big deal that I'd call on the media. You only call on the media when something is *really* bad. This wasn't bad; they just wanted to keep themselves safe. After all, the buckle of the Bible belt was tightest in this quiet southern town.

"And you need to call the conference program chairs and ask them to remove your affiliation with our school district."

More nodding. Wider eyes. For safety. For safety, I nodded in agreement.

"I've spoken to the district's lawyer, and you are to write the following statement on all of your slides and handouts." He slid a piece of paper across the desk to me: *Monroe County Public Schools*[1] *do not support or endorse the work contained in this presentation.* "This is for our safety. It's just not safe for us to support your work."

I stared at the emblem of the school district's proud motto behind his head: "Success for ALL." I held my breath for what seemed like forever and repeated *Success for ALL, Success for ALL, Success for ALL,* over and over in my head as I sat like a shrinking child in his office chair, far on the other side of the desk from him. All I could see were praying hands and serpentine smiles and laughing kids and Bibles on desktops and Success for ALL. *Praying hands and serpentine smiles and laughing kids and Bibles on desktops and Success for ALL.* My face was crinkled now. But I still nodded in agreement. For safety.

In the year they pulled my funding, Success for ALL didn't include queer students or faculty. It didn't include supporting the successful acceptance of my proposal to a national conference. Or supporting my presentation that stemmed from my academic work on children and adolescent literature for and about queer students. In this year that they pulled my funding, queers were the terrorists of success in Monroe County Public Schools, and Success for ALL meant excluding them from success in order to keep the district safe.

But their safety meant my *un*-safety. And hundreds of students' un-safety. And the un-safety of all the (mostly closeted) queer faculty and staff members in the county. So in the year they pulled my funding, I fought back for safety.

I called on a prominent LGBTQ lawyer in the area who reminded me, "Queer folks like us aren't a protected class," and let me know that she supported my "desire for justice."

"It's unethical to pull funding. My work is not illegal, and I am advocating for the success for all students," I pleaded to the human resources department.

My colleagues emailed, "Dana's work is of the highest academic caliber, and she is an expert in best practices in literacy. Her professionalism and care for student success are admirable."

"The presentation proposed by Dana Stachowiak is of upmost importance in advancing the literacy growth and achievement for today's students. Culturally responsive and equitable literacy, such as proposed by Dana, ensures success for all. Denying her equitable access to the conference is a threat to the growth of conference attendees and LGBTQ students in your school district and in districts across the nation," was penned in an official letter from the conference chairs to the school district.

I eventually got the funding reinstated.

"You still need to rebuke your affiliation with the school district," I heard him say. "And you still need to keep the *Monroe County Public Schools do not support or endorse the work contained in this presentation* statement on all of your conference work."

I nodded. For safety. And for success. And because in that carefully crafted statement, the school district *announced* their ties to me and my queer self and work.

At the end of the year that they pulled my funding, I was removed from an administrator position and put back to a teaching position because of a "budget crisis." At the time, I didn't know that the budget crisis wasn't real, that it was just a ~~nice~~ safe way for them to say, "We can't have a queer like you in this kind of a position, and a budget issue is the only way we can remove you without any ~~trouble~~ queer terrorism."

Hello, media? I have a threat of terrorism to report.

ON NOT BEING SURE

I just don't think we are ready for someone like *you**."—University administrator

*see: queer; critical thinker; lesbian; social justice activist; transgender person; Northerner; dyke; young scholar; genderqueer ("Is *that* what you call yourself?"); dog mama; gay; wife; same-sex partner.

AN INVOLUNTARY ACT OF QUEERING

I am queer.

I am genderqueer.

And in the notoriously heteronormative world of academia, I queer it.

It's hard for me to find the line between *being* queer in academia and queer*ing* academia. My *being* queer becomes an involuntary act of queer*ing*.

"We've never had a professor like you before," my students tell me.

And I know they mean that they've never had a(n out) genderqueer (let alone queer) professor. On the day they tell me this, I'm wearing my favorite orange checked button-down, orange chinos, a navy blue tie, and cognac-colored monk strap shoes. They tell me they love this outfit because it "queers the eye" (a phrase I'm positive they've never used before, and one that I am damn proud they're using now).

Just by *being*, I am queer*ing*.

QUEER IDEAS NOT ALLOWED

SCENE 1: In the oversized office of a University upper administrator, mid-January

UPPER ADMINISTRATOR. Dana, I know you're a new faculty member and aren't advised to be on any official committees in your first year, but I think you would be really great as a member of a committee that is creating a Diversity Module for our first-year students. Will you consider joining?

ME, *to Upper Administrator*. Yes[2]! I would love to be a part of the committee. I will run it by my department head, but do count me in unless I let you know otherwise. Thanks for the opportunity!

INTERLUDE: email correspondences; no specific location; several days

February 6
All:
I would like to thank all of you for volunteering your time in order to create the Diversity Module for our first-year students. I will send the day/time/location for our first meeting in the coming days.
See you soon,
Woman-Appointed-in-Charge

March 10 (10:13 a.m.)
Dear Woman-Appointed-in-Charge,
Did the Diversity Module meeting ever come to fruition, and I missed it? Any update would be appreciated; I definitely still want to be a part of this.
Thanks,
Dana

March 10 (1:48 p.m.)
Hello Dana,
I want to apologize for leaving you out of the meetings. I completely forgot about you. The group has only met once thus far. At that meeting, we brainstormed several ideas and reached somewhat of a consensus. The next meeting will be held today at 4:00 p.m. in the

Administration Building, Room 101. I know it is last minute not to mention raining, so I understand if you can't make it. If you could make it, we would welcome your input.
Thanks,
Woman-Appointed-in-Charge

SCENE 2: March 10, 4:00 p.m.; Administration Building, Room 101. Dim lighting, rain on windows. Faculty members gather around a meeting table: one genderqueer; one lesbian; one Black female; one Asian female; one woman-appointed-in-charge; two older white women; two white men; one university diversity officer.

WOMAN-APPOINTED-IN-CHARGE. What should we do during the Diversity Module at orientation to engage our first-year students in discussions about diversity on campus?

OLDER WHITE WOMAN #1. Let's create a video where diverse students say, "I'm a proud [insert university mascot here]!" to show the diversity we have here and that we're all just human beings.

WHITE MAN #1, *eagerly cutting OWW#1 off.* I could be in charge of making the video. I already know the people who would be perfect for this! I know this one student who is disabled—but totally with it—and I also know this lesbian student who started a great group for the gay students here on campus. I know she'd be really excited; this stuff is right up her alley!

Continued exchanges between Older White Woman #1 and White Man #1 for several minutes about how to put the video together and how to share it at orientation. All others listen in but do not interject.

GENDERQUEER (Me). I think we can find a way to fit those great ideas in somewhere during orientation, but I really think that our time should be dedicated to facilitating critical thinking and engaging students in necessary conversations about privilege, power, and difference.
Silence and stares.

WOMAN-APPOINTED-IN-CHARGE. I don't think our students are ready for conversations like that.

WHITE MAN #2. Me either.

WHITE WOMAN #1. They definitely aren't; that's too heavy. We just need to show how our university celebrates the many differences on our campus.

The meeting continues, and I push for more critical work around diversity and social justice. Everyone is amiable to my suggestions, but the video project dominates the conversation.

INTERLUDE: email correspondences; no specific location; 3 group meetings later (that were similar to the meeting in SCENE 2, but without the one Black female, one Asian female, and one university diversity officer)

April 13 (2:03 p.m.)
Hello Dana,
If it is at all possible, I would like to speak with you. There is something I need to run by you concerning the diversity module. I promise not to take up too much of your time. Can you please let me know when would be a good time for me to stop by your office?
Thanks,
Woman-Appointed-in-Charge

April 13 (several minutes later)
Hi Woman-Appointed-in-Charge,
I am happy to meet with you and give my input! I am available any time after 1 p.m. on Tuesdays and Thursdays. Just come by!
Looking forward to our conversation,
Dana

(At this point, I am hopeful that this is an invitation to further discuss some of the ideas I have shared for the Diversity Module that other members of the committee have been hesitant to consider. I'm hopeful that the privacy of this meeting might allow the two of us to engage in a discussion about how to raise the critical consciousness of our first-year students around privilege, power, and difference.)

SCENE 3: My office; a few days later
Small talk ensues about the weather, the size of my office, and the wedding pictures of my wife and me.

WOMAN-APPOINTED-IN-CHARGE. While I think your ideas for the Diversity Module are good, I think they are too hard to implement right now. Our current students aren't even ready for these conversations, so I don't think our first-year students will be able to handle it on the first day. We're going to do the video and then a question-and-answer session for orientation. Your ideas are just too hard, and we're running out of time. Maybe it's something you can pitch to another group, like one that works with faculty members and diversity issues.

ME. *staring, silence*

WOMAN-APPOINTED-IN-CHARGE, *looking away.* I just wanted to tell you those things. I didn't think this was a conversation the rest of the group needed to be a part of. We're running out of time, so we need to use the meetings to talk about the video and the question-and-answer part only.

ME. So, what did you want to run by me?

WOMAN-APPOINTED-IN-CHARGE. Oh, I think we should have some "Diversity Fun Facts" rolling on the screen as the students come in. For example, did you know that international students can't work while they are here on campus?

ME. I did not know that.

WOMAN-APPOINTED-IN-CHARGE. Isn't that interesting? That's the kind of fun fact I think we should include.

ME. I actually think that's kind of an oppressive fact, not fun. But we could talk about how that fact is alarming to hear and how not allowing our international students to work is oppressive.

WOMAN-APPOINTED-IN-CHARGE, *confused look; slight pause.* I also told the group I would allow them to add fun facts about homosexuals. I think that is such a popular topic with young students right now.

ME. Okay. I'll send you some fun facts. Thanks for coming by!

WOMAN-APPOINTED-IN-CHARGE, *getting up to leave.* I just love the pictures of you and your friend—at y'all's wedding. She's just so beautiful.

I usher Woman-Appointed-in-Charge out of my office.

END: email correspondence; several days later

Dear University Upper Administrator,
I would like to let you know that, upon a lot of reflection, I have decided to relinquish my spot on the committee for the Diversity Module. Your reminder that I don't always have to say, "yes," especially when I'm overwhelmed, evoked my decision. Right now, I am very overwhelmed as a new faculty member.[3] *I am very happy to support the group "behind-the-scenes" leading up to and during orientation as they (and you) see fit, as I wish to support you and honor my commitment to volunteer my time during those two days. Many thanks to you for this eye-opening opportunity and for your faith in me as a young academic.*
All the best,
Dana

POSTLUDE:

In addition to honoring my commitment to the Diversity Module, I signed up to teach a section of the intro course required of all first-year students. As long as the learning outcomes of my section were not altered, the course topic could be of my choosing; I could queer it any way I wanted. So I chose to develop a section titled Developing a Social Justice Mindset. I set out with the intention to tackle this idea that our students weren't ready for critical conversations about diversity issues. I most certainly wanted to have some "data" to prove that our students were already having and were ready to dive even deeper into conversations about privilege, power, and difference. Within this, I wanted to show that social justice work could be done, and done well, and this work *should* be done. Second, I wanted to create a space for those students who were already committed, or just really interested in topics of social justice and equity, to be able to engage in these discussions, create community, and participate in a revolution.

The first class meeting was held on the morning of the first orientation day. The students' first assignment? Critique the hell out of the Diversity Module video.

QUEERING THE CLASSROOM

Since I spend the majority of my time in the classroom, that is where I most queer academia. The first-year students in my Developing a Social Justice Mindset course experienced this. There were no set course materials. There were no grades. And sometimes we didn't meet in the classroom. Some class meetings made more sense sitting under the live oaks lining the university grounds or at the campus swamp; while sipping on coffee at the nearest coffeehouse; or while sitting in our pajamas in a Google Hangout.

There were no grades because I think they do more harm than good. I only give letter grades at the end of the semester, as the university requires. Instead of putting letter grades or percentages on assignments, I offer substantial feedback that allows time for reflection, growth, and deeper understanding by the student. If students want to know their grade on an assignment, they need to schedule a meeting with me. They have to come prepared with specific questions, and be able to tell me what grade they think they received and why. Before getting their grade, I have the students set goals and establish ways to strengthen their understanding of the course content. I do this so that we de-center the focus of a final grade and center the mind-body-soul connection on a conversation about learning and growth. More often than not, a student will forego knowing his or her grade and walk away with goals for growth, a stronger connection to their work, and a deeper sense of success.

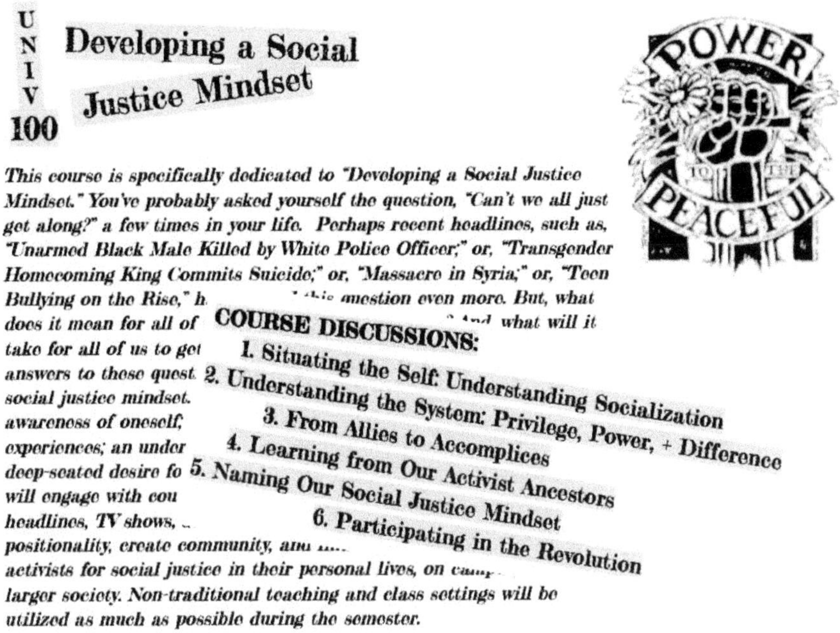

Figure 20.1.

There were no set course materials because, instead of choosing them *for* my students, I let them choose *with* me. I gave them the topic for discussion, provided a handful of relevant readings or films, and together, we picked which ones to analyze and learn with. Poems, photographs, artwork, podcasts, documentaries, academic (and not-so academic) articles, music, and other forms of media all became our bodies of study.

The first two topics for discussion (see topic titles in figure 20.1) laid the groundwork for the course. Here, students had to do the difficult work of troubling their socialization and positionality in critically conscious ways before troubling institutional and systemic modes of oppression, power, and difference. Artwork, slam poetry, collages, and music were just some of the ways the students conveyed how they grasped these topics. The next two topics pushed students to move beyond allyship to defining solidarity. They did this through creating working definitions of social justice and activism, by studying current and past work of social justice activists, and by naming and defining their social justice mindset.

Finally, the students became social justice activists; they participated in a revolution. Some students staged a protest at a large retail chain to raise awareness of wage inequity. One group of students created an interactive booth to promote the #BlackLivesMatter movement. There was a short documentary on LGBTQ life on campus. Signs from a "If you could, move your hood" campaign littered parking lots where the fronts of cars blocked access to sidewalks for students experiencing visual and/or physical impairments. And another group of students launched a university-wide movement to eliminate campus rape culture.

Not only were my students already having conversations about privilege, power, and difference, they were ready to go deeper. And going deeper didn't just mean engaging more critically in these conversations. My students were ready to make waves, ready to change minds, ready to engage in real social action. My students were ready to queer the world. And they did.

FINAL THOUGHTS: DON'T FEAR THE QUEER(ING)

I haven't always been an out queer and genderqueer, and I haven't always named my ways of being, of living, of educating, as an act of queering. For too long, I feared (my) queerness—what it meant, what I could do with it, what others could do with it. But there's power in naming/embodying/doing queer that eliminates those fears. Today, I don't think I could be an academic if I didn't queer academia. I fear silence and disembodiment and idleness more than I fear queering.

NOTES

1. Monroe County Public Schools is a pseudonym.
2. Because you always say yes to invites like this from Upper Administration, no matter how busy you are as a new academic or that it's against an unwritten university "code."
3. Because you never want to disappointment a University Upper Administrator when you are new in academia with *"But, a large part of my decision has to do with the disjointedness of the committee (lack of communication and collaboration), as well as some decisions that have been made that I don't necessarily want to have my name attached to, to be quite honest, some general feelings of unwelcomeness and my own 'reading between the lines' on things. I feel as though any further participation in meetings would not be a beneficial use of my time, nor beneficial to the other committee members."*

CHAPTER TWENTY-ONE

The Constant in My Life

WILLIAM F. PINAR

In a 1934 essay, Eiland and Jennings (2014) remind, Walter Benjamin characterized Kafka's gift for "study" as an "oblique attentiveness to aspects of a forgotten 'pre-world,' a sphere of inchoate myth whose laws determine the course of daily existence" (p. 601). Is sexuality such a "pre-world," hardly "forgotten" but maybe mythic, unacknowledged—except as scandal—in academic life? I am not suggesting any homology between sexuality and scholarship, but a reverberation perhaps? My generational, class, gendered, and racial locations—and my efforts to contradict them—must have been in play in the apparent promiscuity[1] of my intellectual and sexual life.

Coming of age in politically conservative Westerville, Ohio—in the 1950s a small town, now a sprawling suburb of Columbus—contributed to my sexual-subject formation. I dated Sue Smith in junior high school, Patsy Bean and Judi Wood during high school. These were appealing girls whom I wanted. Alas, they were respectable girls—I could bring home to my parents no other kind—and I graduated from high school a virgin. I dated Sue Wakefield and Betsy Bowers[2] my college freshmen year, both of whom were also appealing and, yes, respectable.[3] Not until a year later—in summer 1966 I transferred from the Conservatory of Music at Capital University in Columbus to study history at Ohio State—did I bed a girl.[4] As I reflect on those years from today's queer perspective I recall that there were boys whose bodies I noticed but sex didn't occur to me, not until Jeff Girard.

It was fall quarter 1968, my junior year at Ohio State. One very early morning after a night of heavy drinking I pulled my still drunk but pretending-to-be-asleep best friend and roommate on top of me. There might have been a kiss or two, but no entries or orgasms. Jeff didn't share my enthusiasm, and so we went our separate ways, me back to my girlfriend—his ex-girlfriend Cindi (how gay was that?)—and he onto yet another girl. Sometime afterward I had sex with someone I must have met at a gay bar but I didn't like it (the bar or sex with the guy), so I set "gay" aside. My senior year I spent with Karen, with whom I enjoyed fantastic sex over and over again.[5] Karen had a son—David—maybe four years of age; we were somewhat of a "family." When I moved to Long Island, New York, that August, I said goodbye. If there's determinism—as Benjamin seemed to think—it is implied in "decisions" I made contra common sense, seemingly in the service of some "law" I did not divine. Leaving Karen and Columbus qualifies as one of those.

After teaching English at Paul D. Schreiber High School in Port Washington, New York—where I was privileged to have a passionate affair with Betsy, then developed a crush on Kenny—I returned to Columbus to finish the Ph.D. During that year (1971–1972) I there were women—one affair, several one-night stands—and one sexual experience with Kenny who'd come to Columbus to see me. When in 1972 I moved upstate New York to teach at the University of Rochester, I shared a cottage in the middle of an unfarmed field with two women, both of whom—Marjorie Harper and Nancy Fruchtman[6]—I'd met on Long Island. After that ménage disbanded, I moved into the first of a series of places I shared with others my age—I was then in my mid-twenties—who smoked weed, drank, meditated, and slept around. At one point I had a crush on a guy named Billy Boaz, but he wouldn't budge.

At the Zen Center on Arnold Park in Rochester I met Denah Joseph. I fell hard. On September 15, 1976, our son was born: Gabriel, now married to Jane Virga, the father of four-year-old Olympia, one-year old August, and Rhein, born December 3, 2015. After breaking up with Denah I resolved[7] to be gay, announcing the news to parents and friends. Almost thirty and a son on the side—Denah departed Rochester with him for California where he grew up—my initiation into "gay culture" was fast and furious. I enjoyed the presence of a mentor: Ron Padgham, who taught interior design at the Rochester Institute of Technology and studied for his doctorate with me.[8] The paintings he found for me hang in our home in the northwest Washington woods. Ron became a dear friend and I miss him still.[9]

My parents were distressed at my announcement. Dad's concern seemed limited to its impact on my career. After the tears dried, Mother accompanied me on more than one occasion to gay bars; it was as if the ex-night-club singer suddenly was in her element again. After fooling around (as we used to say)—it was pre-AIDS still, although not for long—I fell for David Parker, a Ph.D. student in the

University of Rochester's History Department. It was a passionate affair that blew apart a year later.[10] After fooling around for a while I met Frank Cordello, with whom I lived for three years, breaking up when I left Rochester for LSU in 1985. In Louisiana I fooled around—again—especially after my son returned to California in 1992, and I moved into the French Quarter in New Orleans.[11]

When I had "come out" in Rochester, it had been to family and friends, not to colleagues at work. No doubt my move was noticed but uncommented on, except by those to whom I was close there: Madeleine Grumet, Peter Taubman, Philip Wexler, Margaret Zaccone. For me coming out had been no acknowledgment of my true but previously repressed identity. Sex with other men for me was an impulse first, then an idea, a political cause, always a subjective experiment, cause and consequence of an inner project of reconstructing what others had made of me.[12] Just as being sexually involved with women had not precluded noticing other guys, being gay did not end being sexually drawn to women. An ambivalence about identity remained, contradicted by the zeal with which I embraced my new gay life.

That overdetermined quality is discernible in my first foray into gay studies, a piece I composed while visiting my son in California, published two years later (1983) in *JCT*. In it I juxtaposed the work of Nancy Chodorow and Guy Hocquenghem—unlikely bedfellows—to argue that any pre-oedipal identification with the maternal body made likely men's internalization of mothers' desire, including heterosexual mothers' desire directed toward men. Even the sons of lesbian mothers know, *au fond*, they are "girls." Infamously Hocquenghem had proclaimed "from behind we're all women," and Chodorow, to my mind, provided the backstory. In 1981, matrifocality and the universality of homosexual desire constituted my "queer" reply to the macho Marxist emphasis on "reproduction theory"[13] then dominating curriculum studies in the United States.

Queer also animated my move back to the study of race during the next two decades. In 1968 I had been astonished by Eldridge Cleaver's insistence that race was also about sex. Along with Richard Wright's *Black Boy* (1945), I chose Cleaver's *Soul on Ice* (1968) for the eight-grade English class I ("practice") taught at Theodore Roosevelt Junior High School in Columbus in spring 1969. Students' somewhat stunned sullen silence persuaded me I was in over my head teaching poor black kids, so I declined the Roosevelt job offer and accepted instead an invitation to teach white, mostly upper-middle-class kids at Schreiber High School. I was in over my head there too.

During those two years I was consumed by teaching, and by studying, as I continued the M.A. work that I'd commenced in Columbus the summer before, undertaking independent studies with Donald Bateman and Paul Klohr (both of whom would serve on my Ph.D. committee). I recall reading *The Greening of America*, which endorsed the country's homosexualization, as well as works by Paul

Goodman, John Holt, George Dennison (who wasn't gay), and Edgar Friedenberg. On Long Island I faced students only three years my junior, many of whom seemed older developmentally than I was. Certainly they were more worldly than I, leaving me astonished, insecure, curious. Somehow I kept my calm, studying as much as teaching them.[14] They studied and taught me, helping me find my way. That fall 1969 I stumbled onto the Grateful Dead at the Café au Go Go on Bleecker Street in Greenwich Village. Maybe there were a dozen of us in that room that night. Not a year later I heard them again at the Fillmore East, surrounded by thousands of loud listeners, including several of my students. I listened to Led Zepplin in Carnegie Hall (of all places). One night I listened to James Taylor (again with half-a-dozen others) and maybe in that same Café au Go Go. I spent out-of-school time with students, with their parents, as well as solitary time with myself, studying, trying to reassemble something subjectively coherent out of what I was experiencing.

Despite Nixon's election in 1968, few of us seemed to notice the end of the 1960s. While circumstances had changed, my self-demand to experiment sexually, intellectually, and with drugs had not. I had tried much of what was available, including marijuana, LSD, even Quaaludes. It was cocaine, not LSD and marijuana, that sent many of us "straight" from the sixties into the eighties, but I didn't become thoroughly acquainted with cocaine until the 1990s when I was living in New Orleans.[15] I get ahead of myself.

The truth is that I used to get ahead of—or was it behind—myself a lot in those days. Maybe studying—the constant in my life—was a sort of scrambling to catch up, to grasp what (or whom) I was chasing (or fleeing) and why I seemed always out-of-sync with myself, sometimes startling myself with what I did (and didn't) think and feel. I hadn't planned to pull Jeff Girard onto me; I couldn't believe I was actually leaving Karen and Columbus for Long Island. As an undergraduate studying the concept of "socialization" helped me understand why there could be noncoincidence between me and my experience; "interpellation" came later. Making something else out of what others had already made of me seemed my ongoing situation, even ethical obligation. Such "subjective reconstruction"[16] involved "talking back" to the internalized "cop" who kept calling me. Coming-of-age is more complicated than what I had sketched in 1984 to University of Rochester undergraduates.[17] Then I referenced the gendered relations among history, the workplace, and the production of personality. Yes, it was a whiff of economic determinism and that not a year (publication-wise) after having snorted "machismo" at the Marxists in my field.[18]

That field—curriculum studies—had been recently resurrected as theoretical, no longer organized around school-based curriculum development, the Kennedy administration's national curriculum reform ending forty years of that. Theory was no match for misogyny, the concept with which I decoded the scapegoating of schoolteachers.[19] Demoting teachers from public to domestic servants was a gendered agenda, intensified later in the name of No Child Left Behind, a poor and probably black child, adding racism to misogyny as the main motivators of the manufactured crisis,[20] a nightmare that became the nightmare of the present for millions of teachers and the children (reduced to "learners" and, bottom-line, test-takers) they taught. From Cold War to cold hard cash, there was always a political problem male politicians were covering up, never taking responsibility for Sputnik or global economic blunders but recoding these as due to an absence of academic "standards" in schools, remedied they said by demanding "accountability" in a "Race to the Top." Corporate greed[21] now takes the form of "technology" in the classroom, educational experience upended by test scores, somehow the symbol of salvation in an era when "numbers" are no longer cute guys but the "bottom line" erasing experience and with it meaning, those concepts now relics of an earlier not yet "post-human" time. In U.S. public schools for one hundred years—first slides, then film, then radio, followed by TV, computers, and now tablets—technology has been a history of hype. It is also a gendered and racialized history: during the Weimar Republic technology was embedded in a fascist mix of masculine mobilization and imagined Aryan (male) superiority.[22]

Given matrifocality maybe there has always been a "crisis of masculinity," the concept to which I went to understand the gender of racial violence in America.[23] There is nothing far-fetched about castration, except that it was enacted, repeatedly, in lynching. "Power" proved an inadequate explanation for this peculiar practice, and the clue came not only at the site of the phallus but its timing: the apex of lynching was 1892, and that was the year the crisis of masculinity was, historians suggest, at its most intense. That history I summarized and juxtaposed to women's engagement in the antilynching campaign and the civil rights struggle more generally; racial violence, it seems, has been a matter between men. "I AM A MAN" said the signs striking sanitation workers held during their 1968 strike that brought Martin Luther King Jr. to Memphis. As "blowback," interracial prison rape was, I noted, also about racialized manhood.[24]

Blowing back may have been in play that mythic night in Noah's tent, but all we know from Genesis 9:24 is that upon waking from too much wine Noah "knew what his son had done unto him." The so-called Curse of Ham had been referenced as the biblically legitimating incident for other sins of the flesh, for example, the sexual assaults that accompanied and structured slavery. Father-son sex seemed the primal scene not only of racialization. In that study[25] of the Curse of Ham I reported anthropological research detailing how older and younger men seemed sexually stitched together. To "book-end" that study of race, religion, and reparation I reviewed maybe the most infamous instance of the father-son sexual sublime: the memoirs of Daniel Paul Schreber, the German judge whose breakdown followed his feminization by none other than God-the-Father himself.[26]

While my interest in queer theory had started subjectively, without institutional support, being affiliated with the Louisiana State University Women's and Gender Studies (WGS) program encouraged it. Through WGS I enjoyed friendships with colleagues across campus; my partner Jeff Turner and I hosted parties at our place not only for Curriculum and Instruction but for Women's and Gender Studies faculty and students as well.[27] After moving to the University of British Columbia (UBC) in 2005 I attended one Women's Studies meeting but quickly concluded that an additional monthly meeting would not do for the aging overcommitted academician I'd become. Overcommitted was also why I withdrew from the Coordinating Committee of the UBC program in Critical Sexuality—it now has Institute status—as I found out fast that the Canada Research Chair is as much promissory note as it is an honor.

But Jeff has come to like it here, "here" being the woods of Northwest Washington State where he gardens and I study. Jeff Turner and I celebrated our twentieth anniversary on September 26, 2015. We were married in our house in November 2013, and then again in December, the second (symbolic) time in a double ceremony with our dear friends Mary Aswell Doll and Marla Morris, an event held in our son's Brooklyn brownstone. Among the guests were our granddaughter Olympia, and our friends and colleagues Janet L. Miller and Elizabeth Macedo.

I met Janet Miller during fall term 1972, about the same time I met Madeleine Grumet, also my M.A. student. It was my first term teaching at the University of Rochester; both women taught me feminist theory and practice, subjects to which I had been introduced by Gabriel's mother Denah. In the late 1970s Peter Taubman was influential[28] for me; he completed his doctoral dissertation on gender politics, inspired by Foucault's recently translated *The Order of Things*. By decade's end Denah and I were split up, I was gay and sleeping my way through Toronto.[29] In the early 1980s I served as external examiner for James Sears, whose doctoral dissertation at Indiana University was not on gay studies—for which he became famous soon after[30]—but on teacher education. In Bloomington I met his pal and fellow student Patti Lather. Also during these first years as an "out" man I met Dennis Carlson, teaching then at Hobart and William Smith Colleges in nearby Geneva, New York.[31] Dennis covered for me at Rochester while I spent a term at Colgate University. As my career comes to a close, I find myself returning[32] to queer theory. I might assemble between two covers queer pieces now scattered here and there, relics of that "pre-world" of scholarship—sexuality—to which I remain attentive. We'll see where study takes me.

NOTES

1. Certainly I've "slept" with several "bodies of knowledge," but not indiscriminately as the term suggests.
2. Betsy contacted me last year; how remarkable to hear from her again! She is now retired from a career in the Ohio public schools.
3. "Respectable" meant passionate kissing and fondling of breasts (and in that order) were possible, but no genital penetration was permissible.
4. We'd met in a bar just off campus; her name I have forgotten.
5. Now an old man, I have reflected on the "best sex" I've ever had in my life: Karen was one of the two. The name of the other person I've now forgotten; I do recall he was a Turkish immigrant to Toronto whom I met there around 1980.
6. Nancy, now Nancy Chatfield and living in New Mexico, has been in touch in the last year.
7. The decision was political and personal, as Denah and I had been involved in discussion groups with other (heterosexually engaged) couples discussing feminism, gay liberation, and the role of gender in American politics. As political protest, thousands of heterosexual women were becoming lesbian, contesting the patriarchy then considered to be the core of American reactionary politics. For me, too, the political became personal.
8. His dissertation research is referenced in Pinar et al., 1995, p. 1135.
9. Ron and his partner, Chuck, died of AIDS in 1988.
10. A year after we split up, David died, his illness undiagnosed. I've wondered if it might have been AIDS. Somehow spared, I remain today HIV-negative.
11. I describe that period in Pinar, 1994, pp. 253–268.
12. "Subjective reconstruction" I call it now (Pinar, 2012, pp. 207ff.).
13. Schools were said to reproduce the socioeconomic order: see Pinar et al., 1995, pp. 244ff.
14. I published the essays they'd composed in one of my classes (Pinar, 1971).
15. I wrote about both: cocaine (Pinar, 2006, pp. 43–70) and New Orleans (Pinar, 2004, p. 260).
16. Pinar, 2012, p. 207ff.; Pinar & Grumet, 2015, pp. 191–219.
17. Who invited me to address that undergraduate forum—women's studies?—I can't recall (Pinar, 1994, pp. 183–189).
18. I remain whipsawed by determinisms, most recently by Penney's (2014) provocative work. Thanks to Nelson Rodriguez for recommending that book.
19. Pinar, 2007, pp. 155–182.
20. Berliner & Biddle, 1995.
21. Moving curriculum online (Pinar, 2013), cuts costs in the short term, teachers recast as auditors confined to contract work, while money previously allocated to services to children rerouted to software and the (de)vices that use them.
22. Pinar, 2012, pp. 170–173.
23. Pinar, 2001.
24. Pinar, 2001, pp. 1012ff.
25. Pinar, 2006.
26. Pinar, 2006, pp. 89ff.
27. At one party Michel Serres chased my handsome guy around the kitchen.
28. Peter remains influential for me, as do Janet and Madeleine.
29. Where I kept, for a while, a pied-à-terre.
30. See Pinar et al., 1995, pp. 396–399.

31. Where Madeleine Grumet would also teach for a time, before moving onto Brooklyn College and, finally, to the University of North Carolina in Chapel Hill.
32. I've spent the last decade working on the internationalization of curriculum studies, with projects on Brazil, China, India, Mexico, and South Africa. The report of each is now available in book form. For a summary, see Pinar, 2015, chap. 3.

REFERENCES

Berliner, D. C., & Biddle, B. J. (1995). *The manufactured crisis*. Cambridge, MA: Perseus.

Chodorow, N. J. (1978). *The reproduction of mothering*. Berkeley: University of California Press.

Cleaver, E. (1968). *Soul on ice*. New York: Dell.

Eiland, H., & Jennings, M. W. (2014). *Walter Benjamin*. Cambridge, MA: Belknap Press of Harvard University Press.

Hocquenghem, G. (1978). *Homosexual desire*. London: Allison & Busby.

Penney, J. (2014). *After queer theory*. London: Pluto.

Pinar, W. F. (1971). *Shadowgraphs: Sketches from a suburb*. New York: Vantage.

Pinar, W. F. (1983). Curriculum as gender text. *JCT, 5*(1), 26–52. [Reprinted in Pinar 1994, 1998]

Pinar, W. F. (1994). *Autobiography, politics, and sexuality*. New York: Peter Lang.

Pinar, W. F. (Ed.). (1998). *Queer theory in education*. Mahwah, NJ: Lawrence Erlbaum.

Pinar, W. F. (2001). *The gender of racial politics and violence in America*. New York: Peter Lang.

Pinar, W. F. (2006a). *The synoptic text today*. New York: Peter Lang.

Pinar, W. F. (2006b). *Race, religion, and a curriculum of reparation*. New York: Palgrave Macmillan.

Pinar, W. F. (2007). Punk'd. In N. M. Rodriguez & W. F. Pinar (Eds.), *Queering straight teachers: Discourse and identity in education* (pp. 155–182). New York: Peter Lang.

Pinar, W. F. (2012). *What is curriculum theory?* (2nd ed.) New York: Routledge.

Pinar, W. F. (2013). *Curriculum studies in the United States*. New York: Palgrave Macmillan.

Pinar, W. F. (2015). *Educational experience as lived: Knowledge, history, alterity*. New York: Routledge.

Pinar, W. F., & Grumet, M. R. (1976/2015). *Toward a poor curriculum* (3rd ed.). Kingston, NY: Educators International.

Pinar, W. F., Reynolds, W., Slattery, P., & Taubman, P. (1995). *Understanding curriculum*. New York: Peter Lang.

Wright, R. (1945). *Black boy*. New York: Harper & Brothers.

Contributors

Michael Borgstrom is associate professor and chair of English and Comparative Literature at San Diego State University, where he also co-directs the university's LGBTQ Research Consortium. He teaches and writes about American literature, sexuality and gender studies, African American literature, and critical race theory—interests that inform his book *Minority Reports: Identity and Social Knowledge in Nineteenth-Century American Literature*, which was published by Palgrave Macmillan as part of their Future of Minority Studies series. Additional work has appeared in journals such as *PMLA*, *African American Review*, *ESQ: A Journal of the American Renaissance*, *Journal of Homosexuality*, and *Pedagogy*.

Douglas Bristol, Ph.D., is an associate professor of History at the University of Southern Mississippi. In 2002, he received his Ph.D. with distinction from the University of Maryland, where he studied under Ira Berlin. He is a scholar of the African American experience and race relations. In his first book, *Knights of the Razor: Black Barbers in Slavery and Freedom* (2009), Bristol examined the relationship between black barbers and the prosperous white men whose throats they shaved with straight-edged razors from the colonial period to the Great Migration. He is currently working on his next book, *The Black Greatest Generation: African American Men and Women in Uniform during World War II*. He is also the Vice-Chair of the Institutional

Diversity Committee and the faculty advisor to the Alliance for Equality, which is a student organization on the Gulf Coast campus of the University of Southern Mississippi.

Ryan Burns has spent nearly a decade as a secondary English educator in Rhode Island. He earned his M.A. in English, applying queer theory and feminist film criticism to conflicting representations of men and masculinities in animated Disney films, and in his M.Ed. in Curriculum and Instruction, honing his practice in developing mindful, learner-focused classrooms. To learn more about Burns's work, follow him on Twitter @TeacherManRI or contact burns.ryanm@gmail.com.

David Lee Carlson, Ed.D., is an associate professor of secondary education in the Mary Lou Fulton Teachers College at Arizona State University.

Adam J. Greteman, Ph.D., is an adjunct assistant professor of Art Education at the School of the Art Institute of Chicago and Affiliate Faculty member in Interdisciplinary Studies at Creighton University. His work centers around issues of sexuality, philosophy of education, and ethics and has been published in various journals including *Educational Theory*, *Educational Philosophy and Theory*, *Discourse: Studies in the Cultural Politics of Education*, and *Studies in Philosophy and Education*. He is currently working on a book-length manuscript on the histories and studies of sexuality and gender in education.

Darrell Cleveland Hucks is an associate professor of Elementary Education at Keene State College. He received his Ph.D. in Teaching & Learning from New York University. His research interests include the schooling experiences of Black and Latino males, collective achievement, teacher education, culturally responsive pedagogy, college student retention and development, and literacy enrichment and technology integration. He is also the author of *New Visions of Collective Achievement: The Cross-Generational Schooling Experiences of African American Males*. He is also one of the editors of *Literacy Enrichment and Technology Integration in Pre-Service Teacher Education*. He was a New York City public school teacher for several years at the Ella Baker School.

Janet D. Johnson is an associate professor of Secondary Education and Co-Director of the URI/RIC Ph.D. Program in Education at Rhode Island College. She uses critical and feminist theories to frame her current research interests, which include yoga as a tool for social justice in schools and teacher agency and advocacy.

Jenny Kassen is a second year Master's student in Applied Psychology at the University of Western Ontario. Her research focuses on the experiences of educators living with mental health and addiction issues. She holds a Bachelor of Education from the University of Western Ontario, and a Bachelor of Design from OCAD University. Kassen is also an Intermediate/Senior teacher with the Thames Valley District School Board.

Alicia Lapointe is a Ph.D. candidate at the University of Western Ontario, where she researches Gay-Straight Alliances (GSAs) and student activism in Ontario public and Catholic schools. Lapointe also created and instructs the undergraduate course, Lesbian, Gay, Bisexual, Trans*, Two-Spirit, Queer/Questioning (LGBT2Q) Issues in Education (2014–present).

Bethy Leonardi is a postdoctoral research associate in the School of Education at the University of Colorado, Boulder. She is co-director of A Queer Endeavor, an initiative that aims to support educational communities to affirm gender and sexual diversity. She completed both her M.A. and Ph.D. at the University of Colorado, Boulder, in Educational Foundations, Policy, and Practice.

Catherine A. Lugg is a professor of education in the Department of Theory, Policy and Administration, Graduate School of Education, at Rutgers University. Her research interests include educational politics and history, and the influences social movements and political ideology have on educational politics and policy. She is the author of three books, *For God & Country: Conservatism and American School Policy* and *Kitsch: From Education to Public Policy*, as well as *U.S. Public Schools and the Politics of Queer Erasure*. Honors include the Paul S. Silver Award for outstanding article in the *Journal of Cases in Educational Leadership* (with Autumn K. Tooms), the Scholar-Activist Award (AERA-Queer Studies SIG), the William J. Davis Award for outstanding article in *Educational Administration Quarterly* (with Autumn K. Tooms and Ira Bogtoch), the UCEA Service Award, and the Jay D. Scribner Award (UCEA), a career award for outstanding mentoring of junior scholars.

Kerrita K. Mayfield, Ph.D. is a radical Renaissance woman who is a teacher, raconteur, and lifelong learner. She has been faculty and developed curriculum at: Upward Bound; Georgetown's Institute of College Preparation; Vassar; UMass Amherst; the University of Wyoming, and the public Science, Math and Technology Magnet High School she helped create. Still a researcher, writer, and state-certified educator, Mayfield currently teaches biology full time in an urban district under state takeover in Massachusetts.

sj Miller is associate professor of Literacy Studies at the University of Colorado, Boulder. Miller has published widely in journals and presented at national conferences on a variety of topics related to teaching young adult literature, antibullying pedagogy, undervalued student literacies and identities, challenging the gender binary, multimodal applications of popular culture in secondary classrooms, and cultivating sociospatial justice dispositions with secondary preservice English teachers. Notably, sj won the 2005 Article of the Year Award from the *English Journal* for "Shattering Images of Violence in Young Adult Literature: Strategies for the Classroom," and co-authored *Unpacking the Loaded Teacher Matrix: Negotiating Space and Time Between University and Secondary English Classrooms*, which received the Richard A. Meade award from NCTE. sj helped draft the Beliefs Statement about Social Justice in English Education and helped pass the NCTE Resolution on Social Justice in Literacy Education, which informed the newly vetted CAEP Social Justice Standard 6—the first-ever standard in the United States that advances social justice work in teacher preparation. sj also co-created the newly vetted CEE Commission and NCTE Resolution, Commission for Dismantling the School-to-Prison Pipeline. sj co-authored *Generation BULLIED 2.0: Prevention and Intervention Strategies for Our Most Vulnerable Students*, and has been awarded Essential Book for Professionals Who Serve Teens, by *Voices of Youth Advocate Magazine*. sj was recently named the 2015 recipient of the Joanne Arnold Courage and Commitment Award for contributions to advocacy and education in the lives of LGBTQ people at CU and beyond and recently published *Teaching, Affirming, and Recognizing Trans and Gender Creative Youth: A Queer Literacy Framework*.

Currently, sj is Executive Committee member of the Conference on English Education (CEE); AERA Division G; Affirmative Action Officer; Co-Chair of the AERA Queer SIG; consultant for the College Board providing best practices to secondary Pre- and Advanced Placement English teachers; AP Literature and Composition Table Leader and AP Grant Mentor; coeditor of *English Education*; coeditor of the inaugural book series with Peter Lang Publishing, *Social Justice Across Contexts in Education*; advisory board member for Routledge's *Critical Studies in Gender and Sexuality in Education*, *Journal of Adolescent and Adult Literacy*; member of the CU's Chancellor's LGBT Committee; and newly appointed by UNESCO as the representative for the United States to develop socially just curriculum in India with the Mohathma Gandhi Institute.

Thabo Msibi is an associate professor in curriculum studies in the School of Education at the University of KwaZulu-Natal, South Africa, where he is also Cluster Leader (Department Chair) for the Education Studies Academic Cluster. Msibi's research is primarily concerned with gender, sexuality, and decolonization in the context of education. He has published numerous academic articles and book chapters in local and international scholarly platforms. His forthcoming book focusses on the "hidden sexualities of South African teachers." Msibi is currently an editorial board member for *Gender and Education*, as well as *Gender and Language*.

Summer Pennell is a doctoral candidate in education at the University of North Carolina at Chapel Hill. Her research interests include queer theory and pedagogy; secondary English education; qualitative methods; social justice education; and intersectionality. Her research, teaching, and service are all connected to social justice and to issues faced by LGBTQIA students, parents, and teachers in particular.

William F. Pinar teaches curriculum theory at the University of British Columbia in Vancouver, Canada. He lives in the woods of Northwest Washington state with his husband Jeff Turner: the two celebrated their twentieth anniversary on September 26, 2015. They are the proud grandparents of four-year-old Olympia, one-year-old August, and two-week-old Rhein.

Pinar is the editor of *Queer Theory in Education* (1998), the coeditor—with Nelson M. Rodriguez—of *Queering Straight Teachers* (2007), and the author of *The Gender of Racial Politics and Violence in America: Lynching, Prison Rape, and the Crisis of Masculinity* (2001), and *Race, Religion and a Curriculum of Reparation* (2006).

Erich N. Pitcher is a Ph.D. candidate at Michigan State University. His dissertation explores the ways that educational organizations shape the experiences of 39 trans* faculty. Through research, teaching, and service Pitcher seeks to improve the lived experiences of lesbian, gay, bisexual, transgender, and queer people within the academy.

Kristen A. Renn is professor of Higher, Adult, & Lifelong Education at Michigan State University. She graduated from Mount Holyoke College and received her Ph.D. in higher education at Boston College. Prior to working at Michigan State University she was a dean in the Office of Student Life at Brown University. Dr. Renn teaches courses on college students and student development, history of higher education, and diversity and equity in postsecondary education. Her research focuses on the intersection of student success with issues of identity in higher education, including studies of mixed-race identities, LGBTQ students, and leaders of identity-based student organizations. She recently completed a landmark study of women's colleges and universities worldwide and is co-PI (with Michael Woodford of Wilfrid Laurier University) of the National Study of LGBTQ Student Success.

Nelson M. Rodriguez teaches sexuality and queer studies in the Women's, Gender, and Sexuality Studies Department at The College of New Jersey. He is coeditor of two series: *Queer Studies and Education* and *Routledge Critical Studies in Gender and Sexuality in Education*. His current research areas span queer studies and education, critical masculinity studies, and Foucault studies. His most recent publications are *Queer Masculinities: A Critical Reader in Education* and *Queering Straight Teachers: Discourse and Identity in Education* (with William F. Pinar). His forthcoming books include *Critical Concepts in Queer Studies and Education: An International Guide for the Twenty-First Century*; *Queer Pedagogies: Theory, Praxis, Politics*; and *Friendship as Ascesis: Michel Foucault, Queer Theory and Education*.

Scotty M. Secrist is a doctoral student at Michigan State University. His research interests include college student success; teaching, learning, and curriculum in postsecondary education; and diversity, equity, and social justice. His current work focuses on how assessment and evaluation are taken up in higher education research and practice.

Stephanie Anne Shelton is a Ph.D. candidate in the Language and Literacy Education Department at the University of Georgia. She is a teaching assistant in the Institute for Women's Studies and serves as the Managing Editor of the *Journal of Language and Literacy Education*. Shelton received the Carol J. Fisher Award for Excellence in Research and the Genelle Morain Award for Excellence in Graduate Teaching from her department, and the Graduate Student Diversity Engagement Award from the university. She currently serves as the co-chair of the Literacy Research Association's Gender and Sexualities Innovative Community Group.

Dana M. Stachowiak, Ph.D., is an assistant professor of Diversity/Multicultural Education at the University of Louisiana at Lafayette. She is also a social justice literacy consultant with the Educator Collaborative. She earned her degree at the University of North Carolina at Greensboro in the Department of Educational Leadership and Cultural Foundations as well as a Graduate Certificate in Women's and Gender Studies. Her primary areas of specialization and research include cultural foundations of education, qualitative research methods, gender studies, social justice education, and equity literacy. Stachowiak has several publications (current and forthcoming) on embodied experiences of genderqueers, a critical social justice framework for literacy, social justice, and equity in higher education, and teaching social justice in teacher education programs.

Sara Staley spent several years in the classroom as a high school English teacher before making her way to graduate school to pursue a Ph.D. in Literacy Studies. Currently, Staley is a postdoctoral research associate in the School of Education at the University of Colorado Boulder. With Bethy Leonardi, she is cofounder and co-director of A Queer Endeavor, an initiative that aims to support educational communities to affirm gender and sexual diversity. Her research explores queer issues in education and the intersections of teacher learning and high-stakes educational policy reform.

Kamden Strunk, Ph.D., is an assistant professor in the Department of Educational Foundations, Leadership, and Technology in the College of Education at Auburn University. He is also a director of the Research Initiative on Social Justice and Equity (RISE). He earned his Ph.D. in Educational Psychology from Oklahoma State University in 2012. Currently, his research focuses on issues of educational equity, particularly for LGBTQ people, as well as motivation in education.

William Takewell is the Director of Campus Life at Millsaps College in Jackson, Mississippi, where he directly works with fraternity and sorority life, orientation, first-year experience, and multicultural programs. Takewell earned his B.A. in organizational communication from Southeastern Louisiana University and his M.Ed. in counseling and personnel services with an emphasis in student affairs from the University of Southern Mississippi. Prior to working at Millsaps, Takewell worked in the Office of Student Activities at Southern Miss as the Student Activities Manager and campus programming advisor.

Michael Wenk has worked in public schools as a secondary English teacher, instructional coach, athletic coach, migrant program educator, and curriculum specialist. He has been honored by students and colleagues for his work in the classroom. Wenk earned his Ph.D. in Curriculum and Instruction (Literacy) at the University of Colorado, Boulder, in 2015, where he taught undergraduate and graduate language and literacy courses for elementary and secondary teacher candidates. His research interests include cross-content literacy instruction, STEM education; professional development; instructional technologies; reading and writing workshop; and critical literacies. He has been published in *English Journal*, *Statement*, and *The*

Colorado Reading Journal, and has a chapter in *Teaching, Affirming, and Honoring Trans and Gender Creative Youth: A Queer Literacy Framework* (2016). Wenk is an active member of the Colorado Language Arts Society (a state affiliate of the National Council Teachers of English), serving over the past ten years as president, webmaster, and affiliate journal editor. In his spare time, he volunteers for his neighborhood association as well as a teen suicide prevention nonprofit. Wenk can be reached at mjwenk@hotmail.com.

sj Miller & Leslie David Burns
GENERAL EDITORS

Social Justice Across Contexts in Education addresses how teaching for social justice, broadly defined, mediates and disrupts systemic and structural inequities across early childhood, K–12 and postsecondary disciplinary, interdisciplinary and/or transdisciplinary educational contexts. This series includes books exploring how theory informs sustainable pedagogies for social justice curriculum and instruction, and how research, methodology, and assessment can inform equitable and responsive teaching. The series constructs, advances, and supports socially just policies and practices for all individuals and groups across the spectrum of our society's education system.

Books in this series provide sustainable models for generating theories, research, practices, and tools for social justice across contexts as a means to leverage the psychological, emotional, and cognitive growth for learners and professionals. They position social justice as a fundamental aspect of schooling, and prepare readers to advocate for and prevent social justice from becoming marginalized by reform movements in favor of the corporatization and deprofessionalization of education. The over-arching aim is to establish a true field of social justice education that offers theory, knowledge, and resources for those who seek to help all learners succeed. It speaks for, about, and to classroom teachers, administrators, teacher educators, education researchers, students, and other key constituents who are committed to transforming the landscape of schools and communities.

Send proposals and manuscripts to the general editors at:

sj Miller sj.Miller@colorado.edu
Leslie David Burns L.Burns@uky.edu

To order other books in this series, please contact our Customer Service Department at:

(800) 770-LANG (within the U.S.)
(212) 647-7706 (outside the U.S.)
(212) 647-7707 FAX

or browse online by series at:

WWW.PETERLANG.COM

www.ingramcontent.com/pod-product-compliance
Ingram Content Group UK Ltd.
Pitfield, Milton Keynes, MK11 3LW, UK
UKHW020200290926
15471UKWH00005B/980